REFORMING SOCIAL SERVICES IN NEW YORK CITY

REFORMING SOCIAL SERVICES IN NEW YORK CITY

How Major Change Happens
in Urban Welfare Policies

Thomas J. Main

CORNELL UNIVERSITY PRESS ITHACA AND LONDON

Copyright © 2025 by Cornell University

All rights reserved. Except for brief quotations in a review, this book, or parts thereof, must not be reproduced in any form without permission in writing from the publisher. For information, address Cornell University Press, Sage House, 512 East State Street, Ithaca, New York 14850. Visit our website at cornellpress.cornell.edu.

First published 2025 by Cornell University Press

Library of Congress Cataloging-in-Publication Data

Names: Main, Thomas James, 1955– author.
Title: Reforming social services in New York City : how major change happens in urban welfare policies / Thomas J. Main.
Description: Ithaca : Cornell University Press, 2025. | Includes bibliographical references and index.
Identifiers: LCCN 2024050784 (print) | LCCN 2024050785 (ebook) | ISBN 9781501782893 (hardcover) | ISBN 9781501783173 (paperback) | ISBN 9781501782916 (epub) | ISBN 9781501782909 (pdf)
Subjects: LCSH: New York (N.Y.). Human Resources Administration—History. | New York (N.Y.). Human Resources Administration—Management. | Public welfare administration—New York (State)—New York—History—20th century. | Public welfare administration—New York (State)—New York—History—21st century. | New York (N.Y.)—Politics and government—1951–
Classification: LCC HV99.N6 H35 2025 (print) | LCC HV99.N6 (ebook) | DDC 361.9747/1—dc23/eng/20250320
LC record available at https://lccn.loc.gov/2024050784
LC ebook record available at https://lccn.loc.gov/2024050785

Contents

Acknowledgments	vii
Introduction: Change and Urban Politics	1
1. The HRA under Lindsay	9
2. The HRA under Giuliani's First Term	21
3. The HRA under Giuliani's Second Term	36
4. Beginnings of de Blasio's Welfare Policies	50
5. Overview of the Career Pathways Employment Programs	64
6. Implementation of Career Pathways Welfare Programs	73
7. Career Pathways and the Drive for Coordination	92
8. Early Challenges to de Blasio's Homelessness Policy	110
9. Later Developments in de Blasio's Homelessness Policy	122
10. De Blasio, Cuomo, and Trump	139
Conclusion: How Change Happens in Urban Politics	146
Notes	167
Index	193

Acknowledgments

I wish to thank the following people and institutions for the assistance that made this book possible. Grants I received from the Achelis & Bodman Foundation, the Howard J. Samuels State and City Policy Center of the Marxe School of Public and International Affairs at Baruch College–CUNY, and a PSC-CUNY Research Award gave me the time and resources I needed to complete this work. People involved with welfare policy in New York City who graciously agreed to be interviewed by me included: Lauren Aaronson, Richard Acosta, David Aguado, Beatriz Baldwin, Steven Banks, Lee Bowes, David Casey, Eileen Cassidy Rivera, Anthony Coles, Patricia M. Connelly, Swati Desai, Diane Edelson, Sheree Ferguson-Cousins, Lisa Fitzpatrick, Jessica Gardner, Annie Garneva, Christian Gonzalez-Rivera, William Grinker, Rebecca Kirszner, Neil Kleiman, John Krinsky, Jesse Laymon, Jacqueline Mallon, Ilene Marcus, Jim Miller, David Neustadt, Demetra Smith Nightingale, Amy Peterson, Vanessa Preston, Cynthia Stuart, Fran Sullivan, Dolores Swirin-Yao, J. Phillip Thompson, Charmaine Williams, and Stacy Woodruff. I also had an email exchange with Jason Turner and spoke with Jack Krauskopf. Professors Bin Chen, Sanders Korenman, and Jonathan Engel of the Marxe School, and Lawrence M. Mead of New York University, offered me advice and saved me from mistakes. Ellen Levine of the New York City Department of Social Services provided me with important data, and Brad Hershbein, of the W. E. Upjohn Institute for Employment Research gave me information about career pathways programs. My editors at Cornell University Press, Mahinder Kingra and Michael J. McGandy, provided excellent help and advice. Laura Poole improved the manuscript with a final edit. I thank two anonymous reviewers of the book's early manuscripts who offered very helpful comments.

Parts of chapters 2 and 3 are based on my article, "Nonincremental Change in an Urban Environment: The Case of New York City's Human Resources Administration," published in *Administration & Society* 37 (2005), 483–503.

My wife, Carla T. Main, helped me with advice on editing and legal issues. I benefited from conversations with my brother, William Main. My sons, Henry Main and Joshua Main, gave me hope for the future and a reason to keep working. My parents, George and Catherine Main, and my grandmother, Catherine Gallacher, supported my education and developed such abilities as I have. Any errors that have ended up in this book despite all the help I received are my own.

REFORMING SOCIAL SERVICES IN NEW YORK CITY

Introduction

CHANGE AND URBAN POLITICS

Can US cities respond effectively to pressing social problems? Or, as many scholars have claimed, are urban politics so mired in stasis, gridlock, and bureaucratic paralysis that dramatic policy change is impossible? This book examines efforts in New York City to respond to its wicked problems of inner-city poverty and homelessness by establishing and periodically restructuring the city's Human Resources Administration (HRA) and related social welfare agencies.

The HRA has been the focus of three nationally significant reform campaigns over several changing mayoralties. Mayor John Lindsay's creation of the HRA in 1966 as a "superagency" was a classic liberal effort to fight poverty with government action. Mayor Rudy Giuliani brought dramatic change to the HRA to implement paternalistic, work-oriented welfare reform. Then came the episode that is this book's main focus: the struggle of Mayor Bill de Blasio and his precedent-breaking HRA leader (and later Department of Social Services commissioner) Steven Banks to execute a dramatic change at the city's social service agencies when they installed a progressive social welfare agenda to reduce inequality. The success of the de Blasio administration in redirecting an entrenched bureaucracy onto an innovative path is a reflection on whether progressives can overcome the widespread assumption that they are ineffective executives. The overall history of the HRA illustrates what works and what does not in urban management.

Much political science and public administration literature has claimed that change, when it takes place in policy making and implementation, occurs slowly and incrementally.[1] Urban policy making especially is held to be slow and incremental. Classic statements of pluralist and corporatist theories of urban politics predict that urban politics, particularly in New York City, will tend toward stasis, as proposed changes are fought against by the many interest groups who defend stakes in the status quo.[2] Later, structuralist accounts of urban politics argued that various sorts of economic, constitutional, and social structures drastically limit the possibilities for change.[3] One textbook on urban politics summed up the consensus of the literature on the nature of urban politics as follows: "Urban political structures change slowly in an incremental, evolutionary fashion."[4]

Urban politics generally, New York City politics particularly, and New York City public bureaucracies especially are held to be resistant to change. In her analysis of the city's agencies, Blanche Blank begins with the observation that "it may be the very essence of any bureaucracy to move cautiously, even ponderously," and she concludes that "change is always incremental as it is too in New York City government."[5] In their updating of Wallace Sayre and Herbert Kaufman's famous pluralist analysis of New York City politics, the authors of *Power Failure: New York City Politics and Policy since 1960* hold that "there is much inertia within the system, which makes change difficult. . . . The major difficulty is in putting forward changes, regardless of the direction of the change."[6] Finally, street-level bureaucracies—that is, public service agencies that employ a significant number of frontline workers who interact with the public with substantial discretion—are held to be very resistant to change. In his classic account of street-level bureaucracies, Michael Lipsky writes, "I have argued that the determinants of street-level practice are deeply rooted in the structure of the work. . . . These observations contribute to our understanding of the stability of the institutions and their unlikely response to significant reform activities."[7]

Another strand of literature takes up the issue of political change and has challenged the picture of slow or very limited change in policy and implementation. The most comprehensive statement of this position is *The New Politics of Public Policy*, edited by Marc K. Landy and Martin A. Levin. The contributors to this volume argue that the combination of a fragmented institutional framework, a divided government, a highly competitive political environment, and the rights revolution encouraged policy entrepreneurs to compete to have the best claim to implementing popular political ideas. The result has been that "a shift has taken place from a 'politics of interests' (which tend to be fixed and thus to change slowly) to a 'politics of values and ideas' (which tend to be more open, fluid, and responsive to change and reason)."[8] Contributors provided convincing accounts of how the new politics led to nonincremental changes in such areas as the environment (Clean Air Act of 1970), education (Education for All Handicapped Children Act of 1975), taxation (Tax Reform Act of 1986), and immigration (Immigration Reform and Control Act of 1986 and the Immigration Act of 1990).

Ideas do not play a major role in theories of urban politics, which more typically focus on interest groups, social structures, regimes, markets, and other material factors. That absence of ideas is one reason current accounts of urban politics underestimate the potential for nonincremental change. Public ideas are a key element in what *New Politics* calls ideational/entrepreneurial politics, which is a principal route through which the highly fragmented and pluralistic US policy-making process is capable of nonincremental change. Public ideas are slogan-like distillations of expert analysis. Thus, in the 1980s, "lower the rates, broaden the base" summed up many years of research on tax economics; in the 1990s, "end welfare as we know it" briefly stated the negative evaluation experts had come to about the United States' welfare policies. Such public ideas can facilitate nonincremental change by galvanizing the public and validating a policy direction. Public ideas shared among policy makers can also engender change, as Eugene Bardach has noted in *Getting Agencies to Work Together: The Practice and Theory of Managerial Craftsmanship*, when they serve as an "interpretative lens" that "provides focus and enables insight," linking objectives and means.[9] In doing so, public ideas can help political actors overcome fragmentation, promote coordination, and thus achieve nonincremental change.

However, *New Politics* and its follow-up volume, *Seeking the Center*,[10] had little to say about subnational or urban politics. Have urban politics evolved from a politics of interests to one of values and ideas? To what extent, if any, can this paradigm of ideational nonincremental change replace or supplement the incremental model usually applied to urban politics?

We must address two conceptual issues before we go further: Why are we interested in the issue of nonincremental urban change at all? And how shall we define nonincremental change so that we can distinguish it from incremental change? The question of whether nonincremental change is possible in urban environments goes to the issue of whether these environments are democratically responsive. In his analysis of the failure of urban movements of the 1960s, Ira Katznelson laments that "the promises of radical or fundamental change have [not] been redeemed."[11] Undoubtedly some types of such change are undesirable, but surely we would be disappointed in a political system that was incapable of deep change altogether. With the object of vindicating the legitimacy of the national political system, Daniel P. Moynihan presented the failure of Richard Nixon's version of welfare reform, the Family Assistance Plan, "as evidence that 'fundamental,' rather than merely 'incremental,' social change *is* a realistic option for American society at this time."[12] Certainly, it could be shown that generations of political scientists (including Sayre and Kaufman, Theodore J. Lowi, Katznelson, Shefter, and John Mollenkopf) ultimately regard the present limits on political change in New York City as a problem in various ways. My purpose here is to begin an inquiry into just how much of a problem the city's alleged imperviousness to change really is.

How, then, do we define nonincremental change? Briefly, incremental change modifies baseline policy but leaves it intact, whereas nonincremental change breaks with baseline policy and creates a new baseline. The history of US welfare policy provides an illuminating example of this distinction. In 1935, the Social Security Act created the program that came to be known as Aid to Families with Dependent Children (AFDC). The creation of AFDC was a nonincremental change; it marked the first federal program consciously designed to specifically address family poverty. Until 1996, AFDC went through many modifications. In the 1960s, the changes were mostly about enforcing various sorts of work mandates on aid recipients. Yet the basic entitlement program endured, providing income support to poor families with few obligations. Throughout the decades from 1935 to 1996, the program saw only incremental change. In 1996, the Personal Responsibility and Work Opportunity Reconciliation Act (PRWORA) was passed, replacing AFDC with Temporary Aid to Needy Families, ending the entitlement aspect of welfare, imposing strong work requirements on recipients, and setting a five-year limit on eligibility.

The PRWORA was as much of a nonincremental change as AFDC was because it eliminated an old policy and created a new one. Nonetheless, AFDC and the PRWORA represent two very different ways in which US politics generates nonincremental change. Landy and Levin's classification of models of political change is useful here. The modal type is the pluralist/incremental model in which every interest group with a stake in the policy baseline fights to hold on to its benefits and change can happen only incrementally, if at all. Under the presidential/majoritarian model, nonincremental change is possible only if the political system is hit with an exogenous shock, such as a war, an economic depression, or an extraordinarily inept opposition. This enables a presidential candidate to run on a platform promising major change, to win overwhelmingly, to bring in majorities of their party in Congress, and to neutralize possible opposition from the Supreme Court. In national politics, the New Deal, including AFDC, and the Great Society are classic examples of this change model; in New York City, examples are Fiorello La Guardia's mayoralty and the consequences of the 1975 fiscal crisis. Such grand changes are exceptions that prove pluralist and structuralist rules. Soon enough, the window of political opportunity shuts, the new economic or governance structures take root, and we are back to an "ordinary" politics of pluralist/incremental change.

The other change process capable of generating nonincremental change is the ideational/entrepreneurial model, which enables the politics of values and ideas.

In this model, a strong professional policy consensus is translated by policy entrepreneurs into a slogan-like public idea and disseminated through mass media, enabling competitive politicians to outbid each other in taking credit for the most radical version of the reform idea. The PRWORA is an example of the ideational/entrepreneurial model on the national level, as Giuliani's welfare reform was at the city level.

The Present Book

This book explores the possibilities of nonincremental change, however achieved, as a vindication of the democratic legitimacy of urban politics. The ideational/entrepreneurial path to change especially interests me because it produces changes that the incrementalist model would predict are not possible during times of ordinary politics. Put in other words, nonincremental change that is the product of the politics of values and ideas, with its key features of expertise, policy entrepreneurs, institutional fragmentation, competitive political environments, and especially public ideas, is especially relevant to the issue of democratic legitimacy. As Steven Kelman has argued, "The best operational test of the importance of public spirit in the political process . . . is the ability of ideas to overcome interests in determining the content of political choices."[13] If "the new model of 'ideational-entrepreneurial politics'"[14] operates in New York City, that indicates greater possibilities for democratic politics than if that path to change is unavailable.

My thirty years of research on urban politics—mostly in New York City—suggest that nonincremental change happens more frequently than scholars have realized. This argument is developed in my previous book, *Homelessness in New York City: Policymaking from Koch to de Blasio*,[15] in which I relate the remarkable story—warts and all—of how the United States' largest city has struggled for more than thirty years to address the crisis of modern homelessness. That book follows New York City's journey through the landmark development, since the *Callahan v. Carey* litigation in 1979, of a municipal shelter system based on a court-enforced right to shelter. My finding there was that, despite some obvious shortcomings—especially considerable cost and still too many homeless people—New York City was able to effectively address a pressing social problem. Developing and managing the shelter system required the city to repeatedly overcome daunting challenges, from dealing with mentally ill street dwellers to confronting community opposition to shelter placement. In the course of these efforts, classic dilemmas in social policy and public administration arose. Does adequate provision for the poor create perverse incentives? Can courts manage recalcitrant bureaucracies? Is poverty rooted in economic structures or personal behavior? The tale of how five mayors—Ed Koch, David Dinkins, Giuliani, Mike Bloomberg, and de Blasio—have wrestled with these problems is one of caution and hope: the task is difficult and success is never unqualified, but positive change is possible.[16]

This book continues this investigation into the possibilities of US urban change by telling the story of New York City's latest struggle with a wicked problem and an unwieldy system: the efforts by de Blasio and Banks to address inequality and remake the city's social welfare system. This topic has not yet received much scholarly attention, and I was able to gain access to key sources in the de Blasio administration. To set this story in context, I look at two previous campaigns to dramatically restructure the city's welfare system: Mayor Lindsay's creation of the HRA in 1966 as a superagency, and Mayor Giuliani's reinvention of the agency during his terms in office to implement paternalistic, work-oriented welfare reform. The key criteria for evaluating these efforts are whether the mayor and his senior management succeeded in bringing a recalcitrant bureaucracy under control and the extent to which they implemented their policy preferences and produced the desired immediate outputs, whether fewer people on the welfare rolls or more low-income people in good jobs. This book examines which strategies (if any) work and which do not work for a mayor of any political orientation who wants to make dramatic changes in urban bureaucracies.

In Lindsay's, Giuliani's, and de Blasio's reform campaigns, we have strikingly different case histories of attempts at nonincremental change. Judged in terms of administrative effectiveness, Lindsay's superagency strategy is usually evaluated as a failure.[17] My research suggests that Giuliani's reinvention of the HRA was effective in its own work-oriented terms.[18] The success or failure of de Blasio's and Banks's struggles to remake the city's social welfare system along progressive lines is more complex. Did their efforts fall short, as Lindsay's is thought to have done, and provoke a conservative reaction? Or did they succeed and address what Richard R. Buery Jr., a de Blasio deputy mayor, called "the biggest challenge progressives face in governing . . . this assumption that we don't know what we're doing, we don't know how to execute"?[19]

Another issue relevant to urban nonincremental change is the unusual position of cities in the US constitutional structure. Under the Dillon rule, cities are entirely creatures of the state, and the state has plenary power over its cities, unless expressly limited by statute. The State of New York became a home rule state in 1963, which allows municipalities to pass legislation for some matters, while the state continues to have legislative power over the affairs of the cities.[20] States are not similarly beholden to the federal government; unlike cities, they have a set of powers and privileges acknowledged in the Constitution. Nonetheless, states necessarily interact with and find their actions limited by the federal government. Thus, cities are the lower authority in the complex structure of US intergovernmental relations, which is another reason urban change can be so hard to achieve.

The relationship between mayors and governors generally is difficult, and nowhere more so than in New York. In two of the three case histories considered here—the creation of the HRA under Lindsay and Career Pathways reforms under de Blasio—mayor-governor relations were especially fraught, to the extent of being considered the worst in the history of the state. Lindsay's conflicts with Governor Nelson Rockefeller and de Blasio's tensions with Governor Andrew Cuomo affected and impeded the welfare policies these mayors tried to implement. Giuliani tried to get aid from the state government in Albany by famously crossing party lines; in 1994, he endorsed the incumbent Democratic governor, Mario Cuomo, for a fourth term over Republican challenger George Pataki. The chapters on these administrations discuss the different strategies the mayors deployed to overcome their weak constitutional position and achieve nonincremental change in welfare policy despite the opposition from state and federal chief executives.

The main audience for the book is anyone with a professional interest in how cities are governed and deliver vital services, including people working in urban affairs, social services, and welfare policy networks. Scholars who study public policy and administration, students (especially graduate students) studying these disciplines, people working in the HRA and similar organizations who want to learn about policy implementation, bureaucrats in other cities looking at New York City as a model, journalists covering urban affairs, and community activists can all read this book with profit. The generally educated public with an interest in cities and their history, and New York City in particular, may also be interested.

Chapters 1 through 3 cover the Lindsay and Giuliani administrations. Chapters 4 through 10 cover various aspects of de Blasio's efforts to make a major change in the city's welfare and workforce policies. After touching on the legacy of Bloomberg that de Blasio confronted, chapter 4 introduces the Career Pathways approach to human resources policy, which he applied to welfare and workforce policy. Chapter 5 evaluates the Career Pathways–oriented programs that de Blasio and Banks introduced at the HRA in terms of their effectiveness in placing welfare clients in jobs. Chapter 6 looks at the implementation of the Career Pathways programs through interviews with executives at the organizations that ran those programs and the HRA's evaluations of those organizations' performance. Chapter 7 goes beyond welfare policy to look at workforce policy. The workforce inquiry was needed because the de Blasio administration made a bold effort to coordinate welfare and workforce policy in a bid to get city agencies and private employers to work together. The goal was to do a better job at placing welfare clients in "good" jobs—presumably better than previous human capital development programs had done. The subject of chapters 8 and 9 is de Blasio's homelessness policy and how he dealt with the rising shelter census he inherited from Bloomberg. Homelessness policy is relevant here because under de Blasio, the Department of Homeless Services was, along with the HRA, placed under the aegis of the Department of Social Services and thus became an integral part of the city's welfare bureaucracy. Chapter 10 considers de Blasio's efforts to deal with opposition from Governor Andrew Cuomo and President Donald Trump. The conclusion sums up the book's findings and provides insights into nonincremental change in urban politics.

1
THE HRA UNDER LINDSAY

The plan for the John Lindsay administration's Human Resources Administration (HRA) was written by its incoming director, Mitchell Sviridoff, and embraced by the administration before Sviridoff arrived in New York. Previously, he had been executive director of Community Progress, a New Haven, Connecticut, antipoverty program that attracted national attention when it found employment for fifteen hundred people in its first thirty months of operation.[1] In 1966, Sviridoff wrote a report for the Institute of Public Administration: "Developing New York City's Human Resources." This was the HRA's foundational document, and it set the agency a daunting task, for, according to Sviridoff, "The objective of the study was to come up with recommendations for improved techniques and administrative arrangements to attack the causes of poverty, expand the range of opportunity and release new productive energies in the City of New York."[2]

The report identified the key to achieving this ambitious objective as coordination. Sviridoff explained in the plan that Mayor Lindsay had proposed a regrouping "of the many proliferating departments and agencies of the city government" to be organized around "related functions."[3] A key area of concern to the mayor was reorganizing human resources, according to Sviridoff's report.

The report characterized the field of human resources in New York City as "broad" and providing a "vast array of separate programs." In Sviridoff's view, this was problematic because the programs were operating in the city "with little or no coordination, sometimes working at cross-purposes." The effect on clients was deleterious because they would become puzzled and frustrated. He proposed the city bring together the "now separate efforts in the field of human resources in a comprehensive program."[4]

Sviridoff was confident that the recommendation of a single HRA for the city would bring clarity, eliminate confusion, and improve performance in delivering services. Integration and coordination with other agencies was the "essence" of the proposal, Sviridoff wrote, suggesting that consolidation would facilitate interagency relationships.[5]

However, the plan of achieving dramatic change through coordination soon ran into problems. One issue even before the establishment of the HRA was the lack of resources available for the job. At the end of the report, Sviridoff remarked, "The fact is that we must move mountains—those that block access to opportunity. We are organizing ourselves for the task. Now we need the resources to carry it out."[6] But it also turned out that bureaucratic coordination was harder to achieve and less effective than had been hoped.

From the beginning, there was skepticism among public administration experts about whether pulling such a wide range of organizations together under the aegis of one agency would work. Well before Lindsay was elected, the idea of subsuming many programs under a single agency had come up and been critiqued by would-be reorganizers. For example, in 1953, a Mayor's Committee on Management Survey issued a report that asserted, "Nobody, however great a management genius, can directly and personally manage such an array of diverse agencies. They exceed the span of management control. This has led some people to advocate grouping all activities under ten or twelve large departments." But the report noted that this approach "would turn many departments into bushel baskets, each with various functions actually unrelated, and would produce within these multi-functional departments many orphan activities."[7]

Social Service Review, a premier journal of social work, reviewed "Developing New York City's Human Resources" and expressed a number of doubts. The journal endorsed bringing under one administrative unit the many antipoverty and community-organizing programs that had developed in the city, especially given their proliferation since the War on Poverty. Yet the article raised some concerns, opining that including traditional welfare (the responsibility of the Department of Public Welfare) with the full roster of education, youth development, labor force, and other programs under one roof was too much of a stretch. In particular, the review was skeptical about merging Public Welfare and Human Resources, with the commissioner of Public Welfare being made administratively responsible to the HRA administrator and no longer reporting directly to the mayor. "It seems quite unlikely that in practice this structure will prevail, for the mayor would certainly need to know at firsthand from his commissioner of welfare the problems and frustrations of administering a program spending more than one-half billion dollars a year," the article reflected. The HRA administrator "could hardly be expected to relay these concerns," the article concluded.[8]

The Early Years of the HRA

Sviridoff became the HRA's first commissioner, but only nine months later, he resigned to become a vice president at the Ford Foundation. Mitchell Ginsberg then became commissioner and replaced many of the people associated with Sviridoff with his own appointees. The agency thus got off to an unstable start and was soon in crisis. One contemporary account noted: "The Human Resources Administration has exhibited a fiscal incompetence of unbelievable proportions. Letters and phone calls concerning vital fiscal matters go unanswered. Vouchers submitted for payment go astray. Checks are mishandled. Payments that should be made are not made. Neighborhood programs miss payrolls and have to borrow from banks."[9]

Under Ginsberg, all sorts of corruption and incompetence became rife at HRA. Ginsberg greatly loosened eligibility and determination rules to the point where a state report found that 13.8 percent of recipients were ineligible.[10] The welfare rolls rose, too. The State Task Force on Social Services described what it perceived as a "welfare explosion" in 1973 when the HRA reported rapid caseload increases during the 1960s and into the 1970s. The HRA reported that the caseload rose rapidly in the early 1960s and accelerated in the middle part of the decade, growing from 328,000 people in 1960 to more than one million by the end of 1969, hitting what was then a peak of 1,275,000 in August 1972 at a cost of $1.2 billion.[11]

Within a few years, the crisis at the HRA had become so acute that expert, activist, and public opinion swung against the organization, and the strategy of coordination through superagencies fell into disrepute. In 1969, only three years after the HRA's creation, the *Proceedings of the Academy of Political Science* devoted an issue to "Challenges and Options for New York," including an article titled "Organizing Community Action" that recommended: "One step that can and should be taken . . . is the dismantling of the Human Resources Administration."

The author reasoned that "in retrospect, it is apparent that while coordination and integration are desirable, it was a mistake to create a new agency and expect it to deal with the three major components assigned to the Human Resources Administration." The *Proceedings* article noted additional problems. Administration of the antipoverty program was an "extremely delicate and difficult job." The commissioner assuming that responsibility "should have direct access to the mayor." Furthermore, a "key error in establishing HRA was to create a new agency to coordinate two almost nonexistent programs (Manpower and Antipoverty) with one that is well-entrenched: Public Assistance." This, the author maintained, makes coordination difficult. It would be better for the antipoverty program to "have maximum freedom."[12]

We see here a clear expression of a dialectic that pervades discussion of bureaucratic organization and has manifested itself in the history of the HRA: that between coordination and entrepreneurialism. Given that the US Constitution and governmental structure are highly fragmented, should bureaucracies be organized so as to facilitate as much coordination as possible, or should coordination be regarded as a chimerical goal and bureaucracies be organized as entrepreneurial, mission-driven, and independent organizations that concentrate on a given task or goal? The HRA came into existence as a quintessential expression of the coordination strategy. When crises hit—as was inevitable given the wicked nature of the problems the HRA addresses, the struggle for resources it has to make against other agencies, and periodic financial problems—the organizational solution most readily available would be to break off various pieces of the HRA to pursue their own tasks and reduce agency repetition and burden. Such was the recommendation to set up antipoverty programs in their own agency, and so were the decisions made in the 1990s to do so with children's and homeless services. Over the years, Head Start and Manpower Training have been moved in and out of the HRA according to whether the imperative for coordination or entrepreneurialism seemed most appropriate.[13]

Thus, when the David Dinkins administration faced a crisis at the HRA over its management of homeless services and called in Andrew Cuomo to devise a solution, Cuomo concluded that the task of running the city's shelter system had gotten lost in the mass of duties performed by the agency and recommended a shift to the entrepreneurial strategy. The Cuomo Commission report to the Dinkins administration, *The Way Home: A New Direction in Social Policy*, concluded that "the primary responsibility for the City's emergency [shelter] system now rests with H.R.A. The expertise required to implement the Commission's plan, however, is beyond the agency's purview." The commission concluded that "a new entity must be created to develop and implement the City's homeless policies and programs." The envisioned entity would be "small, entrepreneurially styled, and function as a 'general contractor' for the system." The report proposed that the necessary funds "would be provided from those saved from the simultaneous downsizing of H.R.A."[14]

The later decision under Bill de Blasio and Steven Banks to bring homeless services and the HRA back under the single umbrella of the Department of Social Services represented the pendulum swinging back in the direction of the coordination strategy.

Lindsay, Rockefeller, and Johnson

No account of Lindsay's efforts to achieve nonincremental reforms in New York City can overlook the barrier he ran into in the form of opposition from the state's governor, Nelson Rockefeller. Lindsay and Rockefeller were representatives of what is today a largely extinct political species: liberal Republicans. Initially, they got along, with the personally wealthy Rockefeller making Lindsay's first campaign for mayor in 1966 possible through a large campaign donation.[15]

As one historian of liberal Republicanism notes, "Rockefeller would come to be a significant rival of Lindsay's, both personally and on account of his office and the perennial tensions between New York City and state."[16] This raises one theory of the conflict, which is that as the two most powerful chief executives in the state, New York's mayors and governors are fated to clash. The Lindsay/Rockefeller conflict has also been attributed to philosophical differences. The argument goes that Lindsay, an idealistic progressive, and the pragmatic, deal-making Rockefeller were bound to lock horns. There are psychological theories as well, with one contemporary observer referencing an "old buck, young buck syndrome," and a historian of Lindsay's mayoralty claiming, "The schism between Lindsay and Rockefeller was based less on politics or policy than on a personality clash between two proud, ambitious politicians."[17]

The main way the Lindsay/Rockefeller conflict affected city welfare policy was through the governor's appointment in 1971 of a Temporary State Commission to Make a Study of Governmental Operation of the City of New York, known as the Scott Commission after its chair, Stuart Scott. This happened after relations between the mayor and governor had been abysmal for years and after a recent conflict over state aid angered both parties. The commission issued a report that brutally criticized the Lindsay administration's welfare politics and the HRA in particular. An account of that document in *Social Services Review* illustrated "the nature and flavor of the task force's assessment of the New York City Social Services system" with the following quotes:[18]

- "No evidence of conviction that social services are important" (83)
- "Episodic rather than continuous services" (2)
- "Coverage and follow-up that is central to the Social Services network is nonexistent" (2)
- Planning is "pointed in the right general direction but is incomplete, has built-in self-destruct mechanisms, and does not have adequate push behind it" (64)
- "HRA is creating endless frustration, potential conflict and, ultimately, a service vacuum" (3)

- "What we now have is not a system or a network but a patchwork of temporary programs designed to meet emergencies and pressures; we have no mechanism that can give disparate programs coherence" (17)
- "New York City suffered when DSS [Department of Social Services] was run by a social leadership without adequate management support; it will not solve its problems by a shift to management and computer leadership without social services input in either" (19)

The Scott Commission's analysis of the Lindsay administration overall, and the HRA in particular, left their reputations in tatters and established in public opinion that New York City was the epitome of welfare policy dysfunction, a sentiment that endured for decades and still is heard in some right-wing circles.

Without the constitutional power of state governments over cities, the Scott Commission would not have been possible. If cordial relations had been maintained between Lindsay and Rockefeller, the commission might never have come into existence. This is true even though the governance of the city under Lindsay was very flawed and merited a critical examination. As executive director of the Scott Commission Steven Berger admitted years later, Lindsay's complaints that the commission was a political vendetta against him were "partly true."[19]

In short, for the present purposes, the important point about the Scott Commission is that it demonstrated the governor's power to oppose by discrediting the initiatives of a New York City mayor in welfare policy. The subordination of city governments to state governments is a potential barrier to urban nonincremental change that Lindsay was unable to overcome.

There is another chief executive with whom New York City mayors must find a way to get along. The US constitutional structure is such that New York City mayors must deal with federal as well as state administrations. Presidents are harder for the city's mayor to influence than governors. New York City is home to millions of voters, and even gubernatorial candidates whose main bases of support are upstate and on Long Island must do tolerably well with the city's voters if they are to win or hold on to their office. Gotham is a much smaller slice of the electorate for the president than it is for the governor. Moreover, under the electoral college system, a candidate with a one-vote majority gets all of a state's electoral votes; the rest of a state's popular vote beyond that is "wasted." This system encourages presidential candidates to court swing states, which do not include New York, rather than large population centers like New York City. Thus, governors have a much stronger incentive than presidents to cater to the city's voters by working with the mayor. In the Constitution's intergovernmental structure, presidents are at the top of the hierarchy and mayors must get their cooperation, but presidents are much less amenable to the mayor's influence than are governors. Presidents therefore represent a potentially much more formidable barrier to nonincremental change. Mayors must find a way to work with (or at least not work against) presidents.

The distinctive features of Lindsay's mayoralty would not have been possible without a sympathetic administration in Washington. The realigning presidential election of 1964 created a unified government under Democratic control and represented a nonincremental change at the federal level in the presidential/majoritarian style. This led to important changes in the relationship between Washington and big city governments. As Martin Shefter points out, the early 1960s' control over the governments of large northern cities was mostly in the hands of "Democratic machine politicians, businessmen, union officials, civil servants and tax conscious homeowners." But it was another part of the Democratic coalition, middle-class professionals, who populated the task forces that drafted the Great Society legislation. Again, according to Shefter, "Middle-class liberals used the influence they enjoyed in the Kennedy and Johnson administrations to influence the policies, practices, and fiscal priorities of city governments." They used their influence, he explains, to propose "that the federal government extend grants-in-aid to local governments on the condition that they adopt 'innovative' programs to deal with the problems of the poor." Middle-class liberals used their access to the executive branch of the federal government—essentially through grants-in-aid programs of the John F. Kennedy and Lyndon B. Johnson administrations—to influence city governments.[20] Federal aid was a key reason the city's operating expenditures were able to increase by more than 50 percent between 1966 and 1969, as were state aid and increasing tax revenues.[21]

Thus, it came about, as Joseph Viteritti writes, "Lindsay responded to President Lyndon Johnson's Great Society agenda with more enthusiasm than any other mayor in the country."[22] Lindsay's agenda, whatever one thinks of it, would have been impossible without a sympathetic president.

Lindsay's HRA in Retrospective

We are left with the question of how to judge the success of the HRA under Lindsay as a product of government reorganization. Not long after the creation of the agency, Howard N. Mantel, an analyst for the Institute of Public Administration, tried to decide how to evaluate the success of Lindsay's reorganization of New York City government (or of any government reorganization). He noted that objective "criteria are hard to establish or prove," and thus suggested that "perhaps the only measures of success are (a) survival of the innovated system and (b) the decibel readings of approval or disapproval by political actors and observers."[23]

By yardstick b, the fortunes of the HRA have gone up and down. In its planning stages and early months of operation, the agency drew considerable (but not universal) praise from progressive politicians, students of urban politics and public administration, and the media. When the agency lurched into crisis under Ginsberg and through the early 1970s, it seemed like the whole world disowned it as a monstrous bureaucracy and a symbol of the failed liberal approach to urban government, welfare, and politics in general. This negative evaluation continued at least through the early twenty-first century when Vincent J. Cannato, in his book *The Ungovernable City*, concluded, "Lindsay proved unable to make a dent in the welfare explosion. This failure harmed his ability to govern New York and crippled his political ambitions."[24]

After Lindsay left office, his reputation and that of the urban liberalism he represented were so damaged that a reaction against them soon set in. After Lindsay came the Abraham Beame administration, which, as Shefter notes "was discredited by the 1975 fiscal crisis . . . in the eyes of the city's electorate."[25] It is telling to note that in the election of 1965, Lindsay defeated Beame and conservative gadfly William F. Buckley, who got 13 percent of the vote. Soon after this defeat, Buckley "mournfully concluded that conservatism would never be a dominant force in American politics because it 'lacked mass appeal.'"[26] Rightly or not, New York City's distress was widely taken as evidence that the liberal project had failed. Charles R. Morris, in his postmortem of the Lindsay years, *The Cost of Good Intentions*, devotes a chapter to "The End of the Liberal Experiment."[27] In 1977, Buckley's book-length account of his 1965 campaign was reissued in a "Vindication Edition," implying that everything conservatives had warned about had come true. Conservatives were quick to fill the vacuum left by the decline of liberalism. From 1978 to 2013, New York City would be governed by three mayors to the right of Lindsay with only a four-year interregnum of the liberal Dinkins. No mayor tried to develop a distinctly liberal welfare policy until Bill de Blasio was elected in 2014. The feedback effect of the failure of Lindsay's welfare policies was very strong.

In recent years, the HRA and Lindsay have gotten better press. In 2014, the distinguished scholar of New York City bureaucracy David Rogers noted that in his second term, Lindsay was able to turn the agency around considerably. Rogers noted that from 1971 to 1972, "the Human Resources Administration made significant productivity gains." The agency, previously beset by a high incidence of fraud in the distribution of welfare checks, established a fraud control program that recovered more than $2.4 million from the issuance of duplicate checks. Furthermore, Rogers noted that the agency established an error accountability program, eliminated a backlog of twenty-eight thousand Medicaid applications, and opened ten new application centers, thus eliminating long waiting lines and reducing fraud. The agency implemented a new state-mandated work relief program, referred more than sixty-two thousand employable welfare recipients to the state employment agency for jobs, placed more than six thousand recipients in work relief positions in city agencies, and implemented the Emergency Employment Act, resulting in employment for four thousand people.[28]

Rogers also correctly notes that "when Lindsay took office, New York's municipal government could best be characterized as a 'slow change' system, operating more to maintain the status quo than to adapt to the vast changes it was confronting."[29] In other words, the city was barely able to generate a bit of incremental change because, as Wallace Sayre and Herbert Kaufman wrote in their iconic 1960 pluralist account, *Governing New York*, the "ordering of the city's political relationships is [such] that every proposal for change must run a gauntlet that is often fatal."[30] Lindsay undertook the necessary task of breaking the logjam, using planning and coordination as his main strategies. He succeeded to a degree that has not been fully appreciated. Rogers is again on point when he writes that "Lindsay was a leading figure in applying rational management techniques to managing big city government, [whose] . . . initiatives in this regard merit closer examination than they have been given in the past." The reforms meriting reexamination, he maintained, include "the superagency, performance-based budgeting, project management, a productivity program, decentralization, and a talent search for people to implement these initiatives. Never before had such an array of management reforms and able people been brought to bear to improve the workings of any city government."[31]

It seems that even the superagency concept, long derided by critics as "far from the administrative panacea it originally appeared to be,"[32] has been vindicated to a certain degree. The diagnosis behind the superagency, which was that the mayor's span of control had to be reduced and greater coordination between agencies had to be achieved, was correct. The superagency concept was a less-than-perfect solution, as the agencies crowded together under a single administrative unit often still worked at cross-purposes. Mayor Ed Koch hit on a better solution to this problem when he expanded the deputy mayor system, with each deputy responsible for a particular functional area in a way that, as one observer put it, "could probably be considered parallel to those of superagency administrators."[33] Under Michael Bloomberg, the position of deputy mayor for Health and Human Services was created, which, one former HRA commissioner noted, "included a somewhat similar array of service programs" as the original HRA superagency.[34]

In terms of criterion b—decibel readings of approval or disapproval—the HRA, though a decided failure early on, looks rather better in historical context. In terms of criterion a—survival of the innovated system—the HRA counts as a success. It celebrated its fiftieth anniversary in 2016 and continues to be the organizational foundation of New York City's extensive human services system. In fact, now that we are well past the shouting and confusion that Lindsay's reorganization effort provoked, we can see that his combination of a large, centralized agency and a decentralized network of community-based antipoverty organizations turned out to be an enduring legacy.[35] If we accept Mantel's plausible claim that "survival in the complex environment of that city [New York] indeed is a legitimate measure of success,"[36] and if we take a long-term perspective, then Lindsay's reorganization of welfare policy counts as a success.

Another reason the HRA merits more respect than it received in the past is that the difficulty of the problems it seeks to address is now better understood than it was in the 1960s. Interestingly, the same year the Scott Commission issued its devastating critique of the HRA, 1973, saw the publication of an iconic article that was one of the first and most influential recognitions of the depth of the challenges faced by welfare and other public agencies. That article was "Dilemmas in a General Theory of Planning," by Horst W. J. Rittel and Melvin M. Webber, and it coined the term *wicked problems*.

The authors argued that the kinds of problems policy seeks to solve, "societal problems . . . are inherently wicked" because "policy problems cannot be definitively described. Moreover, in a pluralistic society there is nothing like the undisputable public good; there is no objective definition of equity; policies that respond to social problems cannot be meaningfully correct or false; and it makes no sense to talk about 'optimal solutions' to social problems unless severe qualifications are imposed first. Even worse, there are no 'solutions' in the sense of definitive and objective answers."[37]

As an example of a problem that is wicked because it defies "definitive formulation," Rittel and Webber pointed to "the poverty problem." They note the many different ways that "problem" might be defined and how each definition suggests a set of plausible causes, which turn out to be interrelated. Merely coming up with an adequate understanding of the problem is so complex in the case of poverty and many other social issues that "the formulation of a wicked problem is the problem!"[38]

The wicked problem argument was one of the first clear formulations of the idea that dealing with social problems such as poverty might be much tougher than it was believed to be in the early days of the Great Society. At some points, Sviridoff's plan for the HRA displayed such overoptimism. Sviridoff was careful to "neither promise nor forecast instant solutions . . . it would be mistaken and dangerous if these proposals gave rise to exaggerated hopes and expectations."[39] Nonetheless, the report reckoned that "realistic planning suggests the need for at least ten years of concerted action," which turned out to be an unrealistic timeline. Quite different from such beginning hopes was the insight reached just a few years later by Rittel and Webber: "Social problems are never solved. At best they are only re-solved—over and over."[40]

Pushed to its limit, the wicked problem concept might seem to end in policy nihilism. One 2015 summary of the research literature on the idea noted: "Followed to its logical conclusion, the intractability of wicked problems, as defined in . . . generic terms, could be taken to mean that grappling with them is a futile endeavor. After all, if they are virtually impossible to comprehend and any solution throws up more problems, then why bother?"[41] Fortunately, few scholars have come to this dismal conclusion. Over the decades, no magic bullet has been found for wicked problems, but research has centered on various ways to manage them through more coordination, continued research, greater innovation, evidence-based policy making, and other means. In the end, wicked problems such as environmental pollution, poverty, crime, and drug abuse are too compelling to simply ignore, but hard experience has shown that miracles are not to be expected. Nathan Glazer devoted considerable effort to documenting the shortcomings of the 1960s social programs, but later in his career, he concluded: "[When] I look at policies that are trying to improve welfare, I think you must keep on trying even if you have not had great success."[42]

My point here is that once expectations of what could be achieved in dealing with poverty and related problems fell to a more realistic level, and the HRA's grosser dysfunctions were overcome, the agency could reasonably be considered more of a success than it had looked to be in its early days.

Can we answer the main question of this book and say that Lindsay's creation of the HRA counts as a nonincremental change and vindicates the legitimacy of urban government by proving change for the better is still possible under the fragmented governmental system of the United States? If we stick with the definition of a nonincremental change as one that breaks a baseline policy and creates a new baseline, rather than simply marginally modifying the old status quo, we can say that the establishment of the HRA was indeed a nonincremental change. A confusing array of antipoverty, welfare, workforce, youth, and education organizations was greatly simplified, and a single agency was put in its place, which has endured for half a century.

However, this nonincremental change was purchased at great cost. Soon after its creation, the HRA descended into chaos, which took a long time to finally resolve. This cast a pall on the reputation of urban reform that has still not entirely died away. If we look at the case histories of nonincremental change recounted in Marc Landy and Martin Levin's *The New Politics of Public Policy*, we do not see such early organizational chaos followed by long periods of recovery. For quite a while, the HRA looked like it might turn out to be at best a pyrrhic victory. If we are looking for a successful change that clearly legitimates the promise of liberal democratic government in big cities, we have to look at the other case histories considered in this book.

2

THE HRA UNDER GIULIANI'S FIRST TERM

This chapter and chapter 3 examine a much-ballyhooed urban policy change: welfare policy in New York City under Rudy Giuliani.[1] Certainly, Giuliani and his supporters thought the mayor had brought about what I call nonincremental change, even though they did not use this term. About midway through his term, Giuliani announced that his goal was nothing less than "to end welfare by the end of this century completely." Even before then, his supporters were hailing the mayor's changes as "the most radical welfare reform New York has ever seen."[2] Critics agreed that great changes had taken place—for the worse. But the point is that there was change. Among the developments most frequently pointed to as evidence of radical change are the following:

- A sharp reduction in the public assistance (PA) caseloads. From the beginning of the Giuliani administration's welfare reform initiative in March 1995 to September 2001, the number of PA recipients declined from 1,160,593 to 463,603, a decline of about 60 percent.[3] By June 2003, the number was down to 421,548.[4]
- The creation of the country's largest work experience program. New York City's Work Experience Program (WEP), with about 21,000 participants in November 1999, became vastly larger than the combined enrollment of the eight other such programs identified by the General Accounting Office in 2000.[5] Before 1996, enrollment in New York City's WEP was fewer than 1,000 clients.

- Organizational restructuring. Like welfare departments across the country, New York City's Human Resources Administration (HRA) strove to transform its critical task from eligibility determination to work promotion. This effort had dramatic organizational consequences. Before 1995, work promotion activities were managed out of what were called employment offices. All other responsibilities, including eligibility determination, were handled by income offices at separate locations. Workers held a collection of titles, including caseworker, eligibility specialist, and principal administrative associate. By 2001, all activities operated out of a single type of office, job centers, and consolidation of workers under the title of job opportunity specialist was well underway.
- The introduction of the Job-Stat system. During the reorganization, HRA managers discovered that their information systems were inadequate for monitoring job center performance. Systems in place at the time generated copious data and statistics, most of it irrelevant to the new task of work promotion, and some of them of dubious quality. A whole new data collection system was developed and used to produce statistics-oriented reviews of how job centers were performing their new tasks. It became possible to accurately measure the percentage of eligible clients who were engaged in some work-related activity. A new agency goal, "full engagement," emerged. Job center directors met regularly with upper agency management and used the new engagement reports to discuss their centers' progress toward full engagement.[6]

In previous years, any one of these changes would have been regarded as a major development. Happening together as they did within a span of about seven years, they present a strong case that a nonincremental change had taken place. But do these changes truly add up to a nonincremental change, that is, one that broke the policy baseline? If yes, how did it take place and what political, economic, and policy developments made such change possible? As we shall see, Giuliani's welfare reforms represented what has been described as an ideational/entrepreneurial model of change, but how does that model work, and how does it differ from other forms of change? What does this story mean for our understanding of urban politics and its potential for major change and democratic legitimacy?

I followed developments at the HRA throughout Giuliani's two terms as mayor. During that time, I interviewed HRA officials, including one commissioner and several assistant commissioners. I also interviewed executives in the mayor's office who oversaw the HRA. I made site visits to local welfare offices and interviewed frontline workers, managers, and office heads. I helped implement a survey of welfare recipients in New York, and this work brought me into frequent contact with HRA staff, management, and clients. I talked with representatives of advocacy organizations that monitor the HRA, including Housing Works, the Welfare Law Center, and Community Food Resources. I consulted court records from various lawsuits brought against the HRA by advocacy organizations, including *Davila v. Hammonds* and *Brukhman v. Giuliani*. I examined city program material on the HRA and reviewed the annual *Mayor's Management Report*. This chapter looks at some history necessary to consider what Giuliani did in welfare policy and the changes he made in his first term. Chapter 3 considers the HRA during Giuliani's second term and evaluates his welfare policy overall.

Before we can understand how Giuliani was able to achieve nonincremental change in welfare policy, we need to look at earlier developments that set the stage for such change to be possible. A revision of the city's charter in the late 1980s, dodging the threat of fiscal constraints imposed by the state, and Mayor David Dinkins's welfare policies are especially important in this regard.

Charter Revision Opens the Door

Giuliani can be thought of as a policy entrepreneur determined to reform welfare and with clear ideas about what that reform should look like. How was he able to realize his ambitions in a city with a highly pluralistic political environment that has classically been thought of as resistant to change? What was it about the city's political environment that made unexpected, nonincremental change in welfare policy possible under Giuliani?

The revision of New York City's charter in 1989 is the key factor here. Before then, for practical purposes, the city's legislative branch consisted of a City Council and a Board of Estimate. The board was composed of the mayor, the comptroller, the City Council president, and the borough presidents; it functioned as the de facto upper house of the legislature.[7] The board was the true center of power and had been described as "the center of gravity in the city's political process" and the "queen" of New York's political chessboard.[8] On the other hand, the City Council, the informal lower house of the legislature, was widely derided as "worse than a rubber stamp because it leaves no impression," and before 1989, it never amounted to a center of significant power.[9] Much of the board's power stemmed from its ability to pass capital and expense budgets, a process in which the City Council played a "merely formal and symbolic" role.[10]

The Board of Estimate's presence and power was the specific institutional manifestation of the propensity of New York City politics to settle into stasis. Wallace Sayre and Herbert Kaufman wrote: "The Board of Estimate is a major conservative force in the city's political contest. The Board . . . has an affinity for the *status quo*. Its dominant characteristic is its capacity to absorb, as if it were a great sponge, the constant stream of proposals for change which flow in upon the Board from the Mayor . . . and from all other sources of dynamism in the city."[11]

The metaphor of the Senate and the House as the saucer and teacup of the national legislature helps illustrate the Board of Estimate's stasis-promoting influence. Whether the board was like the Senate of the city, and the City Council, the lower house, was of little importance; the city effectively had a legislature with only an upper house. Every interest group intent on influencing city legislation had to bring its case, practically speaking, to the Board of Estimate, whose members represented at least borough-wide constituencies and were thus able to play various constituencies against each other. While the board played the "slowing-up" or "cooling-down" function of a saucer-like upper house, there was no effective lower house to be the cup, to concentrate and magnify the heat of local interests.

The Board of Estimate's structure, in which populous Brooklyn and relatively sparse Staten Island each received one vote, brought it afoul of the Supreme Court's "one person, one vote" doctrine.[12] Concern about providing electoral opportunities for minority groups sufficient to satisfy the requirements of the Voting Rights Act dissuaded charter reformers from salvaging the board by weighting borough representation. In 1989, voters approved a set of propositions that established a new charter most striking feature of which was the elimination of the Board of Estimate and a strengthening of the City Council to some extent.[13]

With the elimination of the board, the major conservative—or, more exactly, stasis-promoting—force in the city's political system was removed. If the City Council had been strengthened across the board, New York would have gone from not having a lower house to not having an upper house. In fact, the City Council was strengthened in some respects. It inherited the land use powers of the board, thus becoming the final arbitrator of zoning decisions, and was given great powers over the franchising process. But other important powers, especially concerning budgeting, ended up not with the City Council but with the mayor. The most important of these powers was the ability, or duty, to make official revenue estimates on which the city budgeting process was based. Drafters of the new charter balked at assigning this duty to the localistic council. Memories of the 1975 financial crisis were still in everyone's minds, and the city still had to do its budgeting under the potential scrutiny of the Fiscal Control Board established as a result of that crisis.[14] Eric Lane, the counsel to the 1989 Charter Revision Committee, said, "The commission fully believed that the power to estimate revenues was one that should remain with the Mayor. . . . Legislative bodies tend to be inflationary because you try to satisfy people by providing them with benefits for their constituents. Coming out of the near bankruptcy of the mid-70s, everyone was very wary about creating another opportunity to inflate the budget."[15]

The responsibility and resultant power of making the revenue estimates and thus establishing the departure point of the budget process stayed with the mayor.[16] The full reality of this change only broke upon the City Council during the budget battles of 1997. In his state of the city address of that year, City Council President Peter Vallone pointed to a number of "problem areas in the charter that need to be addressed." Prominent among them was "the budget process, where the executive branch has the sole power to make an officially certified revenue estimate. This undermines, and interferes with the Council's right to enact the budget itself, if necessary—a power any legislative branch must have." Vallone went on to argue that without a new charter revision to shore up the relative strength of the City Council, government in the city "slowly slips into government by executive decree."[17]

The upshot of these charter changes was to empower the mayor. The charter revisions made it possible for an entrepreneurial mayor to implement a popular public idea and face little effective legislative opposition.

Renewed Fiscal Oversight Avoided

In a book devoted to how New York City mayors can sometimes achieve major change, one of the most important sets of constraints on the mayoralty that must be considered are the limits on city finances related to the traumatic fiscal crisis of 1975.

The outlines of that crisis are well known and are only briefly noted here.[18] Demographic and economic changes in the 1950s and 1960s made it difficult for the city to continue to provide services needed by its citizens. The Lindsay administration tried to maintain service levels by borrowing money with short-term notes. As these notes came due, they were refinanced and debt piled up. Eventually, major banks became wary of dealing with the city's debt. It may be too much to accuse the banks of "dumping" city paper. But as Ken Auletta notes, the federal Securities and Exchange Commission concluded, "Moreover certain underwriters determined not to purchase additional city notes for their own accounts and for their fiduciary accounts."[19] That was enough to precipitate a crisis. As a result, the city engaged in massive layoffs and lowered service levels but still could not meet its payroll or pay off its debts. The state set up the Municipal Assistance Corporation (MAC) to refinance $3 billion in city short-term debt into state long-term debt. The MAC also imposed auditing procedures on the city and its agencies. But these actions were insufficient to solve the crisis. Eventually, the federal government had to step in and offer loan guarantees so that New York would be able to reenter the bond market. The Emergency Financial Control Board (FCB) was set up to overlook the city's finances. Thus, the city lost much of its autonomy in fiscal affairs as intergovernmental and private-sector actors gained new power over city revenue and spending decisions. Board approval was needed for all city annual budgets, multiyear financial plans, all contracts, and most financial management practices, such as revenue estimating and accounting systems.

In the end, it took the city ten years to demonstrate, as required by law, that it had achieved a regular budget balance, recovery of market access, and repayment of debt guaranteed by the federal government. By then, the city economy was recovering in the 1980s under Ed Koch. On June 30, 1986, to great fanfare, much of the oversight power of the FCB went into sunset. However, if the city were to incur an operating deficit of more than $100 million in any year, by law, the FCB would reemerge with full powers. Otherwise, the oversight powers of FCB after the sunset were not spelled out in state legislation. The FCB's influence on city budget decisions had to be expressed through persuasion rather than formal authority. Thus, the possibility of renewed FCB power over the city's finances, and the loss of the hard-won renewed autonomy, was a continuing constraint on mayors, including Giuliani.

The looming presence of the FCB nonetheless had certain positive effects. According to Giuliani budget director Abe Lackman, the "threat of a Financial Control Board takeover was a constant source of creativity" driving the administration to find ways to keep finances under control.[20] City Council President Vallone found the specter of the board to be of some use. According to Fred Siegel's history of the Giuliani years, "Vallone . . . was, like Giuliani, almost violently opposed to a Financial Control Board takeover of the city's finances. . . . Vallone recognized that the 'FCB threat' was crucial in selling difficult budget decisions to a reluctant council."[21]

In 1996, partly as a result of a revival of the stock market in 1995, the city's economy began to grow for the first time since 1988. This economic upturn pushed the FCB back into the shadows and freed up the mayor's ability to maneuver. Another Giuliani budget director, Joe Lhorta, observed, "The third quarter of 1996 . . . was the first time we felt we could breathe a little easier. Our credit improved and the Financial Control Board finally backed off."[22] In short, by staying the course and with good fortune, the Giuliani administration avoided the possibility of more fiscal constraints and was able to focus on policy change.

National Professional Consensus and Resulting Policy Ideas

As already mentioned, Giuliani was a policy entrepreneur determined to reform welfare, and he had clear ideas about what that reform should look like. What were these ideas, and where did they come from?

Giuliani came to welfare policy with the strong public ideas of "work first," or "rapid attachment." These ideas had been distilled from the rigorous research of MDRC (formerly known as Manpower Demonstration Research Corporation) on welfare-to-work programs and from the academic analyses of the welfare system by Lawrence Mead, David Ellwood, and other scholars. The evidence suggested that training and education programs seeking to move welfare clients into work by developing their human capital—known as human capital development, or HCD programs—were less effective in terms of job placement than programs that quickly attached clients to the labor force to work at low-skilled jobs they were already qualified for (labor force attachment approach, or LFA). How strong was the research base available to the Giuliani administration when it began the dramatic reorientation of the HRA away from an HCD philosophy and toward an LFA direction?

A good summary of what was known about welfare-to-work programs at the time is found in the "Symposium on Welfare Reform" published in the *Journal of Policy Analysis and Management*. The article was written in 1996 just before the passage of the federal Personal Responsibility and Work Opportunity Reconciliation Act (PRWORA). Judith M. Gueron wrote the lead article in the symposium, "A Research Context for Welfare Reform." Gueron was then president of MDRC, the organization that had produced many of the scientific evaluations of welfare-to-work programs that influenced the PRWORA legislation and its less path-breaking predecessor, the Family Support Act (FSA) of 1988. In the article, Gueron notes that welfare reform is difficult because it aims at three conflicting goals: putting welfare clients to work, protecting their children from extreme poverty, and controlling costs. She reports, "For 25 years, reformers have viewed requiring welfare recipients to participate in work-promoting programs as uniquely able to balance these goals. Numerous studies have shown that this approach modestly increased employment and reduced welfare costs. More substantial gains have been achieved by some 'mixed-strategy' programs, which stress immediate job entry for some recipients and employment-directed education or training for others."[23] In other words, by the mid-1990s, the consensus among welfare policy experts was in favor of the LFA approach. Over time, the professional consensus was simplified into slogan-like public ideas that were used by policy entrepreneurs to push for nonincremental change in welfare policy. At the federal level, the public idea was to "end welfare as we know it," and the policy entrepreneur was Bill Clinton. At the state and local levels, the policy idea was "work first," which was taken up by entrepreneurs such as state governors William Weld in Massachusetts and Tommy Thompson in Wisconsin, and by Mayor Giuliani in New York City.

The fact that Giuliani's proposed policies for the HRA were backed up by firm expert consensus was one reason he was able to achieve such dramatic nonincremental change. Certainly, Giuliani was strong-willed to a fault, but the firm analytic basis of his policies gave him and his staff all the more determination to see them implemented at almost any cost. That powerful evidence could be used to convince holdouts and critics and discredit those who believed otherwise. In short, one reason Giuliani was able to achieve nonincremental change at the HRA was the unusually strong professional consensus and research base that supported his proposed policies.

Policy Legacies and Feedbacks

The structural change in the city's charter made nonincremental change more possible. At the national level, a strong expert consensus supported policy entrepreneurs seeking to implement work-first reform. But there were reasons specific to the city's welfare policy that made this forum particularly susceptible to major change.

In New York City, as elsewhere, current social policy is often, through a process of policy feedback, a reaction to past policy.[24] Part of the answer to the question of how the rapid, dramatic welfare policy changes under Giuliani were possible is that such changes were a policy feedback effect of an earlier, strong service orientation of city policy, which proved to be politically impossible to maintain. To understand this feedback effect, we need to briefly trace the development of New York City's welfare policy from the late Koch era through Giuliani.

The FSA of 1988, sponsored by Senator Daniel Moynihan, mandated that all local welfare departments implement the welfare-to-work requirements of its Job Opportunity and Basic Skills Training Program (JOBS) provision. The FSA reform grew out of what was seen as a "new consensus" on welfare policy that supposedly broke the impasse between conservatives eager to cut back welfare benefits and liberals striving to expand or at least maintain them. In essence, the consensus consisted of conservatives agreeing to expand certain services to recipients of Aid to Families with Dependent Children (AFDC) if recipients were required to make all efforts to find work. The heart of this requirement was the JOBS provision, which required each state to develop a program for placing recipients in employment as soon as possible. As one analyst put the matter, "Behind the JOBS legislation is a philosophy about a social contract: You, the client get financial assistance while you're down and out; but we, the society require you, by way of reciprocity, to make an effort to go to work as soon as possible."[25] This was the reciprocal responsibility idea, which under FSA was embodied in federal legislation, but, as we shall see, it was not immediately implemented in New York City.

As the passage of the FSA approached, the city, in an effort to influence the JOBS legislation the state would be obliged to pass, decided to develop its own blueprint for implementing JOBS.[26] In 1988, Mayor Koch assigned this task to the Inter-Agency Work and Welfare Task Force, chaired by William Grinker, commissioner of the HRA. New York City's implementation of JOBS came to be known as BEGIN. The first blueprint of BEGIN emerged in the May 1989 report of the task force.

In the task force blueprint, BEGIN is a conscious attempt to strike a balance between the goals of work and service to clients. As described by the task force, BEGIN "is a hybrid model that . . . *begins* with a modified up-front job search program for all eligible welfare recipients and is *followed* by a client choice model for those who do not find immediate full-time employment" (emphasis added). The distinguishing feature of the proposed BEGIN model was to be its emphasis on a "mandatory up front job search for all eligible public assistance recipients." "Client choice"; that is, an opportunity for clients to select a training or education program that seemed suited to their needs, was reserved for those who had not found employment *after* the job search. If either goal of the program—work or service—received more emphasis, it was work. The task force report stressed that BEGIN was "to establish close ties between work and welfare" and that "the proposed BEGIN model is a system for delivering income and employment assistance which can be expected to make significant inroads in reducing welfare dependency in New York City."[27] In October 1989, the first two BEGIN offices opened and all AFDC recipients in Manhattan were to participate in the program.

The election of David Dinkins as mayor can be thought of as a local political development that strongly effected the city's JOBS implementation, pushing the program much further toward the service end of the continuum than had been planned under Koch. As part of a conscious effort to break with Koch's social policy in a number of areas,[28] BEGIN underwent a major reorganization during the Dinkins administration. The general direction of it was to deemphasize the mandatory, up-front job search and stress earlier and wider client choice of services.[29] The Dinkins administration's *Mayor's Management Report* of September 1990 described the changes to be made in BEGIN, which it characterized as a new program: "The goal of the new program is to increase the proportion of public assistance clients who voluntarily enter employment and training programs, support greater choice of activities, provide more case management and effective support services (daycare capacity will be expanded by 1,260 slots over the next two years), and reduce the need for sanctions. HRA expects this restructured program to help clients make decisions about their future and select activities that will lead to permanent employment and self-sufficiency. The program will emphasize access to services and informed client choice."[30] The up-front job search, through which, under the Koch plans, almost all clients were to pass before having access to such services as skills training, basic education, and supported work, was, under Dinkins, placed on the same plane with such services, and clients were now invited to construct their own sequence of job search and services.

The Dinkins reorganization further emphasized service provision by weakening BEGIN's sanctioning process. In October 1990, BEGIN policy was changed to "help prevent the reduction of participants' benefits if they do not comply with program requirements." Now "several attempts" were to be made to reach recipients who missed an appointment with a BEGIN worker or who did not show up at assignments, and these clients were offered "several opportunities" to settle their case before sanctions began.[31] The Dinkins reorganization made it easier for clients to pick the services in which they would participate and harder for the city to sanction them when their decisions seemed unlikely to lead to a job.

Of course, at the highest levels, BEGIN executives did not describe their strategy in such terms. When asked exactly what BEGIN clients were expected to do, a top executive replied simply that clients were expected to comply with the requirements of the FSA. Pressed for more detail, the executive responded that clients should be in motion, not at rest, and that when they stop, BEGIN was not doing its job.[32] HRA researchers found that while BEGIN executives stressed that clients should "just find work," they had a very unstructured notion of how BEGIN activities were supposed to guide clients to that work. Researchers concluded that the BEGIN administration focused on processing clients smoothly and were unclear on how the process would guide clients to jobs.[33]

While the Dinkins administration was openly emphasizing the service aspect of welfare policy, city welfare rolls were going up for some reason. The upward trend neither began nor ended with the Dinkins administration but continued throughout his term, with the number of public assistance recipients rising from 813,358 in July 1989 to 1,160,593 in March 1995. In this context of rising welfare rolls, BEGIN's service orientation and its apparent reluctance to move clients rapidly off welfare came under great criticism.

BEGIN's strong process orientation did not go unnoticed. Indeed, as far as BEGIN administrators of the time were concerned, since the program was achieving its operational goal of getting clients to participate in services, the process orientation was not considered something that needed to be hidden. But the general goal of work, while never operationalized by BEGIN, remained fixed in the minds of the public and most political actors as the "real" goal of welfare reform. It almost inevitably happens that programs that achieve their operational goals while leaving unrealized their general goals get accused of "bureaucratic pathology."[34] This is what happened to BEGIN.

BEGIN continued to be held to its general goal by most political actors. Critics of the program described its goal as "to get people off the welfare rolls by training them for private jobs" or even "to get recipients into the labor market."[35] BEGIN responded unpersuasively by arguing that it *had* met its goal, which ought to be understood as the operational goal of service participation. This debate was played out before the New York City Council in 1994 when the staff of the council's Finance Division produced an analysis of BEGIN that conceived of the program's goals as follows: "The Finance Division assumes that effectiveness is measured by the ability of the program to move the welfare client off public assistance and, hopefully, into the labor market *at a rate that is greater than the rate without program participation*."[36] This statement emphasized the general goals of the FSA by unambiguously specifying what should reasonably be expected of JOBS implementations regarding those goals. On the basis of an analysis of a random sample of 927 adult AFDC recipients, approximately half of whom participated in the BEGIN program, while half did not, the study found that "for the sample as a whole, the BEGIN program did not significantly increase a participants' chances of leaving AFDC when compared to a non-participant."[37]

BEGIN was defended against the council's criticism by Meg O'Regan, executive deputy commissioner of the HRA, who testified before the City Council: "If the BEGIN program you studied had originally been designed as a labor force attachment program, evaluating the number of participants who found jobs would be the singularly appropriate way to measure it. But BEGIN was not designed as a labor force attachment program. It was designed, several years ago, as a program to identify and address the barriers welfare recipients face in their struggle to get off public assistance. . . . The focus was preparing for the workforce, not getting a job."[38]

In other words, BEGIN's defense against the charge that it had not helped put its clients to work was that this had never been the goal of the program. Preparing for work, not work itself, had been the objective all along. This was not a response that could withstand much political pressure.

Well before Giuliani became mayor, welfare policy in New York City had become even more unpopular than welfare usually is—a sitting duck for an ambitious mayor to react against. Now we can address how Giuliani took advantage of this situation and achieved nonincremental change.

What Changed and What Did Not

As is well known, welfare policy at both the national and state levels changed dramatically in the 1990s. At the national level, the passage of the PRWORA in 1996 was both widely hailed and decried as a landmark in social policy legislation. Before 1996 several states—Wisconsin and Massachusetts among them—in effect broke with national policy by negotiating waivers with the federal Department of Health and Human Services (HHS) and passing state welfare legislation that anticipated many of the innovations of PRWORA. It has been argued that these developments represent nonincremental change in a very specific sense: PRWORA and its state precursors broke with the previous policy of the Social Security Act of 1935 and ended the entitlement status of federal welfare (previously known as AFDC and now Temporary Aid for Needy Families).[39] The story behind PRWORA and state welfare reforms is well known: When expert opinion turned against AFDC, President Bill Clinton successfully reduced that consensus to the slogan or public idea "end welfare as we know it." Congressional Republicans and various governors wanted credit for the reform idea, which by a bidding-up process led to a radical policy outcome, one that broke with (rather than simply modified) the former policy. Told this way, national and state welfare reform is a story with all the elements of the analysis from Marc Landy and Martin Levin's *The New Politics of Public Policy*: expertise, public ideas, policy entrepreneurs, divided government, institutional fragmentation, and nonincremental change.

To understand what happened in New York City, it is important to distinguish that city's welfare reform process from PRWORA and state reforms. Undoubtedly, welfare reform was part of the intellectual climate of the mid-1990s, but New York City took a very different path to reform than did the nation or the early reforming states. At the national and state levels, new welfare legislation dramatically broke with baseline policy, as we have seen. Both nationally and in some states, divided or nearly divided government played an important role in encouraging dramatic change.[40] Neither party wanted to let the other be identified with the popular cause of welfare reform, and legislatures of one party outbid executives of the other to frame the most thorough reform legislation. This bidding-up process was one of the engines that resulted in a nonincremental outcome.

Reform came about differently in New York City. Giuliani began the process in February and March 1995, about a year before PRWORA was passed. His administration deliberately did not request a waiver from the HHS. According to one high administration official, "The Moynihan structure [i.e., FSA, the national welfare law previous to PRWORA] was all that we needed" to implement welfare reform.[41] In other words, New York City's welfare reform did not break with baseline legislation and in fact deliberately declined to do so through the waiver process. Nor was there a bidding-up war between the mayor and the City Council, even though they were controlled by different parties. Throughout the period discussed here, the City Council remained in Democratic hands and fixedly in the antireform corner, while the Republican mayor championed the cause of dramatic, immediate change. With the City Council opposed to welfare reform in the style of PRWORA, Giuliani needed to demonstrate only modest support for the idea in order to claim credit as the city's foremost welfare reformer. Yet, as we have seen, from the beginning to the end of his administration, Giuliani pushed for dramatic changes, some of which (e.g., WEP) were the most radical in the country. What explains his commitment to welfare reform over and above the call of ordinary politics?

To answer this question, we must note that the welfare reform process in New York City can be distinguished from another, more traditional model of change: the executive-majoritarian model.[42] In this model, dramatic change happens when exogenous events—a depression, an extraordinarily weak opposition—result in overwhelming, simultaneous executive and legislative victories for one party, which then has a brief window of opportunity to pass long-delayed proposals. The New Deal and Great Society initiatives are classic examples of this model. Giuliani's victory over Dinkins in 1993 was not overwhelming, nor was it precipitated by some extraordinary shock or opportunity, and again, the City Council stayed in Democratic hands through Giuliani's administrations.

Yet the Giuliani victory was obviously essential to the success of welfare reform in New York City. This is not simply because the win represented the displacement of a "service-demanding" coalition by a coalition of "money providers," although this change was in itself likely to have an effect on the direction of welfare reform. Yet the specific dynamic of this particular election was to reinforce that impact. Dinkins narrowly defeated Giuliani in the general election of 1989 with a coalition of a highly mobilized Black community, Latino voters who were skeptical of a Republican candidate, and a significant minority of the white population that responded to Dinkins's call for racial and social depolarization.[43] By 1993, after the city had had the experience of its first Black mayor under its belt, voter concerns changed somewhat. Giuliani won in that year by winning over just enough former Dinkins supporters who now had "a desire to see more toughness and competence in the mayor."[44] It makes sense to see the mayoral election as a replay of the choice between reconciliation on one hand and toughness and competence on the other, with toughness and competence coming out as the winners after reconciliation had its chance.

Thus, one result of the specific dynamics of the 1993 mayoral election was that key officials in the Giuliani administration interpreted the election as a vote against poor management and a mandate for administrative reform. Indeed, the new administration's sense that it had a mandate to reverse the trends of the Dinkins years and that this could be done through improved administration cannot be overstated. One official specifically blamed Dinkins's inaction for the steady rise in the welfare caseload during his term.[45] Another official believed that when Giuliani came to office, there was a general sense that the city had grown beyond the ability of any administration to manage it. But this official said that "the mayor [i.e., Giuliani] believes that the city can be managed" and that early in his term he had concluded that a reduction of the welfare caseload was an important management goal.[46] Both officials expressed disdain for the idea that policy outputs should be attributed to forces outside administrative control. How could anyone who expected to make a difference through government believe that?[47] This conviction that administration was the key variable in effecting outcomes found expression in Giuliani's decision not to ask for federal waivers from FSA requirements. As far as Giuliani administration officials were concerned, the important thing to change was not welfare law but welfare administration.

Furthermore, the specific political dynamics of the 1993 election also partly account for the nature of the administrative initiatives through which the Giuliani administration sought to reform welfare. In interviews, city officials said they thought of local welfare reform as a matter of renegotiating the social contract around the core idea that one who takes something from the city must give something back. This notion of "reciprocal obligation" had been developed long before Giuliani and outside of a specifically New York context by welfare policy analysts and in the FSA.[48] There were, however, political reasons specific to the New York City of the early 1990s that reciprocal obligation became the keystone of the Giuliani welfare reform effort.

As discussed elsewhere, the perceived "failure of liberal homeless policy" in New York City played a significant role in the defeat of David Dinkins and the decline of New York City's progressive coalition.[49] Very briefly, the Dinkins administration's policy of making refurbished apartments more easily available to families in homeless shelters was widely seen as causing an increase in the number of families entering shelters in 1990. Many political actors believed that the city's "right to shelter" policy had produced unwanted side effects. This feeling was reinforced when, in 1992, a mayoral task force headed by Andrew Cuomo (son of then-governor Mario Cuomo and later governor himself) issued its report, *The Way Home*. The report concluded that "the facts about homelessness, combined with the indisputable evidence of policy failure, strongly suggest that the City's current strategy, however well intended, must change.... Radical, structural change of the system is necessary."[50] The report made many specific suggestions, but the idea at the heart of them all was the following: "The emergency shelter system must incorporate a balance of rights and responsibilities. A social contract and a mutuality of obligation must exist between those receiving help and society-at-large."[51]

Thus was born a policy idea: "balance rights and responsibilities." It was not likely to be ignored because, in the highly competitive political environment of New York, all parties had strong incentives to "claim" a potentially popular policy idea.[52] Who would take it up? Though he had organized the Cuomo commission, Dinkins chose not to sponsor its main idea, probably because he had been a prominent supporter of the strictly rights-based approach the commission was implicitly criticizing. And so a political opportunity was handed to Giuliani, who pounced on the ideas developed in *The Way Home*. Giuliani campaigned on a platform of introducing a "mutual responsibility" model in the shelter system. Thus, this conception of social policy reform came with Giuliani to City Hall, where it shaped the specific outline welfare reform was to take. That outline heavily and almost uniquely emphasized work experience as the most obvious way welfare clients could "give something back."

Thus, Giuliani can be thought of as a political entrepreneur, marketing the public idea of balancing rights and responsibilities and winning electoral support with it. As discussed, this idea was broached in New York City in the context of homeless policy. Indeed, under Giuliani, the idea of reciprocal responsibilities was implemented in the homeless shelter system through a plan involving privatizing shelters.[53] How did the reciprocal responsibilities idea come to be applied to welfare policy, and why did it take the form of perhaps the strictest workfare policy in the country?

The more than usually unpopular and apparently discredited welfare policy Giuliani inherited made it an enticing target for an ambitious mayor seeking to institute and take credit for a major reform. The elimination of the Board of Estimate gave him the power to make the attempt.

In short, Giuliani's success as a policy entrepreneur with the public idea of reciprocal obligations, the mandate for strong administrative competency he believed he had received in the election, and the negative policy feedback that set up the city's welfare policy as politically weak and especially vulnerable to challenge, all worked together to produce a mayor determined to reform welfare in a way that no one before him had been. But the most radical changes in city welfare policy came during Giuliani's second administration, discussed in chapter 3.

3

THE HRA UNDER GIULIANI'S SECOND TERM

Jason Turner and the Development of Job Centers

Welfare reform during Rudy Giuliani's first term focused mostly on placing welfare clients into work programs, especially in the city's Work Experience Program (WEP). The reform process continued apace in his second term. Indeed, in some respects, reform in the second term was even more radical as Giuliani took on the formidable task of converting welfare offices—which at one point had been called "Income Maintenance Centers"—into "Job Centers" and changing the critical task of frontline workers from eligibility determination to job development. In substance, Giuliani set out to accomplish one of the most difficult types of bureaucratic reform: changing the organizational culture of a large public agency. Realizing this major change became the job of Jason Turner, who had helped Wisconsin governor Tommy Thompson implement welfare reform. He became Human Resources Administration commissioner in 1997.

Another way of thinking about nonincremental change at the agency level is to see the baseline practice of an agency as its culture, defined as a strong sense of mission focused on performing a key critical task. Nonincremental change at this level would be the repudiation of the old culture and its critical task, coupled with the refocusing on a new task supported by a new sense of mission. To accomplish this, Giuliani threw his administration into changing the critical task of the Human Resources Administration (HRA) from eligibility determination to work placement with unusual zeal.

William Grinker and Dennis Smith wrote about the transformation of the HRA under Giuliani and described the depth of the change. They observed that before national legislation was passed, the Giuliani administration "embraced that welfare reform agenda whole heartedly, some would say with a vengeance." Grinker and Smith noted that the "change is clearly captured in the language used" in the Mayor's Management Report (MMR) to introduce the agency. They noted that in 1993, the MMR had stated: "The Human Resources Administration provides income support and social services to New York City's needy residents." In comparison, Smith and Grinker observed that by 1998, it had been changed: "The Human Resources Administration protects the health and welfare of the City's neediest residents by providing temporary economic and social service support and assisting them, whenever possible, to achieve economic independence." They also observed that the HRA had embraced a new critical task and that "getting people 'off welfare' served the management of HRA," much as reducing crime became the (mostly) unquestioned and galvanizing goal of the police department.[1]

The change in organizational culture at the HRA under Giuliani went much deeper than simply a new mission statement. The critical task of an organization is performed by its frontline operators, and when that task is strongly embraced and supported by the organization, one can say the organization has a sense of mission, as James Q. Wilson convincingly argues in his classic account *Bureaucracy: What Government Agencies Do and Why They Do It*. Wilson notes that the tasks performed by operators are rooted in the situational imperatives and naturally occurring incentives they face and are not easily changed by directives from higher-level executives alone.[2] Without major changes in the way operators are rewarded and sanctioned and in their overall environment, a real change in mission, as opposed to a rewritten mission statement, is hard to achieve.

Under Giuliani, the goal was real mission change away from eligibility determination to work placement. This required changing the responsibilities of frontline operators by eliminating two positions—eligibility specialist and employment specialist—and combining their responsibilities in a new job classification, the job opportunity specialist (JOS). The idea was to achieve unified case management, under which "one frontline worker is able to provide several different services for a client: screening for eligibility, social-service counseling and job placement."[3] Not all parties were enthusiastic about the new JOS position. When workers were offered additional pay as an incentive to convert to the new classification, some unions objected because not all workers were being offered a raise.[4] Some who converted from eligibility or employment specialist to JOS reported that "the work is more satisfying and the ability to help clients is greater."[5] Others, while they "seemed to agree with the general shift in policy and programs toward employment," were "disappointed that their primarily [sic] role in this area is to make sure clients know they have to work and then refer them elsewhere for services."[6] Whether the new critical task of job development was performed by the JOS workers or by the vendors to which they referred clients, the shift in mission from eligibility determination to work placement was accomplished. Giuliani's welfare reform broke the baseline in terms of organizational culture.

At the HRA, the process of implementing that change was traumatic. The agency's local offices were to be transformed from income support centers to job centers. HRA staff had long embraced eligibility determination and benefit provision as their critical task and were backed up by federal requirements that mandated that applicants for food stamps and Medicaid be processed for benefits on their first visit. Under Commissioner Turner, job center staff were told not to accept such applications until a later visit; day one was to be devoted to evaluating an applicant's work prospects and filling out a job profile.[7] Lisa Fitzpatrick, a chief program officer at the HRA and eventually administrator of the agency under the Eric Adams administration, had worked at the agency for more than three decades. In an interview, she described the "sea change" that happened under Giuliani:

> MAIN: Tell me about the history of HRA and changes at HRA over this thirty-year period of time. I'm eager to hear.
>
> FITZPATRICK: I think the most dramatic change that we saw was under the Giuliani administration. Because all before that, we had income support/income maintenance centers . . . the focus was primarily on just providing financial assistance to clients. So it was really under the Giuliani administration when . . . we moved to the focus [of] not necessarily just . . . making sure that people got benefits, but looking at their employability and then trying to make sure that they were matched to work. . . . That was in my time, thirty-plus years with HRA, that was the biggest change in how we did business. . . . Absolutely, that was absolutely the biggest.
>
> MAIN: What's it like to go through a big change like that? How did it affect you?
>
> FITZPATRICK: I think for a lot of us it was tumultuous. It was stressful. It was difficult to change the mindset of employees who were driven [by] benefits-first. I remember we had this one employee, and when they came and they said we weren't going to give the [benefits] application on day one, and first day we're going to give this job profile, she absolutely said, "No way, it's not going to happen. You have to give the application on the first day." And [the] administration didn't

want to hear that. As a matter of fact, I think I remember them giving us a book. It was called "First Break All the Rules" . . . this was under Turner's administration. So you do what you're told to do first, you do what the agency wants to do, and then we'll work it all out. . . . Well, we got sued, and we've been dealing with the lawsuits ever since.[8]

The lawsuit alluded to was *Reynolds v. Giuliani*, in which a federal district court concluded that, just as the HRA staffer had said at the beginning, the application process developed under Turner violated federal food stamp and Medicaid regulations. In 1999, the court stopped the conversion of income support centers to job centers. The injunction on the conversion was lifted two years later in March 2001, but other provisions of the court's decision remained in place to prevent the agency from illegally discouraging clients from applying for benefits.[9] In this and other matters, the administration's failure to heed its employees' concerns made implementation of welfare reform unnecessarily rocky.

The point is that nonincremental change, in the sense of changing the baseline task-based organizational culture and establishing a new one, was achieved at the HRA. But the experience was traumatic. Years later, when Mayor Bill de Blasio and Commissioner Steven Banks tried their hand at achieving major change at the agency, they endeavored to avoid the trauma with a more cooperative approach to reform.

The Mayor, the Governor, and the President

As noted in the introduction, the dependence of cities on state governments is a potential barrier to urban change. Reforming mayors need the cooperation (or at least passive acquiescence) of the governor. Something must be said here about how Giuliani dealt with this barrier, which John Lindsay and other mayors never overcame.

Giuliani's relations with the two governors he served under—Mario Cuomo from January to December 1994 and George Pataki from January 1995 to December 2001—had their ups and downs but generally were not as infamously hostile as were those between Nelson Rockefeller and Lindsay or Andrew Cuomo and Bill de Blasio. To manage the city's budget and with regard to homeless policy, Giuliani needed Cuomo's cooperation. Given that these men were of opposing parties, cooperation would not necessarily be forthcoming.

Wayne Barrett depicts Cuomo as having an informal "understanding" with and offering quiet support to Giuliani and expecting to receive no more than the same from the mayor in his reelection campaign of 1994 for a fourth term as governor. Apparently, Cuomo would have been satisfied if Giuliani had simply been neutral in his race against Republican gubernatorial candidate George Pataki.[10] But in October 1994, falling tax receipts, overly optimistic economic projections, and other problems opened up an $800 million gap in the city's budget.[11] Giuliani needed a lot of money, and fast, from the governor.

To get what he needed, Giuliani deployed a bold stratagem: he crossed party lines with much fanfare and endorsed the Democrat Cuomo rather than the relatively unknown and bland Republican Pataki. At the time, an enormous fuss was made of this maneuver, with state political operatives saying that Giuliani was "trying out a new political doctrine" and "defining a new national role for a big-city Republican. He's endorsing policies, not people."[12] Similarly, Giuliani claimed that he was shattering political paradigms, saying the "voters want the gridlock and the partisan politics to come to an end."[13]

In a certain sense, Giuliani's gambit failed. At first, Cuomo received a big bump in the polls after the mayor's endorsement, but he lost his reelection bid, and Giuliani had to deal with Pataki—after he had spurned him. Pataki reportedly would not speak to the mayor for weeks.[14] Given that Giuliani's dramatic party crossover bore no electoral fruit, no new era of bipartisanship began.

Even so, Giuliani got what he was looking for out of his Cuomo endorsement. Cuomo had the Municipal Assistance Corporation—a state authority that had been established after the 1975 fiscal crisis—finance a $230 million severance package that allowed Giuliani to cut thousands of workers from the city payroll through early retirement buyouts rather than massive layoffs, thus greatly helping the mayor resolve his budget problems.[15]

The departing Cuomo also helped Giuliani resolve a problem he had been facing in homeless policy. A regulation promulgated in 1983 by the State Department of Social Service (SDSS) required that eligible homeless applicants for shelter be provided with emergency housing "immediately." If there was no space in the shelter system and no other housing could be found, having applicants stay overnight in an intake office was not considered "emergency housing" and thus was a violation of the regulation. The high demand for and frequent shortage of available shelter spaces meant that overnight stays in offices were frequent. This phenomenon repeatedly opened the city to court action by advocates for the homeless. Justice Helen Freedman, who heard such cases, was unsympathetic to the city's necessity arguments. After years of frustration, the city received some relief from Mario Cuomo who, on almost his last day in office, had the Office of Temporary and Disability Assistance (the renamed SDSS) promulgate a new regulation specifying that emergency housing was to be provided not immediately but "within 48 hours of application." Steven Banks, the city's leading homeless legal advocate who eventually served as de Blasio's commissioner of the HRA, plausibly charged that the more lenient regulation was part of a "political payoff" by the governor to the mayor.[16]

Giuliani gained some material advantages from endorsing Cuomo, and then dealing with the victorious Pataki did not turn out to be so difficult. As the *Economist* pointed out, "But for all his [Giuliani's] and Mr. Pataki's obvious discomfiture, each needs the other's help in controlling the state's and the city's spiraling budget deficits."[17] Very tellingly, when it turned out that the new regulation that Cuomo issued did not convince the courts that the city really did have forty-eight hours to find emergency housing for shelter applicants, Pataki helped the city by promulgating yet another regulation that was even more lenient in terms of deadlines. Unlike the wealthy, nationally famous, and patrician Rockefeller, the mild and low-profile Pataki saw no point in nursing a grievance against a New York City mayor of his own party. Giuliani's apparently risky strategy for dealing with a governor turned out to have no downside.

The point here is that Giuliani successfully used a strategy for overcoming the constitutionally weak position of mayors and getting unexpected support from the governor. Bipartisan cooperation is one way to overcome barriers to change, and we often hear laments about how lacking it is in today's political environment. In this case, *bipartisanship* meant only that two politicians of different parties were willing to cooperate for their mutual benefit, not that partisan differences had melted away. But Giuliani's risky support of Cuomo shows that bipartisanship of a limited sort is still possible and can sometimes overcome constitutional barriers to change, such as the often fraught relationship between mayors and governors.

The other chief executive whom New York City mayors must find a way to work with is the president. Like Lindsay, whose progressive agenda at first dovetailed nicely with Lyndon Johnson's Great Society program, Giuliani's work-first welfare reforms were a local variation on Bill Clinton's drive to end welfare as we know it. Giuliani and Clinton were both policy entrepreneurs selling the idea of welfare reform. Thus, Giuliani's push for nonincremental change in welfare policy met no opposition from Clinton.

Alternative Accounts

The most important conclusion to be drawn from the foregoing analysis is that in this case, nonincremental change in a highly constrained urban environment was possible. Indeed, it was possible in precisely the urban environment that historically has been characterized as one of stasis, ungovernability, or structural imperatives: New York City. The key factors that made this change possible were the city's highly competitive political environment in the early 1990s; a professional consensus and strong research base supporting work-first welfare reforms; the development, nationally and locally, of a popular set of public ideas related to welfare reform and reciprocal obligations; a policy feedback effect of the welfare policy of the Dinkins years, which left the public and policy elites skeptical of alternative approaches to welfare reform; and the emergence of a skillful policy entrepreneur who was committed to institutional reform through executive power. Another crucial factor was the unforeseen impact of the 1989 city charter revision, which eliminated the only institution that had historically been a counterbalance to the mayor's power. The revision placed the power of making authoritative revenue estimates in the hands of the mayor, which allowed a skillful executive to outmaneuver the legislature in the budgetary process, and thus undermined the legislature's power over the city bureaucracy. A mayor determined to restructure that bureaucracy faced little opposition. Also significant was Giuliani's deft political maneuvering that mostly kept the governors he served under from blocking the changes he sought.

In general, this analysis is similar to that put forward by Marc Landy and Martin Levin's *The New Politics of Public Policy*. It may therefore suggest that the nonincrementalist theory of political change can be usefully applied not only at the federal but also the local level of US politics. Before we draw this conclusion, several qualifications are in order.

First, from the perspective of the ideational-nonincremental model, the importance of charter revision is unexpected. Charter revision was essentially a formal amendment of the city's constitution. Formal constitutional amendments do not play much of a role in the case studies of change in *New Politics*. Charter revision is really a type of structural change, and thus the reform of the HRA represents not a pure example of an ideational-nonincremental change but a mixed, ideational-structural case. But charter revision alone would not have resulted in the HRA reforms described here. The development of the public idea of "reciprocal obligations," the emergence of a policy entrepreneur willing to promote that public idea, and the negative feedback of what was perceived as the welfare policy failures of the Dinkins administration were not the result of charter revision. Charter revision was a structural change that unexpectedly strengthened the office of the mayor vis-à-vis the legislature and was thus a crucial prolegomenon to change. The process by which that office came to be occupied by a policy entrepreneur with a well-developed idea applicable to welfare policy otherwise closely follows the ideational-entrepreneurial model.

Thus far, we have been using the ideational-entrepreneurial model from *New Politics* as a way of understanding urban nonincremental change. But there is another school of political analysis that was developed to account for political change at the city level (among other reasons). Regime analysis specifically seeks to "give politics analytic weight equal to that of economic structure . . . (without) returning to a voluntaristic pluralism." John Mollenkopf develops such a "'regime' or 'dominant coalition'" analysis to explain "the rise and fall of the Koch coalition in New York City politics."[18] Regime analysis represents another way of accounting for certain types of change in urban politics.

An alternative account of the HRA reform involves extending Mollenkopf's regime analysis of New York City politics through the Giuliani years. Such an extension might run as follows: the forces led by Ed Koch represented the essentially conservative "dominant governing coalition" that more often is in power in New York. The rise of Dinkins represented the success of the rival, "progressive" regime that included Black and Hispanic people, liberal white people, and unions. Dinkins's defeat four years later by Giuliani represented the reemergence of the old, conservative, dominant governing coalition, which had been waiting, phoenix-like, to rule once again. When the dominant governing coalition was back in power under Giuliani, it went about making policy changes that were consistent with its essentially conservative nature, which included restructuring the HRA to implement a work-oriented welfare reform. It might be claimed that the changes we have documented at the HRA were due not to public ideas, policy entrepreneurs, and so forth but to the victory of a political regime with the will and capacity to remake policy in its conservative image.

The best response to this counterclaim would be to acknowledge the essential accuracy of Mollenkopf's regime analysis and recognize that the fall of Dinkins and rise of Giuliani was indeed a regime change. However, the political change we are seeking to explain here is not the transition from Dinkins to Giuliani but the transformation of the HRA under Giuliani. From the fact that the conservative dominant governing coalition was back in power, we cannot conclude that nonincremental change at the HRA was inevitable. That same conservative coalition was in power under Koch, yet Koch never undertook the kind of dramatic reorganization of the HRA that we have seen here. Regime theory and ideational-entrepreneurialism seem to be complementary (not rival) theories of urban political change. They explain different types of political change. At the city level, regime theory makes the important point that "politics counts" and that the defeat of one regime coalition by another can significantly affect the lives and interests of many people. Regime change accounts for the general direction of change, with a conservative regime catalyzing conservative change and a progressive regime making progressive change. The ideational-entrepreneurial paradigm, in contrast, illuminates policy-level (rather than overall city-level) change. It explains why, for example, under Giuliani, change came to the HRA rather than, say, the Department of Housing Preservation and Development (no strong public ideas about housing policy had been developed and disseminated, no policy entrepreneur made housing policy the center of their campaign, no policy legacies left housing policies especially vulnerable). The ideational-entrepreneurial paradigm also tells us about the magnitude of change. Regime analysis can tell us whether change will be in a conservative or progressive direction, but whether such change will mark a sharp break in baseline policy and whether it will involve dramatic reorganizations, including shifts in the culture of prominent bureaucracies, depends on whether the various elements of the new politics described above are in play.

Another account of Giuliani's brand of welfare reform that deserves some attention is *Free Labor: Workfare and the Contested Language of Neoliberalism* by John Krinsky. Krinsky's work offers a potential challenge to the main project of this book, which is to identify how nonincremental change is possible in urban politics. In effect, Krinsky argues that besides the barriers to change discussed here, there are thick webs of cultural/linguistic "trenches" that prevent progressives from successfully contesting the hegemonic claims of neoliberal elites about welfare and work.

To document these trenches, Krinsky relies on an elaborate block model analysis that produces complex diagrams that he claims show the interconnections between ideas, actors, and contexts in the debate over the WEP from mid-1993 through mid-2004 as it was recorded in the pages of the *New York Times* and the *Daily News*. In this, Krinsky draws on Antonio Gramsci's idea of "trench warfare."

Gramsci held that the liberal democracies of the West had a deeply dug set of defenses, a whole set of social structures, to absorb and resist change. Krinsky believes such a set of trenches existed in New York City under Giuliani in the form of networks of speakers and discursive practices that made it difficult for progressives to contest work-first welfare reform. Krinsky suggests that an accurate map of these trenches could inform new strategies that would eventually achieve victory. He hopes to produce such a map with his elaborate block model diagrams. At several points, he notes the similarity between his diagrams of blocks and connections and Gramsci's vocabulary of blocs and trenches.[19]

How convincing is Krinsky's elaborate documentation of an apparently formidable network of city trenches? The question is hard to answer because the block model diagrams are extremely difficult to understand.[20] Other scholars have found the block modeling analysis of contentious politics to be sometimes obscure.[21] And one reviewer of *Free Labor*, though he praised its diagrams for illustrating the mechanisms postulated by the social network school of analysis at work, found them "not easy to grasp."[22]

In articles on welfare reform under Giuliani that do not rely on the block model methodology, Krinsky makes some points that are easier to understand.

In one he claims, "New York City's entire welfare reform program—from 1994 onward—took place in a milieu of rent-seeking and corruption."[23] Krinsky notes that the Giuliani administration negotiated a contract with union leaders that allowed work placement of WEP participants in unionized city agencies. When the contract was offered to the membership for approval, the leaders stuffed the ballot boxes to get it approved. Krinsky convincingly judges that "a clean union could not have passed the contract and likely would not have acceded to the expansion of WEP."[24] However, he does not show that union corruption was essential to welfare reform implementation in New York City.

Similarly, Krinsky discusses corruption charges against some figures in the welfare reform policy network. Giuliani's HRA commissioner, Jason Turner, was accused by the city comptroller, Alan Hevesi, of a conflict of interest regarding his handling of a city work program contract with Maximus, a private government services firm. An article in the *Village Voice* reported, "An appellate court panel had ruled in October 2000 that the allegations presented to it weren't enough to block the contracts," but it noted other concerning relations between Turner and Maximus.[25] Krinsky acknowledges: "The rent-seeking and corruption that occurred within these networks, however, could generally be isolated and not taint the cores of the policy networks ... the programs themselves—including cutting assistance for poor people and privatization—remain largely untainted as well."[26]

In another article, Krinsky argues that certain concepts central to the conflicts over workfare had a two-edged or dialectical nature that presented dilemmas for progressives campaigning against welfare reform. For example, "Were WEP workers 'workers' or 'welfare recipients'?"[27] Considering WEP participants as workers and using standard unionizing techniques to organize them presented problems. "The pragmatics of worksite organizing were fraught with obstacles. The regular high turnover in welfare rolls and thus at workfare worksites was compounded by the flexibility with which WEP workers were deployed. Once organized, workers in a worksite organizing committee might be transferred to different worksites."[28]

On the other hand, if WEP participants were welfare clients, then the progressive response would seem to be to reject work-first policies and call for better training and other human capital development programs. Krinsky sees a problem with this response, which is that "the rhetoric of human capital is consistent with neoliberal theory of labor pricing, whereby workers are paid what they deserve based on the value they add to the labor process." Demanding skill training in welfare programs is not an optimal progressive response, according to Krinsky, because "training for skills does not, by itself, lead to better placement into labor markets," though he allows that it is "potentially important in individual cases." Labor markets "must be structured to have higher- and lower-skilled positions that reward skill," he writes. Skill is defined by the "relative scarcity of specialized savoir-faire" and kept scarce by closed networks of workers who control part of the production process.[29] Thus, Krinsky maintains that "as criticism of workfare's failure to provide adequate education and training became a dominant discursive strategy among regime opponents, their political claims grew ever closer to the foundational, individualist ideas of neoliberal theory."[30] An opposition that starts out progressive is dialectically transformed to accommodate neoliberalism. Krinsky resolves this dilemma by concluding that however inadequate human capital development welfare strategies might be from a left-progressive viewpoint, "in this context, claims for education and training function as a critique of neoliberal policy."[31]

Therefore, Krinsky's elaborate critique of welfare reform under Giuliani comes down to an endorsement of the human capital development alternative to work-first policies, which would get its chance under de Blasio and Banks.

In short, despite great effort and theoretical sophistication, Krinsky's network-analytic techniques do not convincingly document a set of social structures formidable enough to reinforce the view that urban politics are resistant to nonincremental change.

Qualifications and Conclusion

This chapter has emphasized how the strong research base behind work-first labor force attachment programs was one factor that allowed policy entrepreneurs in the 1990s—including Giuliani in New York City—to make nonincremental change in welfare policy. However, that research base, while very real and consequential, was more nuanced than is sometimes recognized. Research also showed that labor force attachment (LFA) welfare reform had clear limits, which later experts and politicians would seek to address. As we shall see, de Blasio and Banks were among the actors who would seek to go beyond the work-first welfare policy.

In general, LFA programs—focused on moving clients rapidly into the labor force, even at low wages—were found to be more effective than human capital development programs that concentrated on first giving clients basic education or training with the hope that eventually they would get better jobs. But the most effective of the LFA programs did offer some basic education to those most in need of it and thus could be called mixed-strategy programs. Most effective of all the programs discussed by Judith M. Gueron was the version of GAIN (Greater Avenues for Independence) implemented in Riverside, California, a mixed-strategy LFA program that was widely touted as the "Riverside miracle." Thus, the expert consensus for LFA did not imply that education and training were useless, only that such services had to be integrated into an approach that stressed finding some job quickly.

Another important nuance in the consensus in favor of LFA was that it did not extend to what Gueron calls work-for-benefits or workfare programs. LFA programs that put clients in wage-paying jobs—mostly low-wage jobs—had been found to more than pay for themselves (through reduced AFDC, Medicaid, and food stamp expenditures, and increased tax payments) within five years. But what about programs that placed clients not in wage-paying jobs but in unpaid community service positions, which were conceived as part of their reciprocal obligation for receiving welfare? There were "few studies and no strong evidence" that such workfare programs paid for themselves or achieved anything besides satisfying the public's demand that recipients at least do something and perhaps sending a "more socially acceptable, pro-work signal to parents."[32] The WEP, which expanded under Giuliani to include thousands of clients, was such a workfare program, one that he touted as a great achievement of his reforms at the HRA. At the time Giuliani was dramatically expanding WEP, Gueron found that "reliable knowledge about workfare-type programs is limited."[33]

It is important to understand the substance of the consensus behind LFA in the mid-1990s. What was taken as established by most welfare policy experts was not that LFA-oriented reforms could significantly reduce poverty, raise clients' income, or place them in "good jobs." Gueron summarizes the benefits of one of the most effective LFA programs, the Riverside GAIN program: "Riverside produced dramatic results for all groups in the caseload. . . . Although these findings are impressive, the GAIN program has not transformed the earnings potential of welfare recipients. More people got jobs than would have gotten them without the program, and got them sooner, but these were usually not "better" jobs, and families were rarely boosted out of poverty."[34] Thus, it should be noted that what these evaluations found was not that work-first was more effective at moving clients out of poverty. Rapid attachment was more effective than skill-building simply at putting clients to some kind of work; neither approach did much in the way of moving clients into "good jobs" or out of poverty. So the welfare reformers of the late twentieth century could persuasively argue their changes would likely result in more clients working. In fact, more clients did end up doing some kind of work after the changes of the mid-1990s. But even this success was limited. In commenting on an evaluation of work-first welfare programs in New York City, welfare scholar Mary Jo Bane commented on the "sobering finding" that of the more than twenty thousand welfare clients assigned to LFA programs during the study, "only 6 percent were placed in jobs and still employed six months after placement." Of the clients who actually showed up to the programs, almost half were placed and retained in jobs six months later.[35] It has also been found that although nationwide many welfare clients left the rolls, about 40 to 50 percent of these leavers were poor.[36] A work-first welfare policy in New York City was successful on its own terms but left much to be desired. As one author commented: "Fighting poverty among leavers today, therefore, will require finding better ways to help people boost their earnings potential, balance work and family, and achieve greater sustained employment."[37]

For these reasons, it is fair to say that the expert consensus in favor of work-first welfare programs, while it was very real from the late 1980s through the 1990s, sometimes exaggerated what that approach could accomplish. R. Kent Weaver writes: "It is also clear in retrospect that evaluation research on welfare-to-work was interpreted in an overly optimistic manner in the debate on the Family Support Act. Debate focused on the positive results rather than on the small magnitude of those results because that fit the policy and political interests of politicians. . . . In short, even when policy research offers consistent findings and fosters an agreement on a particular direction to policy change, the agreement may be neither deep nor durable."[38] The consensus on work-first programs also influenced the debate on the Personal Responsibility and Work Opportunity Reconciliation Act (PRWORA) in the 1990s, although by that time, other policy options, such as time limits on eligibility for welfare, also gained support and were incorporated into the legislation. The point is that an expert consensus in favor of work-first did exist and was essential to the achievement of nonincremental change in welfare policy. This is so even though in retrospect, the evidence base for that consensus was more mixed than experts and policy entrepreneurs let on. Here I touch on a limitation of the ideational/entrepreneurial model of nonincremental change. That model requires an expert consensus and action by policy entrepreneurs. But experts and entrepreneurs can be mistaken, and their interpretation of research results can be influenced by politics and ideology. As Landy and Levin note, the "existence of such consensus should not be taken to imply that the merits of . . . expert-endorsed reforms are unassailable." Indeed, the "achievement of consensus within the relevant reform professional community is not the same as a 'scientific' consensus. It is less an intellectual than a political and cultural phenomenon."[39]

Giuliani's nonincremental changes at the HRA achieved much but had limits, and in recognition of these limitations, a new direction in human capital development–oriented welfare policy—Career Pathways—was developed by a later generation of experts and entrepreneurs and taken up by de Blasio and Banks. I mentioned earlier that the question of whether nonincremental change is possible in urban environments is relevant to the question of how democratically responsive and public spirited such environments are. If our findings are typical of New York and perhaps other cities, we might be able to argue that urban nonincremental change is more frequent than most of the literature realizes and that city politics are therefore more responsive and public spirited than has been thought.

4

BEGINNINGS OF DE BLASIO'S WELFARE POLICIES

Prolegomenon to de Blasio: The Bloomberg Legacy

Chapter 3 notes that Rudy Giuliani reacted against David Dinkins's version of governance, which he perceived as progressive, and this reaction played out in Giuliani's work-first welfare policy. Similarly, Bill de Blasio reacted against Michael Bloomberg's vision of politics with important consequences for de Blasio's welfare policies. A few things should be said about the Bloomberg baseline that de Blasio sought to replace.

Chris McNickle convincingly describes Bloomberg's attachment to the concept of an entrepreneurial city, explaining that the mayor believed creating a favorable business environment was "one of a mayor's most important tasks." The entrepreneurial city idea emerged out of the United States' "painful restructuring" from the 1960s to the 1990s. That period saw the "financial and spiritual" decline of many Northeastern and Midwestern cities, McNickle notes. The key to the revival lies in a city leader who will "think like an entrepreneur." Since people have a choice of where to live, a city must attract residents. The way to do so, in this analysis, is with a broad tax base "to enhance services" for residents and to attract more people.[1]

But like the progressive paradigm, the entrepreneurial city idea had limitations, which a successful mayor has to acknowledge and manage. McNickle observes that "Democratic sensibilities meant to value every citizen's intrinsic worth equally," no matter how rich or poor, can "live awkwardly in entrepreneurial cities." McNickle noted that Bloomberg had to reconcile goals for market-driven development programs with "the imperative" he faced as mayor "to treat all members of its impossibly diverse population fairly. His approach contained inherent tensions."[2]

By 2013, New Yorkers were exhausted by many years of what has been called "the creative destruction of New York City"[3] and came to believe that the conservative regime was no longer effectively managing the tensions in its political vision. The city's progressive coalition reasserted itself and made de Blasio the first progressive mayor in two decades. Now that the de Blasio years are over, it is time to investigate how well he managed to balance democratic sensibilities and entrepreneurial dynamics.

In the face of the drawn-out paradigm shift from the progressive reform regime to the entrepreneurial city,[4] the incoming de Blasio administration had two options. One was to deny the legitimacy of the shift and fight to restore the glory days of progressivism. The other option was to accept the inevitability of entrepreneurialism and pay better attention to democratic concerns than the conservative dominant coalition had.

Joseph P. Viteritti convincingly argues that de Blasio sought to moderate, not reject, entrepreneurialism. The title of his book, *The Pragmatist: Bill de Blasio's Quest to Save the Soul of New York*, expresses a seeming tension in its overall thesis. "New York City does have a progressive soul," Viteritti writes.[5] If de Blasio's quest was to save that soul, the implication is that the mayor was a progressive. But the title also asserts that de Blasio was a pragmatist. So the claim is that de Blasio was a pragmatic progressive. There is no contradiction in that label. The quintessential pragmatist himself, John Dewey, was a great progressive. But in recent decades, when used as a political label, the term *pragmatist* usually means someone who is guided by immediate practical considerations rather than progressive or other ideals. What Viteritti has to do to make his claim stick is prove that "pragmatism is not an antonym of conviction" and especially not of progressive conviction.[6]

The Pragmatist argues persuasively that de Blasio's policies for developing affordable housing, although they did not abandon the previous administration's strategy of cooperating with private developers, were not a mere "doubling down" on Bloomberg's approach, as some have claimed.[7] What are we to make of de Blasio's welfare policies? Leading the charge to execute what antipoverty advocates described as a "180-degree change"[8] in this area was Steven Banks, de Blasio's pick for commissioner of the Human Resources Administration (HRA), later made commissioner of the Department of Social Services with responsibility for the HRA and the Department of Homeless Services. Prior to those appointments, Banks was well known as a longtime lawyer for and then director of the Legal Aid Society where he directed a litigation campaign against the city that established a right to shelter for homeless families. His designation to lead New York's social service bureaucracy provoked "an audible gasp" among HRA staff when they heard it announced on television.[9] The rest of this chapter discusses how de Blasio and Banks approached the challenge of nonincremental change and their overall philosophy of welfare policy, known as Career Pathways. Later chapters describe and evaluate the implementation of de Blasio's policies.

Paths to Nonincremental Change

In US politics, there are essentially two types of change: incremental and nonincremental. Incremental change is the modal type, where a policy baseline is accepted and, over time, a series of small changes is made to it. Nonincremental change is when the baseline policy is broken and another policy, one that is fundamentally new, is established. At the federal level, welfare policy developed incrementally after the baseline policy of Aid to Families with Dependent Children (AFDC) was created under the New Deal in 1935. From then until 1996, AFDC endured as an entitlement program that supplemented the income of poor families. AFDC did not do a great deal in regard to work obligations or training, although some work requirements were added over the years. In 1996, a nonincremental change occurred. AFDC was replaced with Temporary Aid to Needy Families (TANF), and striking changes were made. AFDC had been an entitlement program, meaning federal expenditures for it were open-ended and continued until all eligible applicants in a year were covered. Under TANF, yearly federal expenditures were fixed. Thus, in a rare development, the entitlement status of an important (but small) welfare state program was ended. In addition, work requirements were greatly strengthened and eligibility for benefits was limited in most cases to five years, marking major shifts in policy.

In New York City, the administration of these welfare programs changed incrementally over the years with only one nonincremental change taking place since the development of the entrepreneurial city during the years following the fiscal crisis of 1975. That change occurred when Giuliani contributed to the national wave of welfare reform in the mid-1990s by dramatically restructuring the HRA to shift its critical task from determining applicants' eligibility for benefits to putting clients to work as quickly as possible.

By 2014, Giuliani's once baseline-breaking welfare policies had become a new baseline, with Bloomberg making only incremental changes to them through his three terms. Just as the early poor performance of the HRA, the so-called welfare explosion of the 1960s, and the fiscal crisis of 1975 provoked a long reaction against urban liberalism in general and its welfare policies in particular, the long reign of the relatively conservative mayors Ed Koch, Giuliani, and Bloomberg provoked a backlash. Bloomberg precipitated this reaction through his consistently neoliberal policies and by maneuvering to serve a third term despite the twice-expressed desire of the electorate to limit mayors to two terms. After that episode, a *New York Times* poll of August 2012 found that 65 percent of New Yorkers would not vote for Bloomberg again.[10] A year later, another *Times* poll found that "most New Yorkers say Mr. Bloomberg's policies have favored the rich over the middle class and the poor" and offered a "portrait of a long-term relationship between mayor and city that remains deeply conflicted and contradictory, marked by almost loveless admiration and an unmistakable yearning for change as Mr. Bloomberg's third and final term winds to a close."[11] A combination of Bloomberg fatigue and disenchantment with conservative policies set up the possibility of a break with the neoliberal baseline.

Once in office, de Blasio attempted to bring about another sea change in city welfare policy but under different circumstances and in a very different way than had been the case with Giuliani. De Blasio elevated addressing economic inequality to the main plank of his election campaign. Eric Alterman of the *Nation* noted that de Blasio made economic inequality "the central issue in his campaign." The candidate attempted "to tie nearly every issue he addressed to that problem . . . repeat[ing] a version of this message in virtually every speech he gave and in every debate." The messaging was so consistent that Alterman concluded it was "hard to imagine that any voter who pulled the lever for or against him could have been unaware of his central theme."[12]

De Blasio's electoral victory was overwhelming, enabling him to plausibly claim a mandate to address economic inequality. Though he tied that theme to many issues, it was especially relevant to welfare policy. De Blasio won in a landslide and garnered a City Council that was not merely Democratic (as the city's legislature always was) but also especially progressive. Viteritti noted that after de Blasio's election, "at no time in recent history has the city had both a mayor and a Council with such a strong progressive orientation aimed at reducing economic and social inequalities," which made for a "cooperative relation between the two branches," something very different than the hostility between the council and Giuliani.[13]

De Blasio's 2013 win was like that of President Lyndon Johnson, who in 1964 ran on a platform rejecting conservativism and endorsing progressive change. His sweeping win produced a unified government with Democratic control of Congress and set the stage for the transformative Great Society programs. Such situations exemplify the presidential/majoritarian route to nonincremental change. This is a very different path than the ideational/entrepreneurial process, discussed in chapters 2 and 3, that was characteristic of Giuliani's welfare reforms. The legitimacy of Giuliani's welfare policies rested on an expert consensus and much-touted public ideas rather than an overwhelming electoral mandate. At no point did Giuliani have a Republican or otherwise sympathetic City Council.

In short, de Blasio's welfare overhaul was the product of an entirely different political process than that of Giuliani and resulted in a very different set of policies.

One big difference in how the Giuliani and de Blasio administrations sought to achieve change at the HRA was that the former deliberately precipitated a crisis at the agency that consciously broke all the rules. In contrast, Banks was a consensus builder who emphasized continuity. He did not assume that critics and opponents had been discredited by virtue of the election and should be overridden. He approached whatever skepticism he found among HRA staff not as debunked resistance but as the legitimate concerns of a constituency that had to be won over.

Lisa Fitzpatrick, the chief program officer at the HRA under Banks, had three decades of experience at the agency. She described a conversation she had with Banks when she first met him as HRA commissioner:

> And so, in my conversation with Commissioner Banks, I asked him, "Are you going to run this like a project?" Because I felt somewhat that that was like what happened under the Giuliani administration with Turner. I felt like they were going to break everything . . . tear it down . . . and then they were going to walk away from it. . . . That's why I asked [Banks] . . . was he here to run HRA as a project or was he in it for the long haul? . . . He was honest about what his ambitions were. . . . His priority was trying to change everything that we're doing that is having an adverse impact on the client. . . . So it wasn't that these changes were going to make our lives miserable. [It] was just [a] change in your perspective. Instead of being focused on one thing, it was a very client-centric perspective, but also it was a worker-centric perspective.[14]

Fitzpatrick described the change process at the HRA under Giuliani as "tumultuous" and "stressful" and compared that experience to what happened under de Blasio and Banks.

> This was a sea change, but it was a more tailored change. So, the focus wasn't on stopping something that we knew was right to do. I think that we all still want clients to get jobs . . . not to just get a temporary job, but a job that's going to be permanent and keep them off of Cash Assistance. So, there has been nothing under this administration, that I can see, that has been contrary to what we, I, know policy to be. They're not saying to break rules that we know shouldn't be broken. So what

we're doing is looking at, examining our processes and trying to say is this the best way.[15]

Banks discussed his approach to change at the HRA and explained that "the process of making change was as important as the substance of the change because the process helps ensure that the substance will take root. So, between February 28 [2014], when I was appointed, and April 1, when I took office, I conducted a series of meetings within the agency with leaders about the kinds of changes they thought were needed in their areas and focus groups with advocates and client groups."[16] This extensive consultation process continued after Banks took office when one of his first tasks was to submit a required employment plan to the State Office of Temporary and Disability Assistance. Putting together the plan "involved, meeting with frontline staff throughout the agency, forty different kinds of focus groups, a staff survey, setting [up] workgroups, continuing core groups and clients for maximum input for our fundamental change in the way that we operated our benefit programs under the umbrella programs of our employment plan."[17]

Banks's methods of consensus building and consultation were antithetical to Giuliani's management approach. Giuliani consciously refused to consult anyone until the changes he sought were a fait accompli and insisted on "utter secrecy."

"'My philosophy,' he said, 'has been, first make the changes and have them moving in a very, very strong way—then, announce them.' At that point, 'there isn't terribly much that people that oppose it can do,'" Giuliani said. The *Times* reported, "The welfare program is filled with lore of the Mayor (and his former assistant, Richard Schwartz) making high-decibel demands for faster, more aggressive action."[18]

Thus, the de Blasio/Banks change strategy did not involve the sharp, tumultuous break with the past, bulldozing staff opposition, and legal battles that took place under Giuliani and Turner. De Blasio and Banks sought a significant change but with less disruption and discontinuity. De Blasio may have wanted a nonincremental change not through a dramatic break but through an accelerated series of incremental changes. The object was not to suddenly shift the HRA's critical task from eligibility determination to work promotion but to stay committed to both tasks and rapidly get better at them by improving staff morale and client satisfaction.

Under de Blasio, change at the HRA happened in a chief executive–majoritarian, rather than an ideational-entrepreneurial, fashion. This book has defined nonincremental change as one that breaks with baseline policy and establishes a new baseline. The de Blasio/Banks strategy for nonincremental change challenged that definition as it involved accepting the baseline but getting better at implementing it and making important, logical extensions of it.

In fact, some of de Blasio's most significant changes in social policy were mostly in the nature of making obvious but potentially significant extensions of policy baselines he inherited from Bloomberg. De Blasio's signature achievement, universal pre-K, was really "no more" than the pre-K program that existed under Bloomberg, now offered to all, full time, with more attention devoted to staff quality. A less frequently noted de Blasio achievement, providing counsel to all defendants in Housing Court, can also be thought of as "just" a logical extension of a Bloomberg policy. Bloomberg made a big shift in the organizational culture of the Department of Homeless Services when he expanded the agency's critical tasks from sheltering the unhoused to also preventing homelessness. Bloomberg's Home Base program, which offered various interventions to poor families at risk of homelessness, was controversial when it was first implemented; eventually, sophisticated analysis demonstrated that it was effective.[19]

Bloomberg did not take the seemingly natural step of preventing homelessness by guaranteeing legal assistance to families facing eviction. Perhaps Bloomberg's private-sector sympathies made him hesitant to do anything that could be interpreted as antilandlord. De Blasio took that obvious step, which involved "just" accepting an already existing institution, the Housing Court and its adversarial mode of operation, and making sure that both parties had representation. Thus an established baseline was accepted rather than broken, and the change made to it has potentially far-reaching implications and amounts to more than "just another" incremental change.

In this respect, de Blasio's change strategy resembled the approach recommended to progressives by A. O. Hirschman in *The Rhetoric of Reaction*. Hirschman argues that a particularly persuasive argument for progressive change is one that presents the newest reform proposal as building on and reinforcing earlier (now accepted) changes. He writes of the "*complementarity, harmony, synergy,* or *mutual support* argument" that emphasizes "how two successive reforms lend strength to each other."[20]

A comparison of Giuliani's and de Blasio's approaches to achieving nonincremental change suggests there are two different ways to make change, one distinctly conservative and the other progressive. Giuliani used an ideational-entrepreneurial model, justifying major change by appealing to a seemingly powerful expert consensus; he saw opposition as a rearguard action by proponents of an outdated paradigm. He was willing to accept disruption as an inevitable part of an essentially healthy process of creative destruction and looked at "moving the needle" on an indicator of a social problem as the ultimate vindication. De Blasio and Banks used a chief executive–majoritarian model, one that justified change as having been democratically mandated, saw opponents as another constituency to be won over, avoided disruption as much as possible, and believed client satisfaction was the decisive indicator of success.

McNickle's biography of Bloomberg has an especially interesting chapter, "Creative Destruction in the School System," that is relevant here. McNickle describes how these two contrasting paradigms of change came into conflict when Bloomberg's Schools Chancellor Joel Klein butted heads with the United Federation of Teachers (UFT) chief Randi Weingarten. According to McNickle, the relationship between Klein and Weingarten "got off to a bad start during a lunch meeting" that occurred shortly after Klein's appointment. As McNickle relates, Klein asked the UFT leader how she thought they could work together "to fix the school system." Her response was "continuous, incremental change." Weingarten believed that other approaches to improving government bureaucracies "invariably proved unsustainable." In contrast, Klein favored radical reform to cure the ills of the city's schools, according to McNickle. He took his bold agenda to the public, declaring that the union contract's "three pillars of mediocracy: life tenure, lock-step pay, and seniority-based decision making" were the greatest impediments to developing excellent schools.[21]

Here we observe Klein as a disruption-embracing, big idea–oriented reform conservative. He is an outsider looking to jump-start nonincremental change by breaking a constraining baseline—nothing less than essential terms of the union contract. Weingarten is a progressive. While she admits the system needs fixing, and she seeks more than incremental change, she is concerned that a break-all-the-rules approach will be resisted by school staff and prove unsustainable. So Weingarten seeks continuous incremental change—quite a lot of changes fast but with each one complementary to the last and perhaps more likely to take root. With de Blasio's overwhelming electoral victory, this progressive approach to nonincremental change got its shot, particularly in regard to social service policy.

A potential weakness in the de Blasio strategy lay in grounding the legitimacy of the proposed changes in popular will rather than in tested expert consensus. Reliance on the popular will risked taking on reform strategies that, however sustainable they seem to be, could eventually prove ineffective. The effort to refocus welfare policy away from work first and toward a new approach to human capital building ran that risk. This new approach was the Career Pathways model, and it sought to do a better job than in the past at helping welfare clients develop the skills necessary to succeed at higher-quality jobs.

The Career Pathways Idea

An administration planning document explained de Blasio's plans for welfare policy as follows: "The Human Resources Administration (HRA) is dramatically changing its approach from a single rapid-attachment model to a population-specific menu of services emphasizing education and employment skills."[22] Commissioner Banks called this new direction an abandonment of "one-size-fits-all" policy. In his testimony to the City Council on September 22, 2015, Banks described the proposed reforms in more detail, sharing that the HRA had "spent the last 18 months focused on improving" the agency's Employment Program. The goal, he said, is "providing services to clients more effectively to help move them off our caseload and out of poverty." He elucidated the administration's sense of mission. "Overall, we are attempting to right a system that has been broken for decades [because] it treated clients as a monolithic group." The system failed to consider why people seek help from the HRA. In making this shift to a "client first approach while complying with all federal and state rules and regulations," Banks said, the HRA would work with clients to close gaps in skill and education so they could compete for a livable wage.[23]

On November 16, 2016, the HRA announced it had awarded contracts to a range of private vendors to provide services for welfare clients under three new programs. Career Compass and Youth Pathways were to provide adults and youth, respectively, with in-depth evaluations to determine what further training would be most appropriate for each particular client. Career Advance would follow up on those evaluations by providing referrals to training, education, and retention services appropriate to a client's needs. The idea was that such intensive evaluation and individualized training would develop clients' human capital and eventually move them into good jobs, off welfare, and out of poverty more effectively than rapidly attaching them to unskilled positions. Another key feature of the new programs was that they would be part of a broad effort to coordinate city education, training, and workforce programs so that clients learned skills that were in demand by private-sector employers.

Overall, this approach, which stressed human capital development (HCD) rather than rapid labor force attachment (LFA), was known as the Career Pathways strategy. In a report titled *Building the Workforce of the Future*, the progressive New York City think tank Center for an Urban Future described the Career Pathways model that was embraced by the de Blasio administration in all aspects of workforce policy, including welfare-work programs. The report observed that, unlike the previous model, which prioritized connecting workers to jobs as quickly as possible, the Career Pathways framework prioritized helping job seekers and workers build the skills required to be more competitive in the labor force. The report also noted the broad range of stakeholders involved in Career Pathways—employers, providers of workforce services, government officials, labor union representatives, educational institutions, and private philanthropy. The new model emphasizes training and education, the report observed, as well as deeper connections with the city's employers and a commitment to improving working conditions for lower-wage workers.[24]

Some questions remained. What evidence showed that the renewed emphasis on developing clients' human capital would produce these desirable outcomes any better than similar programs did before welfare reform or than work-first programs? Was that evidence convincing enough to win over skeptics, build support, facilitate change, and justify de Blasio's expenditure of political capital on it?

As discussed in chapter 3, the expert consensus in favor of the 1990s' work-first welfare policies was overly optimistic about whether that approach would find good jobs for clients and move them off welfare. Were de Blasio's supporters also unduly optimistic in thinking revamped human capital programs would be any more effective at reducing poverty? Furthermore, to justify a reasonable degree of optimism, how convincing did the evidence have to be for the Career Pathways approach? The appropriate comparison is to the last evidence base that helped precipitate a nonincremental change in welfare policy, which would be the evidence that backed up the mid-1990s transition to the LFA orientation.

When the de Blasio administration embraced Career Pathways, there had not been rigorous evaluations of that approach as it related to welfare policy. Indeed, even today, there has not been an independent, rigorous evaluation of the de Blasio/Banks Career Compass, Career Advance, and Youth Pathways. However, there have been many evaluations of the Career Pathways workforce programs that prepare clients for work in specific employment sectors. Most of the results have been positive when programs are compared with traditional federally sponsored workforce training and job programs.[25]

Thus there is evidence (discussed in chap. 7) that Career Pathways provides a promising approach to workforce development policy. Whether the approach is effective in welfare job placement programs has not been shown. For present purposes, the main points are that when de Blasio and Banks deployed Career Pathways programs at the HRA, that philosophy did not have the sort of evidence supporting it that the rapid LFA approach had when Giuliani imposed it. The strong evidence base behind LFA was one reason Giuliani was able to take his bull-in-a-china-shop approach to implementing reform. He had reason to believe he was on the right track, was confident to the point of overconfidence in pushing work-first on the agency, and could rebut critics with independent proof of his direction. Moreover, the positive evaluations of work-first programs in other states created a kind of nationwide craze for LFA welfare-work programs that came together when Congress passed the pathbreaking PRWORA legislation in 1996. The zeitgeist seemed to be behind work-oriented welfare reform and justifying dramatic change to see it implemented. Partly for these reasons, nonincremental change came to the HRA under Giuliani in the late 1990s.

When de Blasio was elected, Career Pathways was a well-known policy direction, but mostly in the workforce rather than welfare policy. Career Pathways lacked as strong an evidence base in welfare as LFA reform historically had. Moreover, Career Pathways had not received the imprimatur of being taken up in federal legislation. Banks did well when he did not try to shove Career Pathways welfare policy down the HRA's throat. Based on his own managerial philosophy and out of necessity, he did not and could not take Giuliani's break-all-the-rules approach to implementation. Banks made important and positive changes at the HRA. But for better or worse, he did not create nonincremental change. When there is a strong professional consensus behind a policy proposal, nonincremental change may be possible, but the de Blasio years demonstrate that without such an apparent evidence base, dramatic change is harder to achieve.

It is worth noting that the research base for work-first was actually stronger than that for Career Pathways by the time de Blasio was elected than it had been when Giuliani implemented his reforms. The Giuliani administration did not undertake an evaluation of its work-first reforms, but the data-conscious Bloomberg administration, which had mostly left Giuliani's reforms in place, did allow such a rigorous evaluation. From 2004 to 2006, Andrew R. Feldman analyzed the twenty-six welfare-to-work programs to which the city's welfare clients were randomly assigned. Although all programs were of the work-first type, the organizations implementing them were "given broad discretion by the city's welfare department to design and operate their own programs," and as a result, Feldman noted, "their strategies and practices differ."[26] According to Feldman, "Some providers have more urgency about getting people into jobs quickly and offer only a few days of job-readiness training. Others make job-readiness a central part of their programs, including encouraging short-term training opportunities and providing substantial case management and multi-week workshops about thriving in the workplace."[27] Providers varied in that some worked under fully performance-based contracts while others worked under hybrid contracts that were partly performance-based and partly expense-based. (These contract structures are discussed in more detail in chap. 6.) In other words, some providers emphasized the work-first and performance-based models more, and other providers emphasized them less. Feldman found that "the results for the full sample suggest that the combined effect of using less training, becoming more focused on quick placement, and moving from partial to full performance-based pay would more than double the share of participants that get and keep jobs for at least six months from 6 percent to almost 14 percent."[28] This shows that among providers who were following a work-first model, those who most embraced the model had higher placement rates than those who introduced HCD elements into the model.

BEGINNINGS OF DE BLASIO'S WELFARE POLICIES

When de Blasio and Banks set out to implement Career Pathways welfare policies, the research base for it as it relates to welfare was not strong and the research base for work-first had actually gotten stronger. The de Blasio administration could not appeal to a strong professional consensus in favor of Career Pathways in welfare policy the way Giuliani was able to do with LAF welfare reform. Therefore, nonincremental change through the ideational/entrepreneurial model, which relies on expert consensus and public ideas derived from it, was not a strategy available to de Blasio and Banks.

I interviewed Banks about what could reasonably be expected of his administration's skill development and education approach. We focused on education interventions, such as high school equivalency and college programs, which are only a few types of HCD services that the HRA reemphasized:

> BANKS: When I came in, you were prohibited from attending four-year college as part of your work requirement for cases that had work requirements. And that flies in the face of the research that shows you get paid progressively more for each credential you get.
> MAIN: What research is there that . . . can point to a program where if you look at . . . the people who got access to college degrees, they were able to get off welfare at a rate that's higher than the people who didn't get the access?
> BANKS: Giving the ability [to] clients to get a high school equivalency, when high school equivalency has been shown to increase your wages, or giving clients an ability to get an associate's degree or a college degree, when all of those things are shown to increase your wages in other states, have shown that education is important.
> MAIN: Is it true, are there gold standard tests, [where] we took a population of people without high school degrees [and] some of them we put in a program where they got GEDs, some of them we didn't? [And] five years down the road we took a look and . . . the people who got GEDs are in fact doing better? . . . My hunch [is] that the literature on that is rather mixed. [The] commonsense intuition that "golly it must make a difference," I don't know that it's well supported.
> BANKS: I think you've got to look at [the] fundamental difference in what we're trying to accomplish and what the prior administration was trying to accomplish. . . . The approach is important, in terms of what impact it's going to have on the client. So the Giuliani approach was just push people off the caseload. And the goal of getting off the caseload was the goal. Our goal is getting them out of poverty. I think you'll find limited research, because it's not the way other ben-

efit programs have been operated. . . . They've been operated to just move people off the caseload as the goal as opposed to move them out of poverty.[29]

A 2008 MDRC overview of the evidence on education programs for welfare clients confirms that "while there is compelling evidence that additional years of schooling and advanced education credentials are associated with higher earnings, evaluations of education and basic skills training programs have yielded mixed results concerning their ability to increase earnings among low-income populations."[30] More recent literature suggests some strategies that could make such education programs more effective. Basing high school equivalency programs at community colleges and organizing them as the beginning of a path leading to employment in a particular sector is promising.[31] Indeed, the de Blasio administration experimented with some of these approaches. La Guardia Community College of the City University of New York implemented a high school equivalency program revamped along these lines. Compared with traditional GED programs, more students completed the La Guardia program, passed the GED, and enrolled in college. But the La Guardia program did not enroll welfare recipients only, and its impact on employment and earnings was not measured.[32]

There is a basic flaw in the argument that since additional years of schooling and additional degrees are associated with higher earnings, it must follow that giving welfare clients more schooling and more degrees will raise their earnings. In society as a whole, people self-select to some extent for how many years of schooling and degrees they will earn. People who are confident of their ability to do well in educational programs are more likely to enter and complete them than people who are not so confident. Greater confidence (and lack thereof) may be based on a reasonable understanding of one's abilities. When people with more schooling earn more than people with less, we must ask if the higher earning comes from what was learned in school or from greater ability going in. Scientific evaluations of the impact of education programs on earnings control for this self-selection by random assignment of clients or by statistical analysis that controls for other relevant differences among people with different levels of education. When these controls are made, it turns out, the impact of education programs on the earnings of low-income clients is mixed.

In 2011, Mary Jo Bane, a distinguished welfare policy scholar, summed up the results of evaluations from the 1980s and 1990s of education-oriented welfare-work programs: "Another important finding of these evaluations was that mandatory education-first approaches had pretty uniformly negative effects both on government budgets and participants' incomes, at least in the short- to medium-term time frame of the evaluations. This finding seems counter intuitive to many service providers, but it is quite well documented and consistent across studies, and has reinforced what has become the conventional wisdom about the superiority of quick-placement strategies."[33] When de Blasio and Banks committed New York City to a new, updated version of HCD welfare-work programs, that approach was not supported by the sort of methodologically sophisticated evaluations that backed up the LFA welfare-work programs of the early 1990s.

The de Blasio/Banks makeover of the city's welfare system may have had certain positive effects. Moving clients out of workfare and into education and training programs might have improved client and staff satisfaction. But moving people out of poverty is a heavy lift—much heavier than pushing them off the welfare rolls or putting them in work assignments. We now know that many of the Great Society programs have been a success in the sense that the poverty rate is lower than it would be if they did not exist. Yet the claim that "we fought a war on poverty and poverty won" persists because early overoptimism was soon dashed and cynicism set in. Chapter 5 considers the effectiveness of de Blasio/Banks's education and training-oriented programs in terms of job placements, and chapter 7 considers the implementation of these programs.

5
OVERVIEW OF THE CAREER PATHWAYS EMPLOYMENT PROGRAMS

Early Critics of de Blasio's Welfare Policies

Early critics of Bill de Blasio and Steven Banks's new direction in welfare policy predicted a large rise in the recipient rolls. In the Manhattan Institute's *City Journal*, Fred Siegel and former Bloomberg HRA commissioner Robert Doar noted that "some critics suggest that de Blasio's proposals would take us back to the bad old peak-welfare days of the late 1980s and early 1990s."[1] A 2015 *New York Post* editorial reported, "The city's welfare rolls in October reached a nine-year high of 373,504, up nearly 8 percent since de Blasio took office" and predicted "with former Legal Aid chief lawyer Steven Banks at the helm of the Human Resources Administration, the odds are pretty good that they'll continue to soar."[2] *Gotham Gazette* weighed in, stating that Rudy Giuliani's former HRA commissioner "Jason Turner . . . is pessimistic about de Blasio's reforms and expects the welfare caseloads to increase dramatically with little or no benefit to families. 'The objective has changed from self-employment, self-reliance, or, rather, self-sufficiency and earned income, to income distribution without mutual obligation,' Turner said."[3]

The *Gazette* also reported that both the American Enterprise Institute's Angela Rachidi and the Manhattan Institute's Alex Armlovivh "think that the significant increase in the raw monthly enrollment as well as the marginal uptick in the unduplicated count provide cause for concern." The paper noted that for both scholars, "the verdict is out on whether Banks' reforms have been or will be successful." According to the *Gazette*, "Rachidi believes the caseloads will pick up slowly over the next year or two. Jason Turner expects this to be a more dramatic increase."[4]

Early on, Heather MacDonald predicted the rolls would rise under the new regime. In 2014, she mocked Banks's testimony to the City Council: "'Policy reforms to address inappropriate denials, case closings, and sanctions may lead to monthly caseload—quote—"growth,"' Human Resources Administration commissioner Steve Banks told the council, visually signaling with his fingers the ironic quotation marks around 'growth' that appeared in his written remarks as well. Growth is not growth when it's 'growth,' apparently."[5]

Early critics predicted that de Blasio and Banks's renewed emphasis on training and human capital development over rapid job attachment would result in fewer welfare clients being placed in jobs. Former HRA commissioner Robert Doar leveled that charge often. In the article he coauthored with Fred Siegel on the subject, Doar wrote that "de Blasio proposes . . . job training and 'seat time' in a classroom will displace the current system of 'rapid placement' into a job . . . [and] a vast new program of job training and enhanced 'education,' on the theory that a new version of the old failure will reduce inequality in New York."[6] Doar also said, "I am concerned that many of the policies being put in place by the de Blasio administration will lead to less employment for New Yorkers on welfare."[7] A 2014 article in the *New York Times* reported that "Robert Doar . . . says that expanding access to education, without insisting on work first, and easing some administrative requirements necessary to get and keep welfare, will send the wrong message. Some welfare recipients may decide to coast instead of finding work, Mr. Doar warned. That could lead to rising caseloads."[8]

Job Placement Results

When the implementation of the Career Pathways job placement programs started in 2014, observers were keenly interested in how many welfare clients would be placed in jobs. Would the number go up, down, or stay the same relative to the placements that had been made under Back to Work, the rapid labor force attachment program of Michael Bloomberg's administration? Since the focus of this analysis is the new job placement programs, the relevant time period is from the start of those programs in 2014 to 2019, which was the last full year under de Blasio and Banks in which those programs were implemented. As the Mayor's Management Report (MMR) of 2020 reported, "In April 2020, HRA suspended in-person employment programs in compliance with New York State's stay-at-home order which, coupled with reduced job opportunities, significantly impacted the Agency's ability to connect clients with employment."[9]

At first, job placements under the new programs went down. In 2016, the Citizens Budget Commission (CBC) made note of that trend. The CBC framed the question: "Is the Human Resources Administration (HRA) increasingly successful at helping people who receive cash assistance gain employment?" The commission found that "a key MMR indicator is therefore the number of cash assistance recipients placed in a job.... The number of clients HRA helped to gain employment declined 41 percent between fiscal year 2009 and 2015 while the overall caseload remained relatively constant."[10]

The CBC attributed the drop in employment placements to "key changes made by the de Blasio Administration in 2014 to the cash assistance programs." Specifically, the commission identified "eligibility restrictions," which "were loosened such that it is now easier for recipients to remain eligible for cash assistance while pursuing training and education." In addition, in 2014 "the Administration shifted away from making placements in short-term jobs towards longer-term, sustainable positions," following recommendations by the "Jobs for New Yorkers Task Force," which the administration had assembled to develop new workforce policies. These reforms, the CBC noted, "depressed the number of short-term job placements but are intended to promote longer-term self-sufficiency."[11] The CBC also noted the results from the preliminary MMR, which "indicated that in the first four months of fiscal year 2016 the decline in placements continued; HRA helped 1,000 fewer individuals gain employment than it did during the same period in 2015. The forthcoming MMR may shed some light on whether the changes in policy, now more than two years old, can move the needle on employment as well as enrollment in education and training."[12] When the final MMR for fiscal year (FY) 2016 appeared, the CBC noted that "placements in employment grew by 0.9 percent in fiscal year 2016 but the overall caseload grew by a larger 2.6 percent," which it characterized as "Ambiguous Results."[13]

In 2018, New York City's Independent Budget Office (IBO) also noted the decline in job placements under the new programs. "The new contracted employment programs placed 15,390 clients into jobs in 2018—a decrease of 34 percent from the 23,278 job placements made by contracted programs in 2016, the last full year under the old contracts," IBO reported. According to the IBO, "The Human Resources Administration attributes the decline to the phase-in of the new employment vendors, and expects job placements to rise substantially in 2019."[14]

In an interview on November 14, 2018, I questioned Steven Banks about the performance of the job placement programs he had implemented at the HRA. According to the MMR of FY 2018, the "Agency helped 38,942 clients obtain jobs in Fiscal 2018, 13.2 percent fewer than during Fiscal 2017."[15] The report and the de Blasio administration attributed this to "the new employment vendors and phase-in of their operations."[16]

In our interview, Banks emphasized that he had made many changes at the HRA that were not immediately related to job placement numbers. He emphasized how the agency had become much less punitive and much more client-friendly. He acknowledged the decline in job placements and attributed it to start-up issues associated with the new programs. He stressed that the most recent numbers as of our interview (as reported by the MMR) showed improvement in May and June 2018 that could continue. He said that the new Career Pathways programs had not really started until April 2018, so that May and June 2018 were the programs' "first two real functional months."[17] I asked Banks if he thought the placement numbers were going to improve, and he responded, "I think you already saw those results in the MMR."[18]

The big question related to the performance of the Career Pathways–related job programs was: Would the improvement in job placements achieved in May and June 2018 continue?

Following are the results reported by the IBO on November 26, 2019. They reference the Career Pathways–oriented programs, which were provided by "new employment vendors" or "new contractors." The "old contracts" refer to the labor force attachment programs operated under Bloomberg.

> The phase-in of the new employment vendors resulted in a 30 percent decrease in job placements by the contracted programs, from 23,278 in fiscal year 2016—the last full year under the old contracts—to 16,208 in 2018. While the number of contracted placements increased by 11 percent in 2019 to 17,983, placements by the new contractors remained 23 percent below the 2016 figure—even as the number of cash assistance recipients remained relatively flat over the period.
>
> Despite last year's increase in contractor placements, the overall number of cash assistance recipients placed into jobs remained flat at 39,856 in 2019 compared with 39,779 in 2018.[19]

The MMR of FY 2019 confirmed that the uptick in job placements registered for May and June 2018 did not portend further substantial improvement. The report noted: "In Fiscal 2019, HRA helped 39,860 clients obtain jobs, 0.2 percent more than during Fiscal 2018," which is to say job placements were essentially flat.[20]

Since the MMR of FY 2018 and Banks both stressed the importance of the increase of job placements in May and June 2018 as compared with May and June of 2017, it is fair to also look at job placements for May and June 2019. There are two different ways to do so.

While the job placement numbers for 2017 and 2018 cited in the MMR of FY 2018 are only for placements made by "the new employment vendors,"[21] when the Department of Social Services (DSS) was asked to provide similar numbers for 2019, the agency at first provided data that included placements made by WeCARE, the agency's employment program for the disabled, as well as placements made by the new programs (Career Compass, Youth Pathways, and Career

Advance). DSS provided these numbers from January 2016 to June 2020. These numbers are not comparable with the data given in the MMR of FY 2018. Even so, these numbers are of interest because it is reasonable to look at the performance of all job placement programs, including WeCARE.

Moreover, according to DSS, there was "a logic flaw in our reporting that was causing us to undercount placements in FY17 and FY18, particularly those for the new Career Services [i.e., Career Pathways] programs."[22] The calculations presented below are based on corrected data provided to the author by DSS.

If we follow the practice of comparing placements for the months of May and June and look at numbers for the new programs plus WeCARE, the results are as shown in table 5.1.

Using the time period chosen by the MMR and pointed out by Banks and following up to see if the rise in placements between 2017 and 2018 was continued between 2018 and 2019, as Banks anticipated, we see that placements in 2019 in fact fell by 8.3 percent. The increase in job placements between May/June 2017 and May/June 2018 turns out to be 39.1 percent. This is looking at total placements by the new programs and WeCARE, which, as the DSS suggested,[23] is reasonable because it covers a wider range of placement programs than just the new programs alone. Using this approach, the uptick in placements that the MMR and Banks emphasized in 2018 did not continue into 2019.

If WeCARE placements are left out and only placements by the Career Pathways programs are considered, as was the practice in the MMR of FY 2018, we have the results shown in table 5.2.

TABLE 5.1 Placements from new employment programs and WeCARE for selected months from 2017 to 2019

TIME PERIOD	NUMBER OF PLACEMENTS
May 2017	1,395
June 2017	984
Total	2,379
May 2018	1,755
June 2018	1,555
Total	3,310 (+39.1%)
May 2019	1,694
June 2019	1,341
Total	3,035 (−8.3%)

Source: Based on data provided by Ellen Levine, Chief Program Planning and Financial Management Officer, New York City Department of Social Services, June 29, 2021.

TABLE 5.2 Placements from new employment programs for selected months from 2017 to 2019

TIME PERIOD	NUMBER OF PLACEMENTS
May 2017	1,026
June 2017	676
Total	1,702
May 2018	1,420
June 2018	1,307
Total	2,727 (+60.2%)
May 2019	1,648
June 2019	1,301
Total	2,949 (+8.1%)

Source: Based on data provided by Ellen Levine, Chief Program Planning and Financial Management Officer, New York City Department of Social Services, June 29, 2021.

Thus we find that from 2017 to 2018, job placements increased by 60.2 percent. Job placements also increased from 2018 to 2019, but only by 8.1 percent, much less than they had increased from 2017 to 2018.

De Blasio and Banks succeeded in making major changes at the HRA, most of which involved moving the agency away from the poor law practices and image developed under Giuliani and Bloomberg. But the Career Pathways programs that were supposed to develop clients' personal capital and move them into better jobs were at first less effective in terms of job placements than were the earlier policies. After an expected decline attributed to phase-in disruption, job placements began to rise, at first dramatically, but then the rate of increase leveled off. If we include WeCARE placements in the picture, the numbers are less impressive. Thus defined, job placements rose by 39.1 percent from 2017 to 2018 but fell by 8.3 percent from 2018 to 2019. Then the COVID-19 pandemic hit and operation of the employment services programs was suspended.

Trends in Welfare Rolls

Besides job placements, another key measure of the success of the de Blasio/Banks reforms is the trends in the welfare rolls. Figure 5.1 shows the number of individuals each month in New York City receiving cash assistance. Figure 5.2 shows the unduplicated number of individuals in the previous twelve months in New York City receiving cash assistance.

Calculating the unduplicated, twelve-month count of people receiving cash assistance was an early decision by Banks. A *Gotham Gazette* article based on

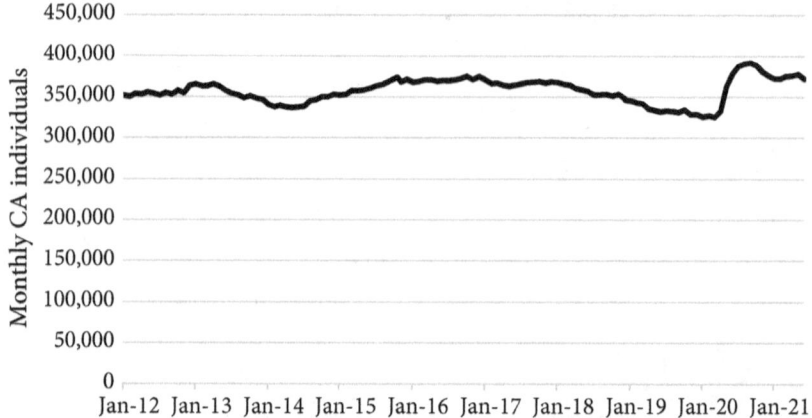

FIGURE 5.1. Number of individuals each month in New York City receiving cash assistance, January 2012–June 2021. Source: New York City Department of Social Services

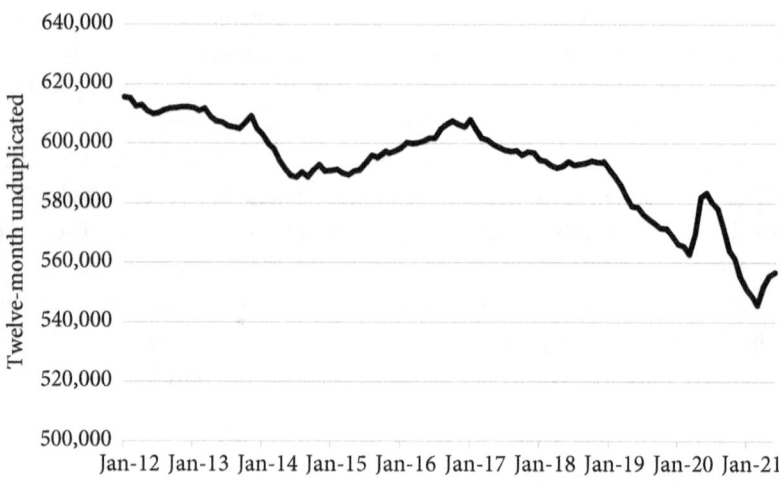

FIGURE 5.2. Number of unduplicated individuals in New York City receiving cash assistance, January 2012–June 2021. Source: New York City Department of Social Services

interviews with Banks explains why he wanted the welfare rolls calculated in this form: "One of the first measures that Banks implemented was creating an annual unduplicated count of cash assistance rolls which displayed a more accurate picture of enrollment in the welfare system. The previous method of relying on monthly enrollment data was often misleading, since it also includes recipients of emergency one-time assistance and does not account for the 'churn' of people going on and off the rolls—roughly one in four welfare recipients would return to the system within twelve months, according to HRA estimates."[24]

Ellen Levine, chief program planning and financial management officer for DSS, explained the decision to calculate the monthly number of individuals receiving cash assistance and the twelve-month unduplicated number:

> Under this administration, the decision was made to share both metrics as there was the thought that policy changes might lead to an increase in the monthly numbers, while the assumption was that the annual unduplicated caseload would either not increase or level off. There have been, for example, changes in the way sanctions are carried out, with more opportunities for clients to "cure" the sanction before it is imposed. This could lead to less "churning" e.g. people falling off the caseload for a period of time but ultimately coming back on in a matter of months. Thus, there would be less change in the annual number than in the monthly numbers.[25]

It is clear from the data that the twelve-month, unduplicated number of people receiving cash assistance, shown in figure 5.2, did decrease during the de Blasio administration. A regression analysis of the unduplicated number by a time indicator shows that number fell by about 425 cases per month on average over the administration's term. That is a modest drop of about 39,000 cases on a load of about 600,000 cases or about 6.5 percent for the term of office. Most of that decline took place during the latter 2010s, which was a period of strong economic growth and declining unemployment in New York City that also saw an increase in the minimum wage. The bulk of this decline was likely driven by the economy and may have happened regardless of the administration's policy changes. There is no statistically significant trend in the monthly figure shown in figure 5.1.[26]

The striking thing about the trend in figure 5.2 is that it shows a modest decline during a time when de Blasio and Banks were implementing policies—such as less punitive sanctioning, more education and training, and less rapid job attachment—that critics believed would encourage more long-term welfare recipients and higher rolls. Predictions of the caseload ticking up, the welfare rolls soaring, or a return to the "bad old peak-welfare days" proved false.

Of course, critics could argue that the decline in the unduplicated number might have been greater had the new, less punitive policies not been put in place, but this possibility is not testable with the current data.

Preface to Implementation Findings

Regarding the trends in job placement, there are two possible interpretations. A pessimistic interpretation would focus on the initial decline, followed by an only modest rise, in job placements under the Career Pathways welfare employment programs of the de Blasio administration. A more optimistic interpretation would emphasize the rise in placements could have continued had not the external shock of the pandemic hit. The question is which of these interpretations is most convincing.

One way to illuminate this issue is to look at the implementation of the Career Pathways programs. Famously, Jeffrey L. Pressman and Aaron B. Wildavsky showed that the absence of riots in late 1960s Oakland, California, could not be attributed to a much-ballyhooed Great Society jobs creation program because the program was hardly implemented there.[27] If Career Compass, Youth Pathways, and Career Advance were implemented smoothly; if the plans that were supposed to produce more job placements were in fact put in place; if administrators, providers, and clients reported that the system was working as expected; then it is plausible that the new policies would eventually make up lost ground. But if implementation was never accomplished, if plans were unrealized, and if key participants were frustrated with how the system worked, there is no reason to believe the desired level of job placement would have eventually been achieved.

To address the question of how effectively the Career Pathways employment programs were implemented, I interviewed executives at the private-sector organizations that operated those programs under contract to the HRA. I also examined HRA evaluations of the provider organizations, which are known as vendor performance evaluations. This material is dealt with in chapter 6.

6
IMPLEMENTATION OF CAREER PATHWAYS WELFARE PROGRAMS

In my research presented here, two types of data were used to evaluate the implementation of the Career Advance, Career Compass, and Youth Pathways programs. One type of data was composed of interviews with executives at private-sector vendors that provided such programs under contract to the Human Resources Administration (HRA): America Works, Grant Associates, Goodwill Industries, and Maximus Human Services. A round of interviews was done in 2018, the first full year of the programs, and a second round was done in 2021. The main goal was to find out what the implementation of the programs was like. I asked what major challenges, if any, the providers encountered; how different the providers felt the new career pathways programs were compared to the old labor force attachment programs offered under Michael Bloomberg; what, if any, were the most striking accomplishments of the new programs; whether, in the end, the programs were successfully implemented; and other questions about running the programs.

The second type of implementation data was vendor performance evaluations (VPEs) made annually by the HRA concerning the private-sector providers of the Career Pathways programs. I looked at one hundred such reports done for ten providers for three Program Years (PYs). These were based on in-person observations of program orientations and classes; a random review of client case records; an analysis of budgets, invoices, and other records; staff interviews; and client job placement. Based on this material, the vendors received an overall evaluation of their implementation of each contract as either unsatisfactory, poor, fair, good, or excellent and were ranked on a scale from 0 to 100.

Together, these data sources provide a great deal of information about the implementation of the Career Pathways programs.

Interviews with Vendors
Client Attitudes

I asked the provider executives I interviewed what they thought were the greatest obstacles in implementing the new employment programs. Interestingly, they often said that the main challenges came not from staff or any other internal factor but from the clients. Many clients, the providers told me, at first did not understand the logic of the new programs, did not see the point of extensive evaluations, did not want to be referred to off-site training programs, and were reluctant to shift from the rapid-attachment approach they were familiar with to the more complex human capital development concept.

Diane Edelson, executive vice president of Grant Associates, made this point in 2018:

> Customers very often don't understand . . . the value of education training. . . . They say they want training, but when it involves coming to a program every day, when it comes to acquiring a credential, possibly taking a test to get that credential, then a lot of their educational deficits come into play. Or they're not sure if they want this training. So the whole value of education training has to be focused on here to help people to see the value of it. That is definitely a challenge that we're running into. . . .
>
> Some people come to us and they don't want to go through an assessment. They don't understand why they need that. It all sounds very nice, but I'm telling you they need a job. So sometimes they're impatient and they are not 100 percent sure this is right. So again, we're educating people on the value of taking the time to think this through.[1]

I was told a similar story by Sheree Ferguson-Cousins, assistant vice president at Goodwill Industries in 2021:

> We had challenges, I think, with clients who were used to the system as it was before. . . . Before it was, you were referred from HRA and you stayed with one vendor until you found employment, or until you came off public assistance. With this new system you were going to one vendor for assessment and then another vendor for training and placement,

and/or you might be going off to an educational institution. So the multiple stops were difficult for some people in the beginning, especially those who had been in the system before. And so they [said]: "This isn't how we used to do it."[2]

The people I interviewed at Maximus in 2021 also spoke of the challenges with client acceptance of the new programs. Vice President for Workforce Services Patricia M. Connelly discussed how clients adapted to the change from the Bloomberg rapid-attachment program Back to Work to the new evaluation and training programs such as Career Compass. "I think in the early days when we first started up, I spent a lot of time going into the rooms where we were meeting with the clients and listening to what we were hearing from them," Connelly said. "And the thing that struck me most was the challenge in getting them to understand the change." Connelly found that "getting the participants to understand, you know, dream the dream . . . where do you want to go?" was difficult. She observed that participants were "kind of slipping back into the old Back to Work model." Maximus had "a lot of work one-on-one with participants to get them to move to that [new] model, because they've been in the Back to Work [model]."[3]

These experiences of client reluctance illustrate the importance of what has been called "coproduction" in public administration. In a classic article on the subject, Gordon P. Whitaker noted, "Citizens influence the content of many public services through their direct participation in service delivery. This is especially the case in services designed to change people directly rather than to change their physical environment. . . . This is particularly the case in human services where change in the client's behavior is the 'product' which is supposed to be delivered."[4]

In the sense of active client participation, coproduction is especially important in education and training-oriented welfare work policies because clients will learn nothing unless they cooperate to some degree. Lawrence Mead has argued that before the advent of work-first welfare reform, policy overemphasized the responsibility of the government to provide services to clients as an entitlement that "threatens coproduction and hence the success of policy in situations where solutions require efforts by the clients as well as government."[5] Mead concluded that the necessary coproduction could be achieved by enforcing an obligation on clients to participate in work programs. In fact, even under the kinder and gentler approach of Bill de Blasio and Steven Banks, clients were still obligated to participate in work programs. The experience of New York City's vendors with the Career Pathways welfare programs suggests that the necessary effort from clients also requires, besides enforcement, patient communication of "the whole value of education training . . . to help people to see the value of it."[6]

Fewer Sanctions

As noted in chapter 5, some early critics of the de Blasio/Banks policies felt that sanctions for noncompliance with work requirements were being gutted and predicted that work activity and job placements would fall off as a result. The staff I spoke with at the private-sector vendors expressed some concern about the de-emphasis on sanctions but overall approved of the kinder and gentler approach.

Staff at Goodwill Industries offered mixed opinions about the sanctioning process under de Blasio and Banks. In 2018, the people I interviewed there included Charmaine Williams, Beatriz Baldwin, Jessica Gardner, and Dolores Swirin-Yao. All interviewees agreed that fewer punitive measures were being taken against clients, and one made the striking observation that "there's no teeth in the system." But they also felt the practices of not financially penalizing clients and allowing them to explain their lack of compliance to staff created "more buy-in" from clients.

> WILLIAMS: I feel like there's nothing punitive about the Blasio plan, in fact. I think it's even where there's no teeth in the system.
> MAIN: [Do] most of you agree with that? Is it the way you look at it?
> BALDWIN: I do agree that there's very few penalties around de Blasio's administration.
> MAIN: There's fewer of those punitive measures under de Blasio than there was under Bloomberg?
> SEVERAL VOICES: Yes. Absolutely.[7]

In my 2021 interviews at Goodwill, the subject of sanctions came up again. Despite recognition that some clients may try to take advantage of the system, the interviewees felt the new approach introduced under de Blasio and Banks did not undermine discipline and was more compatible with Goodwill's organizational culture than was Bloomberg's stricter sanctioning policy.

> MAIN: Did you, or did anybody—I'm talking about Goodwill as a whole—was there a perception that under the new kinder and gentler system, people were abusing the system and, hey, we can't have this?
> FERGUSON-COUSINS: I'm going to say no. And I might be off. It's just my personal opinion. The culture of Goodwill was always to work with clients, even outside of these contracts. You know, we work with other individuals that have barriers to employment. And I think the culture that Goodwill has is very similar to the kinder, gentler [policy]. So it wasn't a big, hard lift for us.[8]

In 2018, Lee Bowes, CEO of America Works, talked about the change in the sanctioning process and the impact it had on her organization. She felt that sanctions were overused under Bloomberg, and she approved of the less punitive approach, even though some of her staff were at first skeptical. She noted that sanctioned clients often appealed to the state for fair hearings. In 2021, she reiterated her support for the softer sanctioning process.

Bowes noted that before the change in policy, when clients were sanctioned more frequently, they "had to spend a period of time where they couldn't participate with us. And they supposedly [lost] their income, but in truth, everyone went and filed for a fair hearing, run by the state." Bowes explained that in "almost all cases—like a hundred percent of the cases," the fair hearings proceeding would result in the sanctions being overturned. Bowes reflected on the position this placed the staff in regarding the clients. "It was a huge administrative hassle for the staff, because then they were [in] an antagonistic relationship with clients," she said. "There wasn't a day that went by where somebody wasn't furious and upset that they were being sanctioned and had to be physically restrained or [we] had to remove them from the building." Bowes saw the change in policy as positive. "To have that taken off of us I think was helpful to us at America Works.[9]

In an important 2011 book, *What Works in Work-First Welfare*, Andrew R. Feldman did a rigorous quantitative analysis of the performance of twenty-six welfare-work programs during 2004–2006. Ferguson found that "the rate at which programs impose sanctions varies considerably among programs . . . yet these rates are not significantly correlated with placement or retention rates."[10] Feldman speculated this may be because in New York, "where the state's sanctioning rules are relatively lenient," providers relied on other means to convey high expectations to clients.[11] This finding backs up the experience of providers like Bowes, who found sanctions to be more trouble than they were worth, and were not sorry to see them further minimized under Banks and de Blasio.

New Contract Structures

In a system that relies on private contractors to deliver services, the structure of the contracts is of central importance. The HRA contracts with work program providers over the years have been of different types. These include performance contracts, in which contractors are paid for specific accomplishments, such as for every client placed in a job or for every client who is retained in that job at specified intervals. Contracts have also been in a line-item or cost-reimbursement format where contractors are paid a set amount based on the expenses they incur with each client they help. Hybrid contracts combining performance standards and line-item payments have also been used, so a contractor would be paid for each client served and for specified accomplishments. Under de Blasio and Banks, in the first year of the new programs, contracts were entirely line-item. In later years, they were hybrid, with 72 percent of the contract being line-item and 28 percent being performance-based.

According to Diane Edelson, this shift from fully performance-based contracts under Bloomberg to hybrid contracts under de Blasio and Banks was due to the different goals of the two administrations. She said under de Blasio and Banks, "there is really an emphasis here on not just placing people in jobs and paying vendors for it, but creating a fuller, broader program that involves variety and diversity of options for customers that are not necessarily paid for through performance, but are paid for as part of contract maintenance. . . . Whereas under the Bloomberg administration . . . everything was really focused on only employment."[12]

The literature on contracting with private vendors to provide welfare services presents simple criteria for deciding between performance-based and cost-reimbursement contracts. Some of that work assumes that for-profit providers, like Maximus, not nonprofits like Goodwill Industries, will prefer performance-based contracts. For example, M. Bryna Sanger said the following regarding contract structures: "Maximus, in particular, has the size and capital to move and gear up quickly in the welfare area. . . . Furthermore, it has the investment capital to survive a long time in a performance-based system, and its corporate representatives are well aware that the smaller for-profits and nonprofits simply do not have the same degree of leverage it takes to manage large caseloads under performance-based contracts."[13] But the interviews I conducted with vendor executives paint a more complex picture of what contract structures are appropriate for different types of contractors.

For example, in 2018, executives at the not-for-profit Goodwill Industries mostly preferred fully performance-based contracts because with good performance, they could earn more money that could be invested in experimental or pilot programs. Thus, Williams noted, "With the performance-based, you performed well, you made money. You can invest into those pilot projects. . . . With the line item that's a little bit harder." Swirin-Yao agreed that a performance-based contract "basically generates funds" that "give you some flexibility to innovate."[14]

Sheree Ferguson-Cousins provided more details on what the organization did with the money it earned under performance-based contracts. "I think with the 100 percent performance that we were used to, it gave us a lot of room to be creative. . . . We have a track record of . . . taking a look at how else we can serve these people. And we were able to do so when we were able to maximize the contract dollars." Ferguson offered ACES as an early program example. "In one of the first Back to Works, we created a program, ACES, that worked with individuals . . . who have been on public assistance for a long period of time. . . . And so we were able to do that because we were working in performance-based. . . . With the hybrid at this time, I think it's okay. But it doesn't give a lot of wiggle room for us to make any extra money, [and] not only extra money, but to really try to think creatively, to create additional programs."[15]

Jim Miller, who was in charge of strategic solutions at Maximus, reported that his company preferred not a pure performance system but hybrid contracts. His comments were consistent with the position that nonprofits ought to feel disadvantaged by performance-based contracts. He said, "If you go to 100 percent performance-based, what you're doing is limiting your supply chain to the people that have the working capital to cover that cost, and I see that that oftentimes eliminates your not-for-profit organizations because they don't have the working capital to do it."[16] But, as noted, the nonprofit Goodwill does not embrace this position and prefers the performance-based model. Despite Sanger's assumption that Maximus would prefer performance-based contracts, Miller said his firm preferred hybrid contracts.

Miller explained that "we articulate and we argue for a hybrid model." Within that model, he said, there are "core costs." He explained this as "a floor that everybody has to cover." An advantage of contracting in the hybrid model is "you normalize that floor," making it "the same for everybody." When the floor is established, Miller explained, then "what you're doing is making your decisions based upon the performance delivered by the contracted entity." When future performance is unknown, and no one can model risk, "you're going to have to lean a little more [toward] cost reimbursement." Then you "end up paying a lot more as a government for a service than you should be." Therefore, at Maximus, Miller said, "We advocate for this hybrid model because it's the most efficient and effective model for government."[17]

Miller's argument is that some costs involved in welfare-work programs are well known and others are more uncertain. Contractors know how much it will cost for them to serve a client, but how many clients will get or retain a job is less certain. If contracts are 100 percent performance-based, contractors do not know how successful they will be in meeting results, so how much they will make is uncertain, and such contracts are risky. Therefore, contractors must charge more to cover that risk. But contracts that partly reimburse for the costs of serving clients reduce that risk, and contractors will be able to charge less because the risk is lower. If part of the contract pays for specified outcomes, contractors will still have an incentive to perform. At any rate, such is how Maximus reckons. Whatever one makes of this argument, the point is that, contrary to what the literature assumes, for-profit organizations do not necessarily prefer pure performance-based contracts.

David Casey, senior vice president of government relations at Maximus, made the illuminating suggestion that performance-based contracts work best when the vendor is allowed to suggest what the performance criteria should be. The idea is that the contractee—the organization that enters into a contract with another entity that provides services—should set the overall goal of the contract, while the vendors should be allowed to devise a plan for achieving the goal and set performance milestones to be met in the process.

"Performance-based contracting works when the vendor or the provider can come back [to the agency] and say, here's . . . the model and how it would work rather than being told [by the agency] how it works," Casey said. For example, "when you get a tender or a [request for proposal] in other countries, performance-based contracting usually entails saying: 'Here's the problem; tell me how you [the vendor] want to fix it.'" In contrast, Casey observed that in the United States, we say, "Here's a problem: Let me tell you [the vendor] how to fix it." Then the agency creates a performance-based contract.[18]

Lee Bowes added another wrinkle to the question of what sort of organizations are most suited for performance-based contracts. She suggested that publicly traded organizations would not find fully performance-based contracts congenial. She said, "I mean, if you can literally earn nothing if you don't perform, it can be a very threatening thing, if you're owned by a publicly traded company and you were applying to a billion vice-presidents and somebody else."[19]

Bowes preferred the fully performance-based contracts because she found the format more flexible. In this regard, she was in agreement with the Goodwill executives. "So I liked the performance model because it's more effective," Bowes said. "It allows flexibility. It allows us to exceed our goals, which we always did. And when we exceed our goals, we do better financially."[20]

Bowes saw that a downside to the hybrid contracts of the de Blasio administration was that 72 percent of the payments were in line-item form. "We share all of our financial earnings with our staff. So for example, a sales person gets a bonus when somebody gets hired and they stay for a certain [amount] . . . of time. The [current mostly] line item [contract with] only [28] percent performance, has meant everybody at America Works has lost the size of their bonuses because I can't pay them out."[21]

Another suggestion regarding contract structure is that if contracts were to be hybrid, the performance-based portion should be based not just on job placements but also on the successful completion of training programs and other milestones. Cousins of Goodwill noted that under the hybrid contracts, "the performance portion is still based on . . . amount of placements and retention, which is okay. . . . However, I feel that . . . a better measure of performance is how many people . . . you've placed through training,"[22] referring to the completion of a training program. Diane Edelson agreed. "Although we have this hybrid method of being paid for developing training and so forth, the performance part of the contract is all about placement," she said. "And I personally—because I think that education, training is very essential for our customers, in a variety of ways—I think it would be good if performance was based on training completion, people getting jobs after those trainings, with those credentials. And I think that that would be a fuller way to assess performance."[23]

The programs Feldman analyzed varied in their profit orientation and contract structure. Some were run by nonprofit and some by for-profit providers. Some programs had contract structures that were entirely performance-based, and others were "based partly on performance," which are described here as hybrid contracts. Regarding contract structure, Feldman found that "moving from a compensation scheme based partly on performance to one that is fully performance-based increases sustained employment by more than half (55 percent) for non-custodial participants [individuals without children] and by more than a third (35 percent) for the full sample."[24] He further notes, "The results imply that stronger incentives for performance produce better overall employment results."[25] This convincing quantitative analysis found that fully performance-based contracts were superior to hybrid contracts in terms of job placement. However, the providers I interviewed who expressed a preference for pure performance contracts did not argue that such a contract structure produced better employment outcomes than hybrid contracts. Instead, they argued that the opportunity to bring in more revenue through better performance allowed greater flexibility to innovate new programs. Nor did supporters of hybrid contracts concede that structure led to fewer job placements. Their claim was that the risk involved with pure performance contracts would drive up costs as all bidders modeled higher costs and thus charged higher rates.

What the providers had to say about contract structures complicates the discussion of that issue. Given the nonprofit Goodwill's preference for performance-based contracts and the for-profit Maximus's preference for hybrid contracts, it seems not to be the case that only large, for-profit organizations will prefer the performance-based formats. And the choice between the performance-based and cost-reimbursement formats is not resolved by simply splitting the difference and using hybrid contracts that incorporate both formats. The question of what performance is to be compensated remains. That question is best resolved when the vendor, which has a better understanding of the work process than the contractee, is given a chance to suggest the performance milestones.

Vendors' Organizational Culture and New Programs

The providers of the Career Pathways programs told an interesting story. The changes introduced under the de Blasio administration were dramatic in the sense of being a clear break with the rapid-attachment approach of Rudy Giuliani and Bloomberg. But the transition from the old policies to the new ones went smoothly, with none of the confusion or tumult associated with the earlier bouts of change of the 1960s and 1990s. The providers attributed this orderly transition partly to the fact that the human capital development approach was more compatible with their established organizational culture than the work-first policies had been.

All the interviewees acknowledged that the shift from work-first to Career Pathways was a major change. Even so, several felt the new programs were more in line with their organizational culture than the old ones. Executives at Goodwill especially felt the new programs were more compatible with their mission of rehabilitating disabled people than the rapid-attachment programs had been. All providers felt that a key reason for the successful implementation of the rapid-attachment programs had always been their staff's devotion of some effort to evaluating clients and placing them in jobs suited to their abilities.

For example, at Goodwill in 2018, Baldwin, reflecting on the Career Pathways model, said, "I would say this model is more aligned with our mission. It gives us the opportunity to really empower the participants to want to be here, as opposed to forcing them to be here."[26] In 2021, Ferguson-Cousins said, "I think the major shift that came about was the kinder, gentler approach to programming and the way participants were treated and options [were] given, etc. And I would say that wasn't a major shift for us. Because as an organization . . . Goodwill employed that [approach] anyways."[27]

In 2018, Diane Edelson said that Grant Associates, like all other employment service vendors, had long before abandoned programs that put the onus of searching for a job on clients. That was the approach of Job Club, a program implemented under David Dinkins in which clients were taught how to look for work and there was no effort by the vendor to do job development. Edelson explained that Grant had incorporated more intensive evaluation, personalized training, and client search even under Back to Work and well before the Career Pathways model was adopted under de Blasio and Banks. "Grant Associates, and other vendors in the system will qualify for this, too," Edelson said, "work like a personnel agency/staffing firm on behalf of our customers. We have a proactive connection with businesses, we set people up on interviews. There's much greater success in that model." After the client is hired, "they're assigned to a career coach who manages and helps them through the initial stages of going to work." The purpose of the coach is "making sure they have the supports they need: carfare, clothing, daycare." Overall, Edelson explained, "It's a lot of proactive work besides just a relationship with a company."[28]

I asked Edelson to compare that approach to the operation of Back to Work. "We did the same model of proactive engagement and reaching out and assigning a person to a career advisor and then to the account managers and the career coaches," she replied. "We did the same model under Back to Work."[29]

In 2021, Vanessa Preston of Grant Associates agreed with Edelson's assessment and explained why the shift to Career Pathways was less dramatic than might have been expected. "Under Back to Work, I would say, a best practice for providers was that oftentimes we would contextualize our adult basic education and workshops," Preston said. "That's part of Grant Associates' model always," she said. "Under Career Pathways that's now an expectation. All providers must contextualize their adult, basic education and bridge programming to the career industry of focus that is in demand in the borough that they operate. So it was, as I said, a best practice before, but now it's a minimum expectation."[30]

In 2021, executives at Maximus, a provider that embraced rapid job placement, agreed that evaluation and individualization of clients were necessary in any program. Patricia Connelly said, "We were not handing people mops and pails in the Back to Work program. We were trying to hook people up with jobs that interested them and that they would qualify for. Because that, at least, got them started halfway." The Back to Work program, according to her, "wasn't just forcing people into any available job that's out there. There was a lot of work that went into [it]," she said, where Maximus "worked with the individual to identify what their interest was and try to connect them to employment to get that started."[31]

The case of America Works and how its organizational culture meshed with the Career Pathways programs is unique. In the early 1990s, America Works received much attention for its reliance on a rapid-attachment model of welfare-work programs. Apparently, partly for this reason, the Dinkins administration turned down several RFP responses by America Works, which eventually won contracts under the more sympathetic Giuliani administration. Under de Blasio and Banks, America Works won seven contracts to provide Career Compass, Youth Pathways, and Career Advance programs. But these new programs were of the human capital development model, supposedly the opposite of the rapid-attachment programs that America Works made its name with. How did a provider with such a different program philosophy end up with many contracts under de Blasio and Banks? Lee Bowes discussed that matter with me in 2018:

I asked Bowes: "America Works had something that was legitimately conceived of as a rapid attachment model. Yet . . . de Blasio and Banks said they wanted to move away from rapid attachment to human capital development. Nonetheless, they came back to America Works. So are you delivering the same stuff that you always delivered?" "Yes and no," she said. "I mean, we had been shifting, because the marketplace has been shifting. So as welfare reform has evolved, we evolved with it. And part of the evolution is that not just here in New York, but around the country, we're doing a lot more Career Pathways."[32]

Bowes also emphasized that even when America Works was providing the Back to Work program and before the de Blasio/Banks administration, the organization developed employer-specific training programs that foreshadowed the Career Pathways approach. "So we started with going out to our employers who have been hiring from us for the past thirty years in New York," she explained. "And we said, we're going to design customized programs that will specifically help prepare, better prepare, people that you're going to be interviewing from us for jobs in your [firm]. So we did that. These were shorter-term training programs, very occupation specific," Bowes explained. "So we did all of that in the context of the old programs." She clarified the timeline under which the de Blasio programs and policies were implemented. "So understand that when Banks came in, it wasn't until the fifth year, basically, that he was able to get these programs up and running," she said, referring to Career Pathways. "It took quite a while. So that gave me a big lead time to put my footprint down in terms of what I saw his direction was going to be, but something that I felt I philosophically could live with and could be proud of."[33]

Bowes's comments are interesting because they suggest that even an organization strongly identified with the work-first philosophy was able to accommodate itself to the Career Pathways programs with their emphasis on human capital development. It is worth recalling that Judith Gueron of MDRC found that the most effective programs were "'mixed-strategy' programs, which stress immediate job entry for some recipients and employment-directed education or training for others."[34] Also, as we shall see in chapter 7, "at the same time work first policies were reducing rates of college enrollment and completion among welfare recipients and unmarried parents generally, they also helped fuel the development of more innovative, accelerated, and employment-focused training approaches."[35] Overall, the vendors' remarks on their organizational cultures suggest that for them, the segue from work-first to Career Pathways was not as dramatic as might be thought.

Data from Vendor Performance Evaluations
Findings from Vendor Performance Evaluations

As mentioned already, the HRA did evaluations for PYs 1–3 of each of its contracts with private organizations to provide the Career Pathways programs to eligible clients. These were known as vendor performance evaluations (VPEs). VPEs were done for three PYs between September 2017 and March 2020. After April 2020, the programs were suspended due to the COVID-19 pandemic. In person observations were not done in PY3 due to COVID-19 restrictions. Over that time, a total of thirty-four contracts were signed with ten different providers, and a total of one hundred VPEs were conducted.

My main concern is how smoothly the Career Pathways programs were implemented. For that purpose, the most important part of the VPEs is the overall score given to each provider for each contract in the form of a number grade from 0 to 100 and a rating of either unsatisfactory, poor, fair, good, or excellent. Table 6.1 shows vendor rankings by number grade, and table 6.2 shows rankings by label.

Several things stand out from the VPEs. First, the majority of ratings were "excellent," at 74 percent, and another 16 percent were "good." The average number grade was 90.5. The evaluators were very positive about the providers' performance. However, 10 percent of grades were either "fair," "poor," or "unsatisfactory," so the evaluators were willing to mark bad grades when they felt that was appropriate.

TABLE 6.1 Vendors ranked by average overall score, Program Years 1–3 with profit status

VENDOR	AVERAGE OVERALL SCORE	NUMBER OF CONTRACTS	NUMBER OF EVALUATIONS	PROFIT STATUS
America Works	98.2	7	21	For profit
ResCare Workforce Services/Equus Workforce Solutions	97.25	2	6	Nonprofit
Goodwill	96.82	4	12	Nonprofit
National Association on Drug Abuse Problems, Inc. (NADAP)	95.52	2	6	Nonprofit
Grant Associates	93.35	4	12	For profit
Maximus	91.6	5	15	For profit
East River Development Alliance, Inc. (ERDA)	88.33	1	3	Nonprofit
Educational Data System, Inc. (EDSI)	86.73	1	3	For profit
FedCap Rehabilitation Services, Inc. (FedCap)	85.84	6	18	Nonprofit
Gay Men's Health Crisis, Inc. (GMHC)	71.38	2	4	Nonprofit
Average	90.5	Total: 34	Total: 100	

Source: HRA Services Contract Monitoring and Compliance Unit, Vendor Performance Evaluations of Career Pathways Contracts 2018–2020.

TABLE 6.2 Vendors ranked by performance label, Program Years 1–3

VENDOR	NUMBER	PERCENT
America Works		
"Excellent" evaluations	20	95.24
"Good" evaluations	1	4.76
Total evaluations	21	100.00
EDSI		
"Excellent" evaluations	1	33.33
"Good" evaluations	2	66.66
Total evaluations	3	100.00
ERDA		
"Excellent" evaluations	1	33.33
"Good" evaluations	2	66.66
Total evaluations	3	99.99
FedCap		
"Excellent" evaluations	9	50.00
"Good" evaluations	4	22.22
"Fair" evaluations	3	16.66
"Poor" evaluations	1	5.55
"Unsatisfactory" evaluations	1	5.55
Total evaluations	18	99.98
GMHC		
"Excellent" evaluations	1	25.00
"Fair" evaluations	1	25.00
"Unsatisfactory" evaluations	2	50.00
Total evaluations	4	100.00
Goodwill		
"Excellent" evaluations	10	83.33
"Good" evaluations	2	16.67
Total evaluations	12	100.00
Grant		
"Excellent" evaluations	10	83.33
"Good" evaluations	2	16.67
Total evaluations	12	100.00
Maximus		
"Excellent" evaluations	11	73.33
"Good" evaluations	2	13.33
"Fair" evaluations	1	6.66
"Poor" evaluations	1	6.66
Total evaluations	15	99.98
NADAP		
"Excellent" evaluations	5	83.33
"Good" evaluations	1	16.67
Total evaluations	6	100.00

TABLE 6.2 (continued)

VENDOR	NUMBER	PERCENT
ResCare/Equus		
"Excellent" evaluations	6	100.00
Total evaluations	6	100.00
All vendors		
"Excellent" evaluations	74	74.00
"Good" evaluations	16	16.00
"Fair" evaluations	5	5.00
"Poor" evaluations	2	2.00
"Unsatisfactory" evaluations	3	3.00
Total evaluations	100	100.00

Source: HRA Services Contract Monitoring and Compliance Unit, Vendor Performance Evaluations of Career Pathways Contracts 2018–2020.

Also interesting is that America Works had the highest average number grade at 98.2. All but one of America Works' twenty-one evaluations were "excellent," with the one exception being "good." I interviewed David Aguado, the CEO of America Works, about what he thought were the causes behind such high evaluations. He shared his thoughts on the subject, explaining much of the success of America Works by noting that there are "from a high level, a couple of things that we've always stuck to and are well known" for. "Number one," he explained, "is treatment of the clients. We are very big on respectful, positive treatment of the clients, of approaching clients from a strength-based perspective." Aguado emphasized that the organization does not focus on clients' "potential barriers or speed bumps" but on their strengths and growing those strengths. "And yes," he said, "how can we turn weaknesses into strengths?"[36]

"Number two, we are big believers in real relationships with employers," Aguado said, which means going beyond looking online for who is hiring. Aguado said it matters "to actually be successful with these placements." "It's not about somebody starting work," he said. "It's about: Is someone working a month later? Are they working six months later? Are they working a year later? That's how we measure success." The way to do this, he explained, is "you have to have a process, a structure in place, a requirement on your staff whose responsibility it is to make relationships with employers and to get our clients hired, that they really have relationships with employers."[37]

The most interesting point here is Aguado's emphasis on "real relationships with employers." America Works was among the first welfare-work organizations to emphasize job development, that is, not just training clients or teaching them how to look for a job but also identifying specific job openings and guiding clients to them. The organization has a staff of marketers who are expected to develop jobs, match them to specific clients, and mentor those clients for their first months on the job until retention goals have been fulfilled. Marketers are paid based on how many clients they place and retain in jobs. This close cooperation between employers and placement organizations amounts to a version of the public/private coordination that the Career Pathways approach seeks to achieve through industry partnerships (described in chap. 7). The main difference is that the job development efforts that America Works developed and continues to emphasize seek coordination on a micro-level, matching individual employers and job seekers. Industry partnerships sought "to ensure that workforce training is directly linked to employers' talent needs,"[38] and to do so by building structures that pipeline potential workers to specific industries, such as a training program to develop the nurse practitioners that the health care industry found in short supply. Chapter 7 discusses how, as a coordination strategy, the industry partnerships met with mixed results. But the practice of developing partnerships with specific employers that America Works pioneered in the welfare context became the best practice for all such welfare-work organizations.

Also interesting is the rating of Maximus, which, at 91.6, was in the lower middle of the pack. Unlike most other providers, Maximus received one "fair" and one "poor" evaluation. This underwhelming performance comes from a company that made a great fuss about how, as a private for-profit entity, it is easily able to outperform public-sector agencies. Maximus was founded by David V. Mastran, who wrote a polemical history of his company titled *Privateer!: Building a Business, Reforming Government*. In this proprivatization tract, Mastran writes: "I was called a privateer by the government employee unions as a slur. As Chief Executive Officer of Maximus, a firm specializing in privatization, I came to regard the name positively—someone who helps government do a better job for the people."[39] Mastran began his career in the early 1970s at the federal Department of Health, Education, and Welfare, where he "observed huge inefficiencies in how poverty programs were being administered by the government.... Since I faced huge obstacles trying to reform these programs inside government, I left government to try to reform these programs in the private sector."[40]

Mastran was critical not only of public agencies but also of nonprofits and New York City nonprofits in particular. Maximus won contracts in the city, he writes, because "Rudy Giuliani . . . wanted to break the hold of nonprofit organizations on the welfare-to-work program contracts in the city since the organizations were not very effective."[41] The Giuliani administration and its HRA commissioner, Jason Turner, were accused of unfairly favoring Maximus in the contract bidding process and were investigated by the city comptroller, Alan G. Hevesi. A suit brought by Hevesi went to the New York Appellate Court, which detected no corruption and found for the administration. Mastran also suggests that nonprofits have limited mandates and cannot compete head-on with for-profits. He writes, "We also frequently competed against nonprofit organizations like the Salvation Army, Catholic Charities, and Goodwill Industries. These nonprofits had noble missions to advance, but tended to bid only on those contracts consistent with their mission statements."[42]

The VPE ratings of the Career Pathways providers do not establish a clear superiority of either for-profit or nonprofit organizations in this case. The highest-rated organization is a for-profit, America Works. But the next three organizations in the top four are all nonprofits: ResCare/Equus, Goodwill Industries, and the National Association for Drug Abuse Problems (NADAP). On average, for-profit organizations received a higher number grade, 92.47, than did nonprofits, whose average score was 89.19. However, the lower average grade of nonprofits was due to the poor performance of Gay Men's Health Crisis (GMHC), which got the lowest score of any organization at 71.38. GMHC differed from the other providers in that its main mission has been providing health services to gay men, not employment services to welfare clients. This may account for the low rating of this organization. When GMHC is excluded, the number grade of the nonprofit organizations rises to 92.752, above the average score of the for-profits. In short, contrary to the claims made in *Privateer!*, the VPEs do not reflect a superiority of for-profits over nonprofits.

The VPEs' ambivalent evidence about the better performance of for-profit providers backs up similar findings from Feldman's *What Works in Work-First Welfare*. Feldman notes, "Overall, for-profits have somewhat better results, measured as the share of all participants who get jobs and are still working at any job six months later."[43] But he also reports that "nonprofits have wider variance in their performance" than for-profits and that "a 'soft and fuzzy' view of nonprofits as necessarily mission driven [rather than profit driven] or necessarily more empathetic, is certainly not accurate."[44] Moreover, the practical significance of the overall better performance of for-profits is debatable. Feldman's analysis found a two percentage point difference between for-profits and nonprofits in the share of all participants that become employed and are still working six months later (10 percent versus 8 percent). Further, the city pays for-profits much more than nonprofits because the for-profits achieve about 36 percent more performance milestones than the nonprofits. Therefore, Feldman remarks, one could argue that "the city pays more for for-profit services despite receiving roughly similar results as nonprofits."[45]

Conclusions from VPE Data

The main concern of this chapter is to document the implementation of the Career Pathways programs. The evidence from the VPEs is that the implementation went well. The only stumble that the evaluators noted was at GMHC during the first year of two Career Advance contracts, on both of which it was rated "unsatisfactory." The next year, the organization's performance improved, and it achieved a "fair" and "excellent" rating on the contracts. A more rigorous evaluation of the Career Pathways programs would have been very helpful. But the VPEs do show that the implementation of the programs went smoothly.

Overall Conclusions

What do these interviews with vendor executives and performance evaluations tell us about the implementation of the Career Pathways welfare work programs? The most important takeaway is that implementation went smoothly for the most part and the programs ended up being implemented as they were intended to be. The early years of the HRA's operation under Lindsay were chaotic, with the organization failing to effectively implement even basic functions such as eligibility determination. The change to work-oriented welfare reform under Giuliani was a traumatic experience, as the administration deliberately embraced a strategy of breaking all the rules. Nothing like these organizational earthquakes took place with the human capital development programs under de Blasio and Banks. This was partly because that administration consciously adopted a change strategy of extensive consultation with involved parties including not only HRA staff but also the vendors who were to deliver the new programs.

The fact that implementation went smoothly is relevant to interpreting the job placement record of the de Blasio/Banks program. As was discussed in chapter 5, in the early stages of those programs, job placement numbers declined, but they started to rise again until the pandemic hit. That trend would likely not have been continued had the Career Pathways programs been chaotic or ineffective. Given how those programs managed to get up and running without too much disruption, it is reasonable to think that the positive trend in job placements would have continued but for the exogenous shock of the COVID-19 crisis, which brought an end to the enforcement of the new programs. What would have happened but for the pandemic is a counterfactual that the available data cannot answer.

What does the experience of the vendors suggest for the main questions of this book—which are whether nonincremental change is possible in New York City government and what is the city's capacity for such change—and imply for the democratic legitimacy of its political environment? Nonincremental change is defined as the abandonment of a baseline policy and the imposition of a new baseline rather than a modification of the status quo.

The creation of the HRA under Lindsay certainly fits that definition, as the baseline situation of many welfare-related agencies reporting directly to the mayor was replaced with a single superagency. The problem with treating this development as a vindication of the democratic potential of city politics is that in its early years, the agency was disorganized and ineffective. A long time passed before the HRA became tolerably well managed and emerged as the necessary centerpiece of the city's welfare system.

Giuliani's version of welfare reform also counts as a nonincremental change, as the baseline policies of income maintenance and service were dramatically abandoned and the new approach of rapid labor force attachment was imposed. The change was a shock for HRA employees, but the agency did not descend into chaos, and management practices that enforced work-first policies were successfully established. These events show that city government is capable of nonincremental change. Whether this whole episode counts as supporting the democratic nature of New York's political system depends partly on what one thinks of the substance of Giuliani's work-first policies.

Whether the de Blasio/Banks programs represent a nonincremental change is less clear. Vendors acknowledged that Career Compass, Career Advance, and Youth Pathways were an important change from Bloomberg's work-first program. The essence of the rapid labor force attachment policies was requiring clients to participate in work assignments, and that practice remained in place under the Career Pathways approach, which could be thought of as an incremental change only, one that simply modified baseline policy. There is also the interesting fact that the vendors who implemented the programs found them more compatible with their organizational cultures of training and rehabilitation than the work-first programs had been. The Career Pathways programs were a change, but to a considerable extent, they represented a return to an earlier baseline that had been broken by the Giuliani/Bloomberg policies. Clients eventually reacted positively to the greater choice and opportunities for training they received under de Blasio and Banks. Vendors appreciated the reduced emphasis on sanctioning clients, a process they found onerous and ineffective. Positive change occurred at the HRA during the de Blasio years, but it was positive incremental change. Voters who elected de Blasio on the strength of his campaign promise to make dramatic changes to reduce economic inequality got a more progressive direction in welfare policy, but not a radical break with the past.

7
CAREER PATHWAYS AND THE DRIVE FOR COORDINATION

Literature on Career Pathways

In a report summarizing its research on Career Pathways, the Manpower Development Research Corporation (MDRC) defined the concept as follows: "Career pathways approaches are efforts to build more 'coherent and easily navigable systems providing skills training, credentials, supports, and employment.'" The report referenced a 2012 Joint Career Pathways Letter from the federal Departments of Education, Health and Human Services, and Labor that defined these programs as "a series of connected education and training strategies and support services that enable individuals to secure industry relevant certification and obtain employment within an occupational area and to advance to higher levels of future education and employment in that area." MDRC further specified that "career pathways strategies focus on *programmatic* innovation, such as a high school career academy, and *systemic* reform, such as aligning occupational curricula across multiple educational systems in a state."[1] With its emphasis on education and training, Career Pathways was partly a reaction to earlier strategies for employing poor people and welfare recipients that emphasized immediate placement in unskilled jobs or work programs. In 2012, David J. Fein wrote an evaluative study of Career Pathways for the federal Department of Health and Human Services. He explained how "work-first," or rapid-attachment programs, dialectically begat Career Pathways.

Fein observed how the changes in welfare policy affect workforce programs, that is, programs that offer training to all workers, not just welfare clients. "In the early 1990s, burgeoning welfare rolls led to national shifts in policies with profound consequences for income support and workforce programs," Fein wrote. "New welfare time limits, financial sanctions for failure to comply with program requirements, and services emphasizing rapid labor force attachment (or 'work first') moved thousands of low-skilled unmarried parents into low-wage jobs with little prospect for economic mobility." According to his study, while many state and local governments implemented "predominantly work first–oriented welfare programs," others adjusted their policies and services to maximize short-term training opportunities to be consistent within the work-first rules.[2]

Thus, Fein found, "to a degree that may not be fully recognized, at the same time work first policies were reducing rates of college enrollment and completion among welfare recipients and unmarried parents generally, they also helped fuel the development of more innovative, accelerated, and employment-focused training approaches." He also reported that "random assignment studies finding work first programs had only modest earning impacts and little effect on overall income increased policy makers' interest in training focused strategies. . . . The career pathways model, in particular, has gained traction among policy makers and practitioners and is arguably the predominant framework guiding development of improved education and training approaches for low-skilled adults and other nontraditional student populations at the moment."[3] When Bill de Blasio took office in January 2014, he and the people who joined his administration were among the policy makers dissatisfied with the work-first approach. Since Career Pathways was the alternative that had crystallized among the workforce/welfare policy network, de Blasio and his commissioners were naturally attracted to the new model.

On June 22, 2014, the new administration announced the creation of a Jobs for New Yorkers Task Force.[4] The initial statement of the task force did not mention Career Pathways, but it raised many themes associated with that policy direction, including the need to "fundamentally . . . shift our workforce paradigm from focusing on transactional outcomes defined by low-wage job placement to building skills that will result in higher wage employment and a stronger workforce" and to "better integrate the $500 million investment in workforce programs and education resources to serve the unemployed and under-employed."[5] An early proponent of Career Pathways in the de Blasio administration was Human Resources Administration (HRA) commissioner Steven Banks. In December 2014, Banks submitted an employment plan to the New York State Office of Temporary and Disability Aid that referenced "HRA's career pathways approach," which "places a special emphasis on training and education that enables clients to progress towards their career goals."[6]

On November 21, 2014, the task force released a report, *Career Pathways: One City Working Together*.[7] The report made clear that the de Blasio administration was embracing Career Pathways as the key to accomplishing the platform of fighting economic equality that the mayor had campaigned on. In his introduction to the report, de Blasio wrote: "My administration is committed to building an economy in which every New Yorker can maintain stable employment and earn a family-supporting wage. . . . To help workers secure good-paying jobs in fast-growing economic sectors, the Task Force recommends an unprecedented full-system shift toward a Career Pathways model and public-private Industry Partnership initiatives to ensure that workforce training is directly linked to employers' talent needs."[8] Two things are particularly striking about the *Career Pathways* report. First, like many of the statements made by administration figures concerning workforce and welfare policy, a dramatic change is envisioned. This is what this book refers to as nonincremental change; that is, a change that breaks with rather than incrementally modifying baseline policy. De Blasio's call for an "unprecedented full-system shift" is typical of his administration's rhetoric about Career Pathways.

A second striking feature is the great emphasis on the need to coordinate the actions of a wide range of policy players. In the report, the main mechanism for achieving this coordination was to be a set of industry partnerships that would harmonize the needs of employers with the skill-building services of public-sector workforce agencies. The report explained: "*Industry Partnerships* will be comprised of teams of industry experts focused on addressing mismatches between labor market supply and demand in six economic sectors. To define and fulfill labor demand in their respective sectors, Industry Partnerships will establish ongoing 'feedback loops,' or a platform for regular interaction with employers . . . Industry Partnerships will collaborate with organized labor, educational institutions, service providers, philanthropy, and City agencies to develop workforce development strategies and mobilize resources in their respective sectors."[9]

Coordination in Public Administration

In emphasizing the need for nonincremental change and greater coordination, the de Blasio administration tackled two of the greatest challenges in US public administration. The introduction to this book reviews the extensive literature that concludes "Urban political structures change slowly in an incremental, evolutionary fashion."[10] Skepticism about the ability of government agencies to coordinate among themselves and then with private-sector actors also runs deep in the literature. A famous expression of that sentiment was made by Harold Seidman and Robert Gilmour. In 1986, they mordantly observed, "The quest for coordination is in many respects the twentieth-century equivalent of the medieval search for the philosopher's stone. If we can only find the right formula for coordination we can reconcile the irreconcilable, harmonize competing and wholly divergent interests, overcome irrationalities in our government structures, and make hard policy decisions to which no one will dissent."[11]

James Q. Wilson, in a classic overview of the US public sector, cited Seidman and Gilmour's comment on coordination and summarized the literature on and experience with coordination. Wilson found that "the problem of coordination is pervasive" due to "the fact that authority in our government is widely shared," and he concluded, "Our system of government makes policy coordination difficult."[12]

The main strategy for achieving coordination has been creating interagency committees or commissions with representatives of the agencies whose activity is to be coordinated. Seidman and Gilmore do not think much of this solution. According to them, "Interagency commissions are the crabgrass in the gardens of government institutions. Nobody wants them, but everybody has them"; they note that such commissions are seldom effective because "the power to coordinate does not normally carry with it the authority to issue binding decisions."[13] Besides authority, other key resources that interagency commissions typically lacked were personnel and money.

An example of an interagency committee with a mandate relevant to the issues discussed here is the Task Force for the Homeless, created by Ronald Reagan's administration in 1983 by administrative action and then superseded by the United States Interagency Council on Homelessness (USICH), created by the Stewart B. McKinney Homeless Assistance Act of 1987. The USICH membership eventually included the heads (or their representatives) of nineteen federal agencies including Housing and Urban Development, Health and Human Services, Justice, and Defense. The McKinney Act also required the council to coordinate federal action with state and local efforts.

For much of its existence, the USICH seemed to confirm the generalizations about the futility of coordinating bodies. One account of the history of homeless policy noted, "The council has an up-and-down history. Congress siphoned off most of its funding in the mid-1990s, and it retreated into HUD, where it nearly died at the end of the Clinton administration."[14] By the early twenty-first century, another overview of national homeless policy found the council had produced little coordination. "Today, a patchwork of federal, state, city, and private money supports more than 40,000 programs—some cheap, others expensive; some staggeringly successful, others struggling; each with its own agenda; and few accountable for the work they perform."[15]

If the USICH had continued along this fruitless path, it would have confirmed the uselessness of interagency coordinating entities and would not merit attention here. But interestingly, the council eventually hit on a strategy that improved its effectiveness and suggests that coordination is not as impossible as much of the literature has found.

The USICH was turned around by Philip Mangano, who became chair in 2002 under President George W. Bush. With few resources, Mangano did not even attempt the impossible task of getting multiple federal bureaucratic behemoths to do what he wanted. Instead, he promoted the latest promising policy ideas about homelessness to state and local governments whose leaders were frustrated by the lack of progress under the status quo. Mangano embraced the analysis of Dennis Culhane, whose research had identified a relatively small subset of the homeless population that took up a greatly disproportionate amount of shelter beds and other resources. These were "chronic stayers who rarely leave the shelter for long periods."[16]

Another body of research Mangano relied on was the Housing First experiments of Sam Tsemberis. Prior to this work, it was widely believed that before street dwellers could be moved into permanent housing, they must be required to "dry out," take medications, and generally reform. The received wisdom was that until street people were "housing ready," they would be unable to stay off the streets for long. In a series of scientifically rigorous experiments, Tsemberis showed that moving these people immediately into permanent housing had two positive results: they were more likely to remain housed longer and more likely to accept rehabilitative services, compared to the old approach.[17]

Mangano appreciated that combining the concepts of chronic homelessness and Housing First resulted in a more optimistic paradigm for homeless policy. The chronically homeless were a relatively small group that could realistically be substantially reduced, thus making a disproportionate impact on the homeless problem. Housing First suggested that moving them permanently off the streets might be more feasible than was previously thought.

Thus Mangano had a new public idea to propose: end chronic homelessness. Rather than wrestling futilely with the federal bureaucracy, Mangano became a policy entrepreneur, selling the idea of ending chronic homelessness to state and local officials who were eager for something new to try. The strategy was effective in some ways. At a minimum, it showed how the USICH could be something other than a fifth wheel and gave the council positive results to claim credit for. In 2006, *Governing* magazine declared Mangano to be "Public Official of the Year," describing him as "President Bush's czar on homelessness. . . . His mission is to cajole governors, mayors and county executives into not just embracing but owning the elusive goal of ending chronic homelessness. . . . Mangano, 58, comes off as one part businessman one part management consultant and one part motivational speaker. . . . Stakeholders in some 224 cities and counties have rallied around Mangano's language by committing to 10-year plans to end chronic homelessness."[18]

The USICH demonstrates how interagency coordinating entities can be more effective than is usually assumed. The works that belittle such efforts focus on their lack of traditional resources: money, authority, personnel. But they overlook another resource: ideas. There is now a considerable literature documenting that ideas can be a political resource.[19] Promoting public ideas can achieve coordination if bureaucracies and political actors take them up, implement them, and move policy change in a specific direction. This possibility raises the question: Was the de Blasio administration able to make use of this ideational strategy to facilitate coordination, or did the industry partnerships and other groups intended to achieve the greater coordination that Career Pathways called for end up as just more crabgrass?

Interviews with de Blasio Administration Officials on Coordination

The de Blasio administration relied on three coordinating entities to implement the Career Pathways initiative. One was the Mayor's Office of Workforce Development (WKDEV), created in April 2014 and originally led by Katie Gaul-Stigge and then Amy Peterson. Another was the industry partnerships, which were based in the Small Business Services agency and led by the agency's first deputy commissioner, Jacqueline Mallon. In February 2018, de Blasio made J. Phillip Thompson, a professor of political science and urban planning at MIT and former deputy general manager at the New York City Housing Authority, deputy mayor for Strategic Initiatives and placed Career Pathways in his portfolio.

Thompson was the leader who most self-consciously relied on the ideational strategy for coordinating some seventeen city agencies and various private-sector actors. When I interviewed him on November 19, 2020, he spontaneously brought up how he used "vision" to achieve coordination.

> MAIN: When de Blasio announced your appointment, he said: "Phillip will make sure our agencies are working together to make New York City the fairest big city in the nation." Can you tell me what it is you are doing . . . to coordinate agencies, to produce or to manifest the Career Pathways initiative?
>
> THOMPSON: So I would say first of all the workforce system is fragmented. And our Workforce Development Office [WKDEV] is trying to coordinate across twenty-seven different workforce programs that exist in various agencies and departments. And they all have different metrics. They all have somewhat different goals and objec-

tives.... And so just the work of building an information system that crosses all the agencies is a mess. And, we're doing, we're in the middle of that.

MAIN: It sounds to me like you're saying, well, yes ... the system is fragmented. But you're working to make it less fragmented.... What other initiatives are you undertaking to try to reduce that fragmentation?

THOMPSON: Well, vision. I would say in America, generally, workforce [policy] is tremendously underdeveloped. Workforce training is underdeveloped.... And so there are huge needs that are still unmet.... In terms of vision, I think there's general unclarity over what the future of work will look like.

MAIN: You've described to me the environment that requires coordination. But what I'm interested in is how you get it. And your response was: vision.... That's very interesting. Tell me what your biggest success was.

THOMPSON: One of them is our Community Hiring Initiative. We got the building trades to agree voluntarily [that] 30 percent of everyone on the job will have to come from a neighborhood [with] 15 percent [or] higher poverty rates or from public housing. And that's a huge turnaround for them.... We are pushing for state legislation so that we can have the same requirement for all city contracts.

MAIN: Are you acting as kind of vision bearer or a policy entrepreneur? Are you trying to sell, to the state legislature, the idea that they need to pass this legislation to enable Community Hiring in other industries?

THOMPSON: Absolutely.

MAIN: If you can step forward and if you've got a good idea ... if you can make a convincing argument that can't be easily rebutted ... the power of ideas can be something. So are we talking about the same thing: vision and ideas?

THOMPSON: I think vision and ideas are the same thing. And I think that in order to really make significant change around coordination that takes vision.

MAIN: I wonder, can bureaucracies live on vision alone? Or maybe they need to be backed up by ... other resources, more concrete resources.... Are you guys going to be able to do what you're trying to do, resting mostly on vision?

THOMPSON: Well, I hope that the Biden administration comes forward with some big workforce programs, so we'll have money.... I think that ... we're at a period of disruption.... We're at the vortex of this disruption being caused by the pandemic. By the revolution in technology. By climate change.... At times like this we're going to have to radically reform and change things.... Ideas at times like this are more important than [at] "normal times."[20]

The WKDEV was another coordinating entity created under de Blasio. A city report on Career Pathways described its mission as follows:

> WKDEV serves as a strategic coordinating body helping to track and guide the efforts of 17 City agencies and entities (such as the Department of Education, the City University of New York, and the Queens Public Library) the NYC Center for Economic Opportunity (CEO), and the Mayor's Office of Operations.... Outside city government, WKDEV engages with private foundations, training and service providers, advocates, the public, and policy and research organizations. As a result, WKDEV is the center point in bringing together the multitude of stakeholders required to enact Career Pathways and build a more effective workforce system leading to opportunities for more New Yorkers to gain, keep, and upgrade employment.[21]

On November 16, 2020, I interviewed the director of WKDEV, Amy Peterson. She faced the challenges typically confronted by heads of coordinating entities. In a testimony to the City Council, a representative of the New York City Employment and Training Coalition noted, "The Mayor's Office of Workforce Development has been tasked with overseeing the progress of Career Pathways, but without the policy making, budgetary, or oversight authority to ensure that these existing workforce entities are achieving that potential."[22] Soon after the creation of the WKDEV, an analyst at the Center for an Urban Future noted, "The experience of other jurisdictions suggests that a central office for workforce is effective only when it includes control over financial resources—which the WKDEV does not have."[23]

I asked Peterson how, despite the lack of authority and other resources, she sought to achieve interagency coordination. She did not explicitly mention ideas and vision as resources for coordination. But she did note the importance of the administration's *Career Pathways* report of 2014 for articulating common goals that served as the basis for bringing disparate parties together

> PETERSON: No, the mayor hasn't said that Amy Peterson gets to figure out how we're spending our workforce dollars overall. However ... I think we are looked to as studying and driving—in partnership with the agencies around the ground that are doing this work—workforce policy.
>
> MAIN: Have you ever had a situation where you met resistance from one of these seventeen city agencies and entities that you are coordinat-

ing? And when you do meet resistance or lack of interest or whatever, what do you do?

PETERSON: I think that overall, we're all kind of working towards the same goals. . . . So I don't think there's a lot of disagreement on the goals. . . . We're all trying to do the same thing, right? It's not like people even have different goals across agencies. Right? Everyone's trying to do the same thing . . .

MAIN: What I hear you saying is . . . I don't have all that much authority. I don't have a lot of money. I don't have an enormous staff. But turns out I don't need all of that stuff to get the agencies to work together, because why? Because they want to cooperate on these goals. . . . You don't need somebody with a chair and a whip to get the agencies to coordinate. All you need is somebody to make sure the agencies are communicating with each other. You need project managers to make sure milestones are being achieved. And those resources are enough to get the coordination that Career Pathways needs. Is that a correct interpretation of what you're saying and how you operate?

PETERSON: Yes . . . I'm a big believer in just that.

MAIN: Yeah, but . . . your approach assumes . . . that the agencies start off and they've all got pretty much common goals. That's not always the case. . . . Tell me why you think they share common goals. Where does this agreement come from?

PETERSON: But I think that is *Career Pathways*, the report, right? The initial report. So I think that the administration in the beginning did a very good job of taking what were those common goals and understanding that different people feed into them in different places, and putting them on paper.

MAIN: You put your finger on an important point. . . . The way you get the common goals is, you put together an extremely convincing report that articulates a vision and that people will buy into. . . . So maybe that's the first thing you need to get this commonality of interests. You need a persuasive statement or a vision statement.

PETERSON: Yeah, I think figuring out what you're trying to achieve, what those overarching goals are, and what ways to get there is important. . . . That's an important part of the workforce system that we're trying to work more towards.[24]

Another important set of coordinating bodies that de Blasio formed were the industry partnerships. These partnerships were based in the Small Business Services (SBS) agency. The most prominent of the industry partnerships were the Tech Talent Pipeline (TTP) and the New York Alliance for Careers in Healthcare (NYACH). The TTP was developed by Jacqueline Mallon, who went on to become the first deputy commissioner of SBS in charge of managing the industry partnerships.

On January 29, 2021, I interviewed Mallon about the partnerships and how she tried to achieve interagency and intersector coordination through them. She emphasized the importance of identifying common interests among various actors and forging a common action agenda. She stressed the importance of having an overriding principle and common goals to achieve systemic change, new processes that would help workers develop their skills, rather than what she called "transactional stuff" that simply slotted workers into low-skilled jobs.

I asked Mallon if industry partnerships work by having representatives of a sector communicate to public workforce service providers in detail exactly what skills they want their workers to have; then the providers could be sure to train workers in those skills. "Is that what happens at an industry partnership?" I asked. She responded:

> MALLON: Nope. . . . That's a transactional type of engagement with employers, right? . . . That is exactly how workforce development was done for a long time. . . . "Rapid attachment" . . . that's an important tool for the city to have in its tool belt because a lot of people need to get to work right away. But there's a limit to how much ahead they're going to get if they don't have any additional skills. And so, the idea, in part, behind Career Pathways is . . . let's go to a complimentary system that is available to people to get more skills so they can find more money and have careers. And let's do that in partnership with industry because they need the skilled labor. . . . Industry partnerships were focused on longer term change. . . . So . . . transactional stuff in an industry? That's easy, in a way. It's much harder to be like, how can we make a more permanent change?
>
> MAIN: You might say a structural change.
>
> MALLON: Yeah, exactly. Exactly. And that's what the partnerships were set up to do.
>
> MAIN: Another way I thought of the industry partnerships is [as] an effort to coordinate with the private sector. . . . Is that a useful way to think about the industry partnerships?
>
> MALLON: Yeah, I do. I do think so. I think . . . it is definitely an attempt to sort of like sit down at the table, figure out what the root problems are and try to work on them together.
>
> MAIN: And what is your, broadly speaking, your basic strategy for improving coordination between the public and the private sectors?

> MALLON: Identifying where we have common interests. They need a skilled labor force, you know. And we need a thriving economy. That's one way.... And then the other thing is, I think, to be transparent where we can. And thirdly, not waste anybody's time. We're not meeting to meet, we're meeting to do things. And if we don't have a thing that we've done or we need input on or whatever, we're not going to meet. Always keep it moving.... We're working with people who share a willingness to work together on a problem. Our job is to make sure that it's a productive and transparent encounter.[25]

In short, when the heads of the de Blasio administration's coordinating entities were asked how they brought a fragmented array of parties together, they spoke of vision and ideas, common goals, and high-level goals rather than short-term transactions. With not much in terms of money, authority, or personnel, the coordinators all brought up the ideational route to achieving their objectives.

Vision, Ideas, and Coordination

In emphasizing the importance of vision or ideas as resources to help achieve coordination, Thompson and the others who worked on Career Pathways reflect concepts developed by Eugene Bardach in his 1998 book *Getting Agencies to Work Together*. In it, Bardach explains how vision or "strategic ideas"—a notion very similar to what this book has called "public ideas"—can promote interagency collaboration:

> Detailed information and technical understanding, however abundant, do not by themselves lead to a workable strategic conception of how to steer better. An interpretive lens is necessary, a lens that provides focus and enables insight. Such a lens is typically a verbal formula or slogan such as "multimedia enforcement" or "preventing wildfires in the buffer zone" or "services integration" or "doing everything in our power to promote [welfare client] self-sufficiency" or "keeping families together and safe." Such verbal symbols suggestively link an idea about objectives and an idea about means, however roughly and indistinctly. That is why I call them *strategic ideas*. My concept of a strategic idea is similar to the concept of *vision* ... I use *strategic idea*, however, because it is more general than *vision*.[26]

In other words, a strong strategic idea, for example, one that is based on abundant research and thus has a clear policy implication, if it is embraced by many organizations or jurisdictions, can generate what Bardach calls a "preexisting purposiveness,"[27] moving them all in the same direction. The participants must buy into the strategic idea, which requires a convincing formulation of the strategic idea. In the de Blasio administration, the strategic idea was Career Pathways, and the convincing formulation was the 2014 report *Career Pathways: One City Working Together*. Thus, one strategy for a policy coordinator can be to act as a policy entrepreneur, selling the strategic idea to various actors and thus achieving a level of coordination. To fulfill their goal, Career Pathways coordinators played the role of policy idea salespeople.

Effectiveness of Coordination by Ideas under de Blasio

The question we come to is: How effective was this ideational strategy for coordination in the case of Career Pathways during the de Blasio administration?

The Career Pathways initiative achieved a number of goals. The new welfare employment service programs instituted at the HRA under Banks were rooted in the Career Pathways philosophy. As we have seen, they were successfully implemented and managed to make the agency's work placement programs much less punitive and thus likely reached a higher level of client satisfaction without inducing a spike in the welfare rolls as critics predicted would happen.

The Community Hiring initiative pushed by Thompson had some success. In August 2020, the city announced it had negotiated new terms to a project labor agreement (PLA) with the Construction Trades Council of Greater New York. Among other things, the PLA would "prioritize the referral of workers from zip codes where at least 15% of the population lives below the federal poverty level and/or are NYCHA [New York City Housing Authority] residents, aiming to reach an overall goal that at least 30 percent of all hours worked under PLA projects are logged by workers from these zip codes."[28] The WKDEV facilitated recruitment events in low-income neighborhoods to line up participants for pre-apprenticeship training provided under the PLA.[29] Deputy Mayor Thompson tried to follow up on this approach by lobbying "the State of New York to act by passing Community Hiring legislation that would require contractors and businesses working with the City to hire New Yorkers from high poverty neighborhoods." But the legislation did not pass.[30]

One early goal of Career Planning was to develop common metrics to be used across all agencies involved in workforce policy to evaluate baseline conditions and progress. By 2019, the WKDEV "developed a set of Common Metrics, 13 performance measures that provide standard terminology and definitions for key milestones (e.g., enrollment in a skills-training program) and outcomes (e.g., full-time job placement) commonly used in workforce programs." By 2020, five city agencies were reporting data from eighteen programs into an integrated platform.[31]

HireNYC: Human Services was a program that required human service providers under contract with participating city agencies to hire one public assistance client for every $250,000 of contract value. The WKDEV helped the providers comply in various ways, including modifying the language of the relevant contract riders. By 2019, the program had placed about eight thousand public assistance recipients in jobs with human services providers.[32]

The Career Pathways coordinating entities were helpful at a task that no one had anticipated: organizing the city's response to the COVID-19 pandemic. The Mayor's Management Report of 2020 noted: "The COVID-19 pandemic dramatically transformed the environment in which City agencies help prepare New Yorkers for and connect them to jobs and careers."[33] The pandemic caused the WKDEV and the Career Pathways initiative overall to shift their emphasis away from coordinating employment services toward helping employers and employees cope with the challenges wrought by the pandemic. The industry partnerships were particularly helpful in this regard. Thus, the NYACH developed a new system to distribute personal protective equipment to home care agencies and facilitated a new process by which food-insecure people could receive food deliveries from these agencies. In response to the collapse of the home health aide pipeline wrought by the pandemic, the NYACH, in cooperation with the WKDEV, set up a process through which home health aide students could be trained virtually.[34] The TTP identified alternative professional experiences for students whose tech internships were canceled due to COVID-19. In conjunction with the industrial/manufacturing industry partnership, the TTP developed the PPE + Reopening Supply Marketplace, "an online platform for matching organizations seeking PPE [personal protective equipment] with local manufacturers that can fabricate it."[35]

Moreover, the Career Pathways job training services under the SBS, the New York City agency responsible for the industry partnerships developed under de Blasio, have received a rigorous analysis. Westat conducted a return-on-investment analysis of six of these programs. Westat compared the costs and benefits for program participants in 2014 and 2015 to an otherwise similar group that did not participate in the trainings. The programs studied included health care sector job trainings designed with the NYACH and other industry partnerships. According to the Mayor's Office of Economic Opportunity, "Westat found that training recipients earned $1,436 to $3,067 more than the matched comparison group members in the second quarter after program exit, resulting in large estimated differences when multiplied across a full year of earnings." In addition, the benefits were projected to five and ten years after program exit with similar results, demonstrating that industry-focused training has a strong, positive effect on earnings.[36]

Other evaluations of Career Pathways programs across the nation have shown more mixed results. In December 2021, researchers at Abt Associates published a report of their meta-analysis of forty-six impact analyses of Career Pathways workforce programs, most of which were provided by community or technical schools or community organizations. The meta-analysis found that "*career pathways programs substantially increase credential completion and employment in targeted industries, but often do not improve earnings* . . . these programs on average substantially increased receipt of postsecondary credentials (by 155 percent) and employment in the industries targeted for training (by 72 percent). . . . However, programs increased earnings by only a small average amount in the short term, and not at all after three or more years."[37]

Furthermore, most independent observers concluded that the Career Pathways initiative in workforce policy did not achieve the "unprecedented full-system shift" to a greatly more coordinated workforce policy system that had been anticipated. Many observers conclude that not much coordination was achieved, and therefore New York City's Career Pathways initiative was not particularly successful.

Early in de Blasio's second term, Annie Garneva of the NYC Employment and Training Coalition (NYCETC), an umbrella organization of some 180 members involved in city workforce services and policy, lamented the lack of progress in de Blasio's first term.

"Career Pathways is the de Blasio administration's 2014 blueprint for workforce development," she wrote. "The lackluster execution of this blueprint over the Mayor's first term has meant New Yorkers living in poverty have been missing out on a real opportunity to rise into the middle class."[38]

In the same article, Garneva pointed out that the Career Pathways report had called for an annual investment of $60 million by 2020 in bridge programs, that is, services for low-income job seekers with weak academic backgrounds to improve their skills so they could participate in more advanced training. But by 2018, the city had allocated only $7 million for bridge programs in its last two budgets.

The industry partnerships met with mixed success. The TTP and NYACH, which were established before the Career Pathways initiative began, remained the most active and effective of the partnerships. The city sought to develop similar partnerships for the industrial/manufacturing, construction, retail, and food service sectors.[39] Partnerships were established in the construction, food service, and industrial sectors. But the city never managed to put together a partnership for the retail sector, which the Center for an Urban Future characterized as "a missed opportunity."[40] An analyst for the center noted the work of the tech and health care partnerships but concluded, "The remaining partnerships have gained little traction or visibility. The Department of Small Business Services (SBS), the city agency that is managing these partnerships, is operating them largely behind closed doors. SBS has not been transparent regarding the goals of each partnership, and few stakeholders outside the agency have engaged substantively with them."[41] On November 27, 2017, in testimony to the City Council Committees on Small Business and Civil Service and Labor, Jesse Laymon gave the following advice regarding SBS, the industry partnerships, and the WKDEV: "Restructure and/or otherwise empower the Mayor's Office of Workforce Development and its relationship with the new Industry Partnerships and the existing workforce agencies (especially SBS). . . . Four new partnerships have struggled to gain any traction, often going unstaffed, and have not produced new programming on any significant scale."[42]

One of the most acute observers of the city's workforce policies and the Career Pathways initiative was Stacy Woodruff. She worked at the WKDEV from 2014 to 2016, and from 2016 to 2020, she was director of the Field Building Hub at Workforce Professionals Training Institute, which is an umbrella organization devoted to "connecting and unifying stakeholders in the workforce development community to plan a more effective system."[43] In talking about her work at the WKDEV, Woodruff described a set of traditional public administration dilemmas not easily resolved through vision or ideas.

> WOODRUFF: Well, we've talked a little bit about the Mayor's Office of Workforce Development, which was probably envisioned perhaps [as] one of the ways to try to tackle those coordination issues. But . . . [there are] some . . . issues [with] offices created with basically no authority, with no budget.
>
> MAIN: That's the eternal dilemma of interagency coordinating commissions.
>
> WOODRUFF: Right. So I will say, in my time there, I got to the office when it was not quite a year old. And one of my objectives, I did some of that: . . . all right, tell me, for the career services program, how many people went through the program during the fiscal year? What was the budget and how many were placed in jobs? And I did that agency by agency, program by program, for the [Career Pathways] update report. But I remember saying to [WKDEV director] Katie Gaul-Stigge at the time and others: If we can't prove our value, the next time we try to collect that information, people aren't going to be as willing. And it's not enough to say "we're the mayor's office,

therefore you have to respond to us." We tried to, when I was there, looking kind of across... how do you foster some of that interagency coordination? Where do you have some examples already and build upon that? And what are, kind of, the holy grails of getting those together? Where do you fight your battles? Where do you think about kind of braiding funding and whatnot?[44]

In 2018, the Field Building Hub issued a report coauthored by Woodruff and based on extensive interviews with actors in the city's workforce policy network. The report described their bottom-line judgment as follows: "Notably, in nearly every interview, stakeholders were able to identify specific examples of successful programs and new initiatives. Yet when asked to step back and assess the larger context of the New York City workforce ecosystem, the broad consensus was that the field's arc of progress is failing to match the rising challenges faced by the City's employers and low-income jobseekers."[45] At the end of her tenure at the Field Building Hub, Woodruff stood by this evaluation of the accomplishments of the Career Pathways initiative: "I accepted the challenge of launching an amorphous entity focused on better coordinating the array of stakeholders, initiatives, and guiding principles of the New York City workforce system.... I am immensely proud of some of the initiatives launched, positions taken, and lessons learned throughout this experience," she said. "And yet," she continued, "I cannot help but lament that the NYC workforce system remains fragmented and continues to struggle with identifying a common vision."[46]

In short, the consensus among the independent members of the city's workforce policy network is that if Thompson's assertion is true that "to really make significant change around coordination that takes vision," then the desired level of coordination was not achieved because the Career Pathways coordinating mechanisms did not manage to infuse a common vision among the many policy players.

This is not to say the coordinating entities did no good work or that they should never have been created. As was discussed already, progress was made in developing common metrics, negotiating PLAs, getting human service contractors to hire welfare clients, creating a nurse residency program, helping businesses respond to the pandemic, and much more. This amounts to a significant record of accomplishment. But this collection of good government accomplishments did not add up to a reconfigured and more effective overall workforce system.

The question is why the entities working on Career Pathways did not achieve the level of coordination that would have produced the breakthroughs in the condition of programs for low-income New Yorkers they were trying for. One could point to the factors that usually frustrate coordinating organizations: lack of authority and especially lack of money. Indeed, in its interviews with workforce professionals, the Field Building Hub found that "unsurprisingly, many program leaders and policy analysts called for greater levels of public and philanthropic funding."[47] But the ideational strategy deployed by Thompson and other coordinators was supposed to compensate for the lack of traditional resources with a strong vision or strategic idea that would catch the imagination of the groups to be coordinated; in being implemented, it would achieve the degree of interagency, intergovernmental, and intersectoral harmony needed. Why did this not happen?

This book has looked at two cases when public ideas played a major role in the reform of human resources: ending chronic homelessness, promoted by Philip Mangano at USICH, and welfare reform under Rudy Giuliani and the idea of work first. The case of the USICH is most immediately on point because it involves a coordinating organization.

One of the most striking things about Mangano's strategic idea of ending chronic homelessness is the degree to which it was grounded in scientific experiments and rigorous quantitative analyses. Culhane's research clearly established that there was a relatively small subgroup among the homeless who took up a disproportionate share of shelter beds and other resources. Tsemberis's gold-standard experiments proved that the Housing First strategy of placing homeless people directly in permanent housing was superior on all fronts. The fact that the ideas Mangano was promoting had met such an unusually high standard of proof was crucial to winning over skeptical service providers who had based their practices on contrary notions. The strategic idea of ending chronic homelessness through Housing First had very straightforward and immediately actionable policy implications. As Mangano explained:

> I was in St. Louis recently . . . I spoke with people doing services there. They had a very difficult group of people they couldn't reach no matter what they offered. So I said, take some of your money and rent some apartments and go out to those people, and literally go out there with the key and say to them, "This is the key to an apartment. If you come with me right now I am going to give it to you, and you are going to have that apartment." And so they did. And one by one those people were coming in.[48]

As a strategic idea backed up with lots of scientific evidence, with clear policy implications and tangible results, ending chronic homelessness was an easy sell and caught on quickly. The ideational strategy for coordination thus "worked" in the case of homeless services, at least in the sense that many jurisdictions and agencies took up the approach, and homelessness was "ended" in the narrow sense that getting many chronically homeless people into a shelter made a disproportionate dent in the size of the homeless population.

The other strategic idea related to welfare policy considered in this book is work first, that is, the drive for "welfare reform" in the late 1990s. In New York City in particular, the idea had an impact in that dramatic decreases in the welfare rolls that could plausibly be attributed to it were achieved. Here again, work first succeeded as a strategic idea partly because the evidentiary base for it was strong. The MDRC's scientific evaluations of work-first implementation in Riverside, California, and elsewhere were convincing. News of the "Riverside miracle" quickly spread nationwide and was embraced by Giuliani in New York. The policy implications of work first were such that jurisdictions taking it up were relieved of certain challenging tasks. Work first counseled against building clients' human capital, something hard to do with people who were usually low skilled and poorly educated. Nor did work first impose the obligation of finding "good jobs" for people with little work experience. The policy implication was to place welfare clients in some job or work program right away and without much concern for job quality. This involved shifting the bureaucratic culture of welfare agencies from eligibility determination to job development, which was a challenge, but not as much of a challenge as human capital development and creating high-quality jobs.

As a strategic idea, Career Pathways did not enjoy the advantages of ending chronic homelessness and work first. There has been a lot of research on Career Pathways, but it produced no scientific consensus around any sort of "miracle." The Career Pathways idea did not point unambiguously to a clear policy prescription. Interestingly, the concepts of "work first" and "end chronic homelessness" were imperatives that expressed an action the agencies were to take. Career Pathways gestured to a structure that was to be built without providing any details on what it should look like and how it would work. It was therefore less compelling as a strategic idea and coordinating force.

It is important to understand that successful strategic ideas are not necessarily the best policy options available to the government or even "better" ones in an absolute sense than their less successful alternatives. This book does not claim to have identified the best possible welfare or workforce policies. My main concern is how urban government can make major changes when the status quo seems suboptimal. Career Pathways was a worthy effort and wrought enough positive change to be considered a success. But it did not achieve the goals of its supporters of achieving nonincremental change and strong interagency coordination.

8
EARLY CHALLENGES TO DE BLASIO'S HOMELESSNESS POLICY

The main concern of this book is when and how New York City mayors were able to achieve nonincremental change in welfare policy. The focus has been on the Human Resources Administration (HRA) and antipoverty programs as well as mayors for whom reforming welfare policy was a major initiative. These concerns have led us to look at the formation of the HRA under John Lindsay and work-oriented welfare reform under Rudy Giuliani. Homelessness was not immediately relevant to welfare policy for these mayors. Homelessness had not emerged as a major social problem under Lindsay, although a minor scandal had broken out when it became public knowledge that the city had been using expensive hotels for lodging families left homeless due to fires or other emergencies.[1] Under Giuliani, homelessness was a distinct concern from welfare reform. They became separate issues because shortly before Giuliani became mayor, homeless services, which had been provided by the HRA, were spun off to a new agency, the Department of Homeless Services (DHS).[2]

The situation changed again under Bill de Blasio because the homeless services that had been lodged at the DHS were reorganized and absorbed into the city's welfare bureaucracy. In 2016, Steven Banks, who had been appointed commissioner of HRA with much fanfare, became commissioner of the Department of Social Services (DSS) with both the HRA and the DHS reporting to him. Thus, homeless services returned to being an integral part of the welfare bureaucracy. Some discussion of homelessness is necessary for the analysis of how change came to welfare policy under de Blasio.

First, some background on homeless policy in New York City is necessary. New York is the only large city in the country with what amounts to a right to shelter. One foundation of that right is the *Callahan v. Carey* consent decree signed in 1981, in which the city committed to providing shelter to virtually all homeless men who requested it. Robert Hayes was the lawyer who brought that suit and helped found the Coalition for the Homeless, an advocacy organization. Other suits brought against the city extended the right to shelter to homeless women (*Eldredge v. Koch*) and homeless families (*McCain v. Koch*). This litigation, laws passed by the City Council, regulations promulgated by state agencies, and the activities of the advocacy organizations created an elaborate set of constraints on city policy and administration concerning the homeless. Before he became HRA and then DSS commissioner, Banks spent decades as a Legal Aid lawyer litigating for the rights of the homeless and helped develop much of this policy structure.

Homelessness circa 2014–2015

When de Blasio assumed office in January 2014, there were 53,615 people in the main municipal shelter system, which was primarily run by the DHS.[3] That number went up fairly steadily until December 2014, when 60,939 people were in the system, an all-time high.[4] By December 2015, the shelter census had dropped to 60,096 people.[5]

Concerning homeless people living on the city streets, the annual enumeration of street dwellers—the Homeless Outreach Population Estimate (HOPE) count—counted 3,183 such people in 2015, down by merely 175 people from 2014.[6] HOPE counts are done in the dead of winter and do not reveal much about what the situation is like in the warmer months, which was when the media started reporting on an apparent surge in street homelessness under de Blasio.

In October 2015, a Quinnipiac University poll reported that 60 percent of city voters believed they were seeing more homeless people on the streets and in the parks and subways.[7] Whether this impression was based on personal experience or sensational media coverage is not clear. For example, stories such as one run by the *New York Post* in July 2015 titled "20 Years of Cleaning Up NYC Pissed Away," illustrated with a photo of a "vagrant" urinating in public, implied that street homelessness had gotten dramatically worse under de Blasio.[8]

The impression of the city's extensive homeless policy network—service providers, shelter operators, advocates, bureaucrats, experts, and media figures—that I talked to at the time was mixed. Some reported an increase in street homelessness. For example, on whether there were more street dwellers, Jeff Foreman, policy director of Care for the Homeless, reported: "Everyone I ask thinks so . . . anecdotally, I agree."[9] Regarding the estimates of the unsheltered homeless, Mary Brosnahan, president of the Coalition for the Homeless stated, "We do know that the city came up with a number between 3,000 and 4,000. Their methodology is so flawed, we believe the number to be easily two to three times that."[10] It is not clear whether this estimate, even if correct, represented an increase since the Mike Bloomberg years.

One hard number that had gone up was the budget of the DHS, whose fiscal year 2016 Preliminary Budget totaled $1.03 billion, an 8.3 percent increase over the 2015 Adopted Budget.[11] Some of this increase came from new rental subsidy programs, known as Living in Communities (LINC), and new efforts at preventing homelessness, which are discussed later. (Eventually, the LINC subsidies and others were consolidated into a single program: City Fighting Homelessness and Eviction Prevention Supplement.) But the DHS budget had hovered around $1 billion since 2013, which is certainly a lot of money to spend on homeless services, but it did not represent an explosion of costs under de Blasio.

The quality and nature of homeless shelters generated criticism in de Blasio's early years in office. Beginning in 2000, under Giuliani, when space in the shelter system was not available, the city had begun placing homeless families in what were known as "cluster apartments," that is, private rental units. What was intended to be a temporary measure soon ballooned, and by August 2015, the city was renting 3,140 cluster units in about four hundred private apartment buildings for almost $2,500 a month in rent and services for each family.[12] In March 2015, the city's Department of Investigations reported that although all types of shelter had their challenges, "the inspected clusters were found to be the worst maintained, the most poorly monitored, and to have provided the least adequate social services to families. . . . DOI investigators observed these buildings to be run down, filthy, and often riddled with rats, mice and/or roaches. Moreover, security was non-existent."[13] This situation generated plenty of negative media coverage and stoked the perception of a homeless policy crisis.[14] Besides cluster apartments, another expedient solution the de Blasio administration relied on was placing homeless families in commercial hotels. Renting hotel rooms was more expensive than other forms of emergency housing, and it generated opposition from the surrounding neighborhoods. Consequently, the practice did nothing to stem the public's sense of a homelessness crisis.[15]

These developments were interpreted by the media and the public as an unremitting homelessness crisis. The tabloid press was filled with articles decrying "the exploding homeless problem [that] began capturing headlines over the summer" of 2015.[16] In October 2015, a Quinnipiac University poll found that 61 percent of city voters disapproved of de Blasio's handling of poverty and homelessness; in August, a similar poll found that a 47 percent plurality believed he did not deserve reelection.[17] Fairly or not, at the end of 2015, the *New York Times* summed up this situation as one where de Blasio had been "under fire for months over a problem that he had promised long ago to solve—but one that he seemed inclined to dismiss or play down, or to blame on others."[18]

In the early de Blasio years, we had a rise in the shelter census, which began under Bloomberg and then declined a bit; widespread public perception (but no hard evidence) of an increase in street homelessness; continued high expenditures; use of low-quality and otherwise suboptimal forms of shelter; and an overall situation that was generally interpreted as a political and policy crisis. How did the city end up in this position, and how did de Blasio deal with it?

How We Got There

In 2004, Mayor Bloomberg announced that he would "make the condition of chronic homelessness effectively extinct in New York."[19] A five-year plan was developed. Preventing homelessness would be emphasized through a "Home Base" program that would intervene with at-risk families to keep them housed. More supportive housing—that is, apartments with services for the mentally ill and other disabled street dwellers—was to be developed. This goal was addressed in 2005 when the city and state signed the New York/New York III Agreement; by 2014, about 90 percent of the nine thousand units called for under the agreement were open or in development.[20] Bloomberg embraced the Housing First philosophy, under which street dwellers would be moved into supportive housing as quickly as possible, an approach that reduced street homelessness and encouraged enrollment in rehabilitation services. Shelter use was to be cut by rehousing long-term shelter stayers.

Bloomberg thus introduced several innovations in homeless policy, some of which—like Home Base and Housing First—were strongly supported by scientific evaluations.[21] Almost overlooked in all this innovation was the administration's initial realization of the need to stick with the policy of providing shelter clients with rent subsidies to move out of the system and into private housing. Bloomberg's five-year plan insisted that "rental assistance resources must continue to be available in shelters to re-house chronically homeless individuals and families."[22] Bloomberg pledged to reduce the shelter census—36,399 people in June 2004[23]—by two-thirds in five years, to about 12,000 persons by 2009.[24]

On October 19, 2004, the Bloomberg administration made a fateful decision. The DHS abandoned its long-term policy of giving shelter residents priority for entering public housing and for federal Section 8 rent vouchers. DHS commissioner Linda Gibbs explained, "We don't want people to think that the best way to get housing is to bundle their children up and take them to the EAU [the Emergency Assistance Unit, the intake point to the family shelter system]."[25] In effect, Gibbs assumed that moving shelter families into public housing would draw new families into the system. But in a groundbreaking analysis, economists Michael Cragg and Brendan O'Flaherty found that "typically, it takes placing at least seven families into subsidized housing to draw one family into the shelter system."[26] In other words, only a very dramatic rise in the placement of shelter users into subsidized housing, far beyond what the city had ever undertaken, would induce a substantial number of families to enter the shelters to qualify for the housing. Thus, shelter families lost preferential access to public housing and Section 8 vouchers based on the refuted notion that perverse incentives were much stronger than they really were. Basing an important decision on a debunked theory when real and relevant scholarship was available was an unfortunate slip for an administration that prided itself on using sophisticated analysis. Shelter clients were offered a temporary, city-funded, five-year rent subsidy, Housing Stability Plus, replaced in 2007 by the Advantage two-year maximum subsidy program.

Unfortunately, the number of shelter residents in June 2009—36,329 people—was virtually unchanged from what it was in June 2004—36,399 people.[27] Yet Bloomberg stuck with the Advantage program for another two years. Things went from bad to worse when Advantage ended in April 2011.[28] There was a city-state dispute over funding the program; when the state finally stopped funding Advantage, the city decided it alone could not fund the program, and it came to an end. At that point, no subsidies of any kind were offered to move families out of the shelter system. In November 2013, the shelter census was at a (then) record high of 53,270 persons.[29]

Bloomberg's failure to follow through on his promising beginnings in homeless policy left the de Blasio administration with an increasing shelter census and a serious homelessness problem. How well did the new mayor respond to this challenge?

As will be shown, the de Blasio administration got off to an unexpectedly slow start on homeless policy. This was surprising given the mayor's emphasis during his campaign on confronting poverty and economic inequality. Part of the reason for the early stumbling may have been that, unlike some of his predecessors, de Blasio came into office with no formal plan for homeless policy. David Dinkins came in with a plan he developed when he was Manhattan borough president. Before entering office, Giuliani had a blueprint for homeless policy in the form of the report of the (Andrew) Cuomo Commission. Two years into his first term, Bloomberg released the plan titled *Uniting for Solutions Beyond Shelter*. De Blasio did not have a written plan when he began as mayor. Three years went by before his administration released such a document, *Turning the Tide on Homelessness*, which was done partly in response to the perceived weaknesses of his early struggles with the issue.

In any case, de Blasio tried to get off to a strong start with the LINC programs, which were rental subsidy programs designed to help various sorts of shelter clients move out of the system. Reinstating rent subsidies was an obvious policy move since the increasing shelter rolls de Blasio was facing were widely and plausibly blamed on the ending of such subsidies under Bloomberg. But how well were the programs implemented? The new administration had problems.

Getting LINC started required cooperation from New York State and Governor Andrew Cuomo. When Advantage ended in 2011, language was put into the state budget that forbade the city from using state money to fund rent subsidies. This was done because the state wanted to prevent the city from redirecting other public assistance money to continue Advantage. This provision had to be changed to get LINC up and running. All that was necessary, according to city officials and homeless advocates, was "a minor legislative change that would cost the state nothing."[30] The necessary cooperation from Albany was not forthcoming in a timely manner, and LINC was not implemented until December 2014. According to the nonpartisan Independent Budget Office: "Despite the expansion of the rental assistance programs, the homeless shelter population has remained stubbornly high this year. This is largely due to a slower than anticipated start to the LINC rental assistance programs. While the city originally planned to use the rental assistance programs to move more than 6,000 households out of the shelter system this year, only around 1,500 have moved out thus far [May 2015]."

Another unfortunate outcome of the ongoing Cuomo/de Blasio tensions was a delay in the development of more supportive housing. Supportive housing had been provided over the decades in the three joint city-state ventures known as the New York/New York agreements. This kind of housing is one of the great successes in homelessness policy and has been demonstrated to keep the disabled off the streets and reduce the cost of their care.[31] Under David Dinkins and Mario Cuomo, Rudy Giuliani and George Pataki, and Bloomberg and Pataki, New York mayors and governors came together in three New York/New York agreements that represented striking cooperation between levels of government that had often been at odds. The last of these agreements was signed in November 2005, and the units it provided were mostly filled by de Blasio's start as mayor.

Andrew Cuomo and de Blasio were unable to strike a fourth New York/New York agreement. Asked why this mayor and this governor, unlike their recent predecessors, were unable to cut a deal, one longtime follower of supportive housing policy who requested anonymity was blunt: "Andrew Cuomo hated Bill de Blasio. Refused to sit down with him and negotiate a New York/New York IV.

Done. That is it." This explanation is corroborated by a plethora of journalism documenting the bad blood between Cuomo and de Blasio.[32] In December 2015, the *Times* reported that "Mr. Cuomo also used a recent radio interview to sneer at Mr. de Blasio's supportive-housing program."[33]

The lack of cooperation from Cuomo came largely as a surprise since the governor had experience with homelessness policy as developer of the private HELP USA shelter network, as leader of a commission that had developed a new homeless policy direction for Dinkins, and as secretary of Housing and Urban Development. As the Institute for Children, Poverty & Homelessness has noted, "Because of his experience working on the issue, some expected more progress when Cuomo became governor in 2011."[34]

Whatever the expectations were, Cuomo and de Blasio were unable to cooperate on a New York/New York IV supportive housing plan. Without a new agreement to provide more supportive housing units, the unsheltered remained on the streets where they attracted the attention of unsympathetic media and the general public, fostering the general perception of a homelessness crisis in the early years of de Blasio's administration.

The Personnel Is Political

A very striking charge wrought by de Blasio's victory was that of personnel: Steven Banks, the Legal Aid lawyer who litigated against the city since 1983 for the right to shelter for homeless families, became commissioner of the HRA. Lilliam Barrios-Paoli, a former Catholic nun who served in the city's social service bureaucracy as HRA commissioner under Giuliani, Department of Aging commissioner under Bloomberg, and other roles, became deputy mayor for Health and Human Services. Gilbert Taylor, formerly executive deputy commissioner for the Administration for Children's Services, was appointed commissioner of the DHS.

Observers were very impressed with the appointment of Barrios-Paoli. Unfortunately, this experienced administrator announced her departure from the de Blasio administration on August 31, 2015, just twenty months after she had joined it with much fanfare. Coming at a point when the media was full of reports on the homelessness problem, Barrios-Paoli's departure was seen as a blow to the administration. The *Times* framed the story as "Mayor de Blasio's Aide on Homeless Is Resigning amid Crisis" and WNYC News reported that there was "shock among social service advocates and frustration among those who track Latino representation at City Hall."[35]

I interviewed Barrios-Paoli in 2016 after she left the de Blasio administration. She never got a chance to play a major role in that mayor's homelessness policy. What she had to say about de Blasio's decision-making process, executive working styles in general, and the different roles of agency commissioners and deputy mayors is significant. I asked Barrios-Paoli why she left the de Blasio administration.

"I felt that my style and the mayor's style, just working style, were very different," she told me. "The way he approached problems, the way he liked to be briefed, the daily work styles," she explained. "Essentially, I felt that they didn't mesh."

"So, how did he like to be briefed?" I inquired.

She replied, "Very briefly. . . . He wanted very brief, very concise. I think some of my problems just did not lend themselves to that. And it was very difficult to get on his calendar."[36]

Access to the mayor and working styles were important issues from Barrios-Paoli's perspective. She said, "I think I underestimated how important it is to know the work style of the person you're working with, particularly if you're working that close with them. . . . The mayor is somebody you see once every three or four months if you're a commissioner of an agency, if that much. Sometimes it was six months. I mean you saw the deputy mayor you reported to."[37]

What Barrios Paoli had to say about different relationships between a mayor and a commissioner in their agency, and a mayor and a deputy mayor working out of City Hall is interesting. She thought a difference between the working styles of a commissioner and mayor are not likely to be a problem. "The mayor's working status is immaterial to a commissioner because they're never there. It's not a daily transaction." But "once you're in City Hall, it's a daily thing. And so that's a different story." She continued:

> I was used to mayors that gave both commissioners and deputy mayors a much wider latitude of decision making. . . . And I think the biggest problem at City Hall [under de Blasio] is that everything is very centralized. Decisions are made by the mayor, and they're not always made on a timely basis because a human being doesn't have enough time in the day to make the number of decisions that have to be made. And there's not enough division in terms of what is just a normal workday decision that not only the deputy mayor, but that the commissioner should be making, and what rises to the level of the mayor. And I think that, at least in my estimation, created many problems that did not have to be created, frankly. And I think he [de Blasio] felt that because he was the mayor . . . it's his prerogative. I really respect that, he wanted to make those decisions. And to me, that was my biggest problem.[38]

Barrios-Paoli's inability to have an impact under de Blasio may partly explain the administration's slow start on homeless issues. Her departure was a blow to the administration, especially in light of how things developed at one of the agencies under her purview, the DHS.

Gilbert Taylor became the commissioner of the DHS in January 2014. His tenure there is not considered a success.

A major issue was the agency's preparation of contracts with service and shelter providers for review by the city comptroller, who was Scott Stringer at the time. Such contracts, which are complex documents and can run to five or six hundred pages, must be approved by the comptroller if payment is to be made in a timely way.

Problems with contract preparation at DHS started developing in March 2015 when the Department of Inspections (DOI) issued a scathing report on conditions in DHS shelters for families with children.[39] The DOI had been asked to undertake this investigation by de Blasio himself,[40] perhaps to document the disrepair into which the shelters had lapsed on Bloomberg's watch. The report set off a chain of events that damaged the new administration.

The report discovered that many shelters and service providers were operating without written contracts, contrary to the requirements of the New York City Administrative Code, the city charter, and the Procurement Policy Board.[41] One former DHS official speaking off the record claimed the agency lost key, seasoned personnel, especially in the procurement department, and that Bloomberg holdovers were replaced too quickly with neophyte de Blasio loyalists. Interestingly, Banks avoided this misstep at the HRA and did not replace his agency's seasoned staff too rapidly. "I think," Banks told me in an interview, "the perception was that when I came [in] I'd make dramatic changes and everybody would be gone. But in fact, there are people here who have dedicated their lives to public service and have great management skills and all we needed was to change the direction."[42]

On September 12, 2015, the *New York Times* reported:

> Millions of dollars in payments to dozens of nonprofits that shelter homeless people in New York are being held up by the city comptroller.
>
> Since . . . Scott M. Stringer, took office in January 2014, the comptroller's office has rejected 33 contracts; in addition, the Homeless Services Department says it has withdrawn another 21 contracts because it believed it would need more documentation to meet the demands of the comptroller's office for registration of the contracts, the requirement for payments.
>
> Mr. Stringer [said] . . . "Get us the documents. I'll register the contracts." . . . Out of the 33 contracts rejected, 18 had open violations, 21 were missing required site reviews and 15 lacked certificates of occu-

pancy, according to the comptroller's office.... "I think it's fair to say that this administration does not get the details," he [Stringer] said.[43]

Eventually, the processing of DHS contracts was taken from the agency and handed over to the HRA,[44] although DHS sources claimed that the HRA merely provided assistance.

Overall, Taylor failed to win the confidence of key constituencies. He did not impress the City Council when he "struggled to answer basic questions about the number of homeless people in the city."[45] It was reported that "Some advocates ... said he was an inexperienced leader who had difficulty supervising staff and navigating the political landscape."[46] The *Times* reported that when his administration's handling of the homeless problem was criticized, de Blasio held a private talk with key advisers on the matter, and Taylor was not in attendance.[47] Taylor's resignation was announced on December 15, 2015.

For about the first two years of his administration, while he was being battered in the press and public opinion over homelessness, de Blasio lacked an effective point person on this crucial issue. With Taylor's departure, HRA Commissioner Banks took temporary charge of the DHS.

Banks's changes in welfare policy at the HRA, which involved moving away from the workfare strategies of the Giuliani and Bloomberg administrations, are discussed in chapters 5–7. Banks saw a connection between homelessness and welfare policies. He believed that strict sanctioning of welfare recipients who, for whatever reason, fall out of compliance with HRA regulations would drive up shelter applications. His agency looked at everyone who applied for homeless shelter from January through March 2014 and did a match to see how many of them had been receiving cash assistance. It found that when looking back six months, 23 percent had a negative case action; looking back twelve months, 35 percent had experienced such an action.[48] This finding was one reason Banks determined a strategy to introduce a less punitive sanctioning policy for welfare clients.

Banks organized all the HRA's homeless prevention efforts into a single Homelessness Prevention Administration. Elevating the prevention of homelessness to a task equal to sheltering the homeless was an initiative of the Bloomberg administration. The former mayor's main prevention initiative was Home Base, a program that offered various sorts of aid to precariously housed families and that scientific analysis has shown to be effective in diverting families from shelters. Instead of having job centers (i.e., welfare offices) refer at-risk families to separate Home Base offices, Banks sensibly located Home Base staff in the centers, thus saving a step. A wide range of other prevention programs were coordinated by the HRA, including the provision of rent arrears and eviction prevention legal services. Given that the average cost of emergency rent help was $3,396 per case and legal assistance cost on average about $2,000 per case, these follow-ups on the prevention strategy are cost-efficient.[49]

Necessity Is Real

With the shelter population failing to decline nearly as much as had been hoped, the de Blasio administration faced a dilemma: How to manage the high inflows and need for space in the shelter system? Past administrations had faced similar crises and were reduced to various catch-as-catch-can expedients. To cope with the rising demand for shelter touched off by the *Callahan* consent decree, Ed Koch's administration rapidly converted government-owned armories—the only sufficiently large facilities readily available—into unpleasant congregate shelters where men slept in hundreds of beds crowded into the armories' large drill floors. When Dinkins had faced an increase in applicant families after successfully reducing the system's reliance on infamous welfare hotels, his administration reluctantly returned to placing them in the hotels. At one point under Bloomberg, the DHS was forced to convert an old jailhouse into a shelter for homeless families.[50] Advocacy groups such as the Coalition for the Homeless and Legal Aid strenuously objected to these desperate measures, while city administrators defended them as unavoidable given that situations were not entirely under their control. Certainly, all of these options were suboptimal at best and thankfully were corrected in the long run. But alternatives were not available in the short run.

The de Blasio administration's turn to wrestle with cruel necessity eventually came. In 2011, there were on average 9,770 families in the DHS shelter system; this number had steadily increased to 14,655 families in December 2014 and then decreased slightly to 12,008 families as of October 29, 2015.[51] Its back against the wall, the city decided to put families in former hotels that served as shelters and did not meet all the provisions of the law on shelter quality. One such offense was that the rooms of the former Pan Am, Westway, and Capri Whitestone Motels in Queens did not have individual kitchenettes, as required under the law.[52] The city defended its use of the Pan Am Motel: "As the number of families with children residing in temporary, emergency shelter grows, we must consider all available options to address our capacity needs and meet our legally mandated right to shelter.... In the short term, DHS is using the Queens Boulevard facility to provide essential shelter and supportive services to families with children."[53] Thus the city entered into temporary contracts with the hotels and service providers and promised Comptroller Stringer that kitchenettes would be installed when permanent contracts were signed. This wise decision made it possible to shelter hundreds of families.

So what was the problem? There was no problem, really, but there was an irony. Back in 1991, Banks, then a Legal Aid lawyer, sued the city to provide better-quality shelter for families. At the time, the city relied on notorious "welfare hotels" to shelter homeless families. Conditions at these hotels were often terrible. The Dinkins administration made a noble effort to stop using those hotels, and by July 1990, it had greatly reduced the number of families placed there. Then, for whatever reasons, the number of families entering the overall system surged from 3,226 in July 1990 to 4,450 by March 1991. The Dinkins administration reluctantly concluded that it had to return to using the welfare hotels, plausibly claiming that the "unexpected influx of families into the shelter system has forced certain policy changes including . . . [re]use of commercial [i.e., welfare] hotels."[54]

Banks—the litigator—did not buy the administration's plea of necessity, arguing that failure to supply enough permanent housing was the real issue, and therefore "the city has only its own poor planning to blame for its problem."[55] Again, many conditions at these hotels were bad, but one issue he cited was, in retrospect, less urgent than others: no kitchenettes in many rooms. Banks argued that a state Department of Social Service regulation forbade housing families in such kitchen-less hotel rooms,[56] despite part of that regulation providing that "hotel/motel accommodations without cooking facilities shall be utilized only when accommodations with such facilities are not available."[57] The judge hearing the case, Justice Helen Freedman, felt she had to "conclude that cooking facilities are mandatory."[58] To its credit, the city scrambled and, despite its alleged propensity for poor planning, eventually found accommodations that complied with the judge's order.

What is the point of this exercise in legal and policy archaeology? I simply want to elucidate that the progressive de Blasio administration ended up making the same necessity arguments that drew scorn from liberal critics when they were made by previous administrations. Of course, weighing the validity of such arguments over time is nearly impossible. Under de Blasio and Banks, the DHS made the right decision in using the kitchen-less Queens hotels, and so did Legal Aid advocates, who decided not to challenge the agency as they did during the Koch and Dinkins years. Finally, everyone, even zealous advocates, realized that the city sometimes deserves to be cut a break. The de Blasio administration learned it had to depend on the forbearance of advocates and other critics, as previous administrations did. Sometimes policy makers have to be flexible and accept the formerly unacceptable in the face of necessity.

9

LATER DEVELOPMENTS IN DE BLASIO'S HOMELESSNESS POLICY

The Effort to Recover

By mid-December 2015, city homeless policy was perhaps not in crisis, but it was less optimal than it might have been. Responsibility for that state of affairs was widespread. Michael Bloomberg had failed to follow up on promising beginnings; he eliminated housing subsidies and consequently drove up the shelter census. Candidate Bill de Blasio then underestimated how difficult it would be to restore the subsidies and plot a new course in this wicked policy area. The conflict between de Blasio and Andrew Cuomo delayed the reinstitution of rent subsidies, and an anticipated drop in the shelter census did not materialize. The feud also put off a fourth New York/New York agreement. This left the city with few supportive housing units for the unsheltered mentally ill, who remained on the streets. The mayor responded slowly to the resulting media flap. His first Department of Homeless Services (DHS) commissioner was not effective and had to step down. Conservative critics were quick to blame the perceived homeless crisis on not just de Blasio but his whole progressive ideology. This charge was summed up in a September 2015 *New York Post* article: "Giuliani: De Blasio's Progressivism Created City's Homeless Crisis."[1] If de Blasio were to prove that a progressive could govern New York City, he would have to pick up his game. He made various efforts to do so.

To deal with the perception that street homelessness was out of control, the administration introduced the Home-Stat program. Sixty field and analytic staffers from the Mayor's Office of Operations helped implement a daily canvass of Manhattan streets. Funding to private outreach nonprofits was slated to be increased so they could expand their street outreach teams from 175 to 312 workers and thus be able to respond to 311 calls within one hour. The police department redeployed forty officers to augment its seventy-officer Homeless Outreach Unit. The city also decided to conduct quarterly nighttime counts of street dwellers. The idea was to identify street dwellers quickly and bring them to shelter rapidly.[2] The administration may have finally realized that more frequent and more accurate enumerations of unhoused people on the street would likely rebut the belief that this population had exploded.

Furthermore, a way around the Cuomo/de Blasio impasse about supportive housing eventually developed. There was no New York/New York IV agreement, but there was what might be called a New York/New York IV *disagreement*. After years of unsuccessfully trying to forge a supportive housing program with Governor Cuomo and being blamed for the apparently growing street homelessness caused by a lack of appropriate housing units, de Blasio decided to strike out on his own. A *New York Times* article on his announcement captured the political dynamics of this move:

> Mayor Bill de Blasio on Wednesday [November 18, 2015] announced a plan to create 15,000 "supportive housing" apartments for chronically homeless New Yorkers. He says he is seriously ramping up the city's response to a crisis that he promised to fix, but that has gotten worse since he took office almost two years ago.
>
> And he wants sole credit. "Let's be clear," Mr. de Blasio said at a news conference. "The City of New York is acting. We are acting decisively. We are not waiting on Albany."
>
> Did you get that? The mayor is not waiting on Albany. That is, on Cuomo.
>
> Mr. de Blasio and Mr. Cuomo have issues that don't seem close to being resolvable anytime soon. Best for the two men to set them aside, and for Mr. Cuomo to respond not with indifference or hostility but a matching or bigger commitment that will swiftly deliver the housing and support that so many New Yorkers desperately need.[3]

The project de Blasio announced here came to be known as the New York City 15/15 Supportive Housing Initiative. The plan was a commitment to develop fifteen thousand units of supportive housing over the next fifteen years. It consciously emulated the three earlier New York/New York agreements that built a total of a bit more than fourteen thousand supportive housing units in the city. NY/NY III included the important innovation of making supportive units available not just to mentally ill homeless individuals but to families and youths aging out of foster care as well. NYC 15/15 followed up on that breakthrough by seeking to develop units for these groups. In January 2016, de Blasio put together a task force of supportive housing policy experts to specify how the initiative was to be implemented. Politically, one of the most interesting things about the task force was its formal title: New York City's Supportive Housing Task Force. That is, NYC 15/15 was entirely the city's show, one in which the state played no role, as was evidenced by the fact that the task force included no representative of the state government.

Once the city had announced this plan, Cuomo quickly decided he would not be outdone. In his State of the State speech of January 13, 2016, he announced plans for the state to develop twenty thousand supportive housing units over fifteen years. In other words, since the mayor and governor could not get along well enough to sign a formal agreement, they each undertook part of the job on their own. Cuomo's plan was dubbed the Empire State Supportive Housing Initiative (ESSHI). Supporters of a New York/New York IV agreement had been calling for thirty thousand more units and were pleased that together the city and state plans committed to developing thirty-five thousand units.

The de Blasio/Cuomo rivalry is often trotted out to explain the delay in developing more supportive housing and as the main reason there was never an NY/NY IV agreement. Political science, especially regarding policy making, usually does not accept individual personalities as causal forces. Yet for some time now, political analysis has accepted gender relations as having explanatory power. It is therefore interesting to note that for the NY/NY I agreement, the main negotiators were both women: Diane Baillargeon of the Human Resources Administration (HRA) for the city and Cindy Freidmutter of the Office of Mental Health for the state. Freidmutter thought having two women do the job was relevant: "Diane and I. . . . We were two women building a consensus rather than trying to win the fight."[4] In contrast, the *New York Times* described Cuomo and de Blasio as "New York's top two political alpha males," who were capable of getting "locked in a contest over something they both agree on."[5] Perhaps there is something to this gender-based analysis even though three earlier NY/NY agreements had been successfully negotiated by male mayors and male governors. It is also possible that the results of the Cuomo/de Blasio rivalry were not all negative. After Cuomo announced ESSHI in response to de Blasio's NY/NY 15, Kevin Corinth, a research fellow in economic policy studies at the American Enterprise Institute, suggested, "While the feud initially stalled action, it is now having the opposite effect as the two leaders race to outdo one another in confronting homelessness."[6] Nonetheless, given that the previous three New York/New York agreements were strikingly successful ventures in intergovernmental cooperation, it was a pity that the process had apparently been abandoned for largely personal reasons.

The de Blasio administration finally found its voice on homelessness policy, and it was that of Steve Banks. Lilliam Barrios-Paoli's replacement—foundation executive Dr. Herminia Palacio, who lacked New York City experience—never became an important force, so Banks ended up as a sort of de facto deputy mayor. When Gilbert Taylor left the DHS, Banks, along with First Deputy Mayor Anthony Shorris, headed up a ninety-day review of city homelessness policy.

Perhaps the most important development to come out of the review was the reintegration of the DHS with the HRA. Homeless services had been spun off from the HRA in 1993. In a 2016 op-ed article for the *New York Times*, Christine Quinn—de Blasio's former rival in the Democratic mayoral primary who became president of the homeless services provider Women In Need—stated, "We need to combine those two agencies. . . . This change would be a recognition that homelessness is not an isolated problem; it interacts with, and is a consequence of, a maelstrom of factors—unaffordable rents, insufficient job training, lack of accessible childcare, untreated mental illness and substance abuse, and too few stable work opportunities."[7]

The argument that consolidation would encourage coordination and solve multifaceted problems is a chestnut of public administration literature.[8] Indeed, such was the logic by which the HRA came into existence under notable progressive Mayor John Lindsay. The agency's official history reports: "Conceived back in 1966, HRA symbolized the mayor's attempts to identify and integrate the gamut of analogous services under one 'superagency.'"[9] As was noted in the introduction, in 1973, a state commission on New York City government operations concluded, "The superagency concept . . . has been far from the administrative panacea it originally appeared to be."[10] Reflecting such disappointment, over the years, the HRA was broken down somewhat. First, the DHS in 1993, then the Administration for Children's Services (ACS) in 1996 became independent agencies.

The merits of merging the DHS and the HRA are debatable. Joan Malin, an influential DHS commissioner under Giuliani who had also managed homeless services when they were at the HRA, argued that an independent DHS "allowed us to focus in the way that we would not [have] been able to do at HRA and I say that because I was at both places." She explained, "As a commissioner, you're at the table with the deputy mayors." This is important, Malin explained, "when they're making changes in the budget, or they're thinking about allocation of resources, or vacancy control." That is the time, she said, when "you can advocate for your organization."[11]

In contrast, when the agencies were merged, Malin explained that the "HRA had to advocate for you along with five other mini-organizations and you never get the priority unless there was something so urgent and so crisis-driven that you had to be able to do it." Consequently, she concluded, "To me it made a huge difference [in] . . . your ability to negotiate with NYCHA, with HPD, and from commissioner to commissioner. And that was significant."[12]

One observer who questioned the wisdom of reintegrating the DHS and HRA was councilwoman Elizabeth Crowley. In 2016, the *New York Times* reported, "She said Mr. Banks, who, as commissioner of the Department of Social Services, oversees both homeless services and the Human Resources Administration, was juggling too much. 'He is well intentioned but completely overwhelmed,' Ms. Crowley said."[13]

Most homeless services are not provided directly by the DHS but by contracted providers. When the reintegration of the DHS was first broached, the private homeless service providers I spoke with were generally not enthusiastic about the idea. Given a choice between dealing with a small agency focused on their specific issue and a very large but possibly more powerful superagency, most providers preferred the first option. Some noted that a merger might make sense given that HRA Commissioner Banks had extraordinary experience with homelessness. Nonetheless, they wondered whether later commissioners lacking such expertise would garner appropriate attention for the agency. Bureaucratic coordination via consolidation is rarely achieved in the fragmented administrative system in the United States. Agency effectiveness can be achieved by smaller, mission-driven, entrepreneurial organizations. On the basis of this logic, the DHS was detached from the HRA in the first place, to universal approval.

I also spoke to former HRA commissioners about de Blasio's and Banks's reorganization of homeless services. William Grinker was HRA commissioner under Ed Koch. A 2005 article coauthored by Grinker endorsed spinning off the DHS and ACS from the HRA.[14] In 2022, I asked Grinker what he thought about the relative merits of a freestanding versus an integrated homeless agency. He told me, "I'm not sure how much difference it makes." He noted that "in the abstract you want the two different agencies to have their own way of doing things, but you also want to have them coordinated. If you have them coordinated out of City Hall it's a little bit harder to do. So if you have them coordinated under one leadership of one person, that that's a major part of his job it's probably better." Overall, he noted the advantages of keeping agencies "close": "I think in the abstract if you've got decent leadership at the operating level it's better to have them closer together."[15]

Grinker introduces a useful distinction for judging how to organize welfare and homeless services. Merging the units under a single commissioner with immediate operational responsibilities for both is defensible. This is what de Blasio and Banks ended up doing. But putting homelessness, housing development, planning, and other responsibilities under the control of a City Hall official, such as a deputy mayor, runs the risk of overstretching the official's attention and effectively demoting the importance of homelessness.

Grinker's insight cuts against proposals such as the one made in the 2021 report *United for Housing from the Ground Up* from the New York Housing Conference, which called for the new Eric Adams administration to "provide leadership at City Hall including a single deputy mayor in charge of housing and homelessness issues" who "oversees a spectrum of housing and economic development agencies that includes close coordination between the Department of Housing Preservation and Development, New York City Housing Authority, Housing Development Corporation, Department of City Planning, and Department of Homeless Services (DHS), to better connect housing opportunity and homelessness."[16]

The concern about overstretch also applies to an equally ambitious reorganization plan from a consortium of homeless advocacy organizations whose report calls for the Adams administration to produce an "Integrated Housing Plan that brings together all the agencies involved in housing, building, and planning to create one coordinated strategy focused on ending homelessness and promoting racial equity. In order to accomplish this, they must create a position of Deputy Mayor for Homelessness, Housing and Planning, and shift responsibility for oversight of and coordination between all relevant agencies, as well as creation of the plan, to this new Deputy Mayor."[17]

Christine Quinn called for City Hall direction of the agencies related to homelessness. She has said, "We cannot have the silos that we have had. . . . It's incredibly ineffective. We need the buck to stop with one person and that person needs to report directly to the mayor."[18] Today, the enemies of silos are as enthusiastic as the champions of agency entrepreneurialism were some twenty years ago. But it seems likely that the benefits of consolidation will mostly be found at the agency level and will diminish when a wide array of agencies are bundled together and managed from City Hall by a deputy mayor with many responsibilities.

Eventually, the city's human resources bureaucracy was reorganized in a way that put both the DHS and the HRA under the control of Banks, who held the title of commissioner of the Department of Social Services (DSS). The HRA was created by Executive Order 28 of August 15, 1966. The Department of Welfare was one of the preexisting city agencies that were subsumed under the new superagency. However, the executive order stated that "nothing in this order shall be construed to impair the functions, powers, and duties of the Commissioner of Welfare or the Department of Welfare as defined by the New York Social Welfare

Law or by any federal statute." The positions of HRA commissioner and the commissioner of the Department of Welfare were merged in 1970. From then on, the agency was more accurately referred to as the NYC Human Resources Administration/Department of Social Services (HRA/DSS).[19] Under the reorganization of 2016, the HRA and DHS became subunits of DSS, with Banks in charge of both as commissioner.

In March 2017, the de Blasio administration finally got around to issuing a comprehensive written homeless policy plan, *Turning the Tide on Homelessness in New York City*. One of the most interesting things about the plan was how realistic it was about the possibilities of major change and how modest its goals were. In the introduction, the plan stated: "We must be clear-eyed: it will take many years to reset the unacceptable status quo we see today. . . . We recognize that none of these measures are sufficient to address this crisis. There are no silver bullets here. We will not solve this crisis overnight. It will be a long, hard fight."[20] This was a marked change from de Blasio's campaign rhetoric and ambitious plans for addressing economic inequality. That change had begun to manifest itself in the document that resulted from the ninety-day review of homeless policy that was published in April 2016. That report stated that the mayor's concern was "to ensure services are delivered as efficiently and effectively as possible in order to prevent, reduce and manage homelessness."[21] After two years of frustrating struggle, no mention is made, as the Bloomberg administration used to do, of ending homelessness; instead, the emphasis is on reducing and managing the problem. *Turning the Tide* followed up on that hard-won realism and set goals that were within reach.

The main objectives were by no means easy, but they were relatively modest: reducing the number of people in the shelters by twenty-five hundred over five years and removing people "from all cluster apartment units by the end of 2021 and commercial hotel facilities by the end of 2023."[22] Again, this acceptance of managing rather than trying to end homelessness represented a backing away from past efforts to make a dramatic change. The Bloomberg administration explicitly embraced the idea of ending homelessness, which it thought was possible through prevention programs such as Home Base, and by concentrating on permanently housing the so-called chronically homeless population, that is, clients who took up a disproportionately high number of shelter bed days. The Bloomberg administration also pledged to dramatically reduce the shelter census. Bloomberg administration officials had scorned the idea of merely managing homelessness; they had swung for the fences and anticipated a major victory. Bloomberg's administration at least expected that it could achieve a nonincremental change in homeless policy. Of course, its plans were frustrated as the census rose and homelessness did not end on its watch. This failure was largely attributed to the end of rental subsidies for shelter clients, which were thought to have made it impossible to move clients out and thus drive down the census. When de Blasio came in, he reinstated rental subsidies, which were probably effective in keeping the census lower than what it would have been in their absence but did not stop the count from going up. The policy mechanism that as much as anything was expected to produce a dramatic change did not meet expectations. This disappointment and the experience of two years of tough struggle just to keep things from getting much worse apparently convinced the de Blasio administration to focus on making incremental progress.

What can we make of the de Blasio/Banks record on homelessness? The principal concern here is whether the administration lived up to its ambition to break sharply with the Bloomberg administration's dread of perverse incentives and make a dramatic change in homeless policy. Near the end of de Blasio's mayoralty, several overviews of his homeless policy were published. These include *Family Homelessness in New York City: What the Adams Administration Can Learn from Previous Mayoralties* from the Institute for Children, Poverty & Homelessness (ICPH); *Assessing De Blasio's Housing Legacy: Why Hasn't the "Most Ambitious Affordable Housing Program" Produced a More Affordable City?* from the Community Service Society; *Right to a Roof: Demands for an Integrated Housing Plan to End Homelessness and Promote Racial Equity*, from a consortium of community organizations; and *Our Homelessness Crisis: The Case for Change*, from the City Council of New York. These accounts, combined with the analysis presented here, make possible a bottom-line evaluation of the de Blasio/Banks record in achieving nonincremental change in homeless policy.

Tellingly, the City Council's report found that under de Blasio, "homelessness has become an accepted reality that the City treats as a crisis to be managed."[23] As was discussed already, this was a fair description of the approach the administration did take up. But apparently, the City Council wished for something more dramatic, as it subtitled its report *The Case for Change*, implying that change was needed but had not yet happened.

In *Family Homelessness in New York City*, ICPH notes several positive accomplishments of the de Blasio administration, especially an increase in the value of the City Fighting Homelessness and Eviction Prevention Supplement rent vouchers and the right to counsel in Housing Court. The institute also notes that at the end of de Blasio's term in December 2021, the number of families in city homeless shelters was lower than it had been at the start of his term, but it observed: "This is no doubt due, in part, to the eviction moratorium put in place as an emergency response to the COVID-19 pandemic."[24] Overall, the institute depicted an administration "with many big ideas and an average of nearly $2 billion spent each year on shelter provision alone" but with uncertain results:

> Out of the gate, Banks and de Blasio struggled to balance their personal beliefs about the shelter system—that we should ease our reliance on the system and do everything in our power to keep families housed—with the reality that they simply had to have enough beds in the system to comply with the Right to Shelter ruling. Their plan to focus on long-term solutions to homelessness—housing production and income equality, being two examples—created a tension with the real and immediate needs of families in and entering shelter. This resulted in enormous expense and the use of unsafe commercial hotels that were a Band-Aid solution from 2015 to 2021.
>
> Over the next year, we will see if the de Blasio years created long-term structural change, or if this current decrease in the family homelessness census is the result of COVID-19-specific solutions that will unravel in the coming months.[25]

So ICPH acknowledges that the de Blasio/Banks administration may have achieved "long-term structural change"—what I call nonincremental change—but whether it has depends on the continued decline in the shelter census, which may be a fluke due to the external shock of COVID-19 and the city's emergency responses. The authors also remark that the administration's "path to this accomplishment was convoluted."[26] Again, we get a record of considerable accomplishment but not a clear-cut case of nonincremental change.

The *Right to a Roof* report acknowledges a record of accomplishment but insists that desired and needed change has not been achieved. "In summary, despite some important steps toward creating and preserving affordability, such as establishing the right to counsel for tenants in housing court, creating and expanding rental assistance programs, and mandating a set-aside of units for formerly homeless New Yorkers in City-subsidized housing, Mayor de Blasio's approach to housing has failed to reduce racial and economic disparities and serve the needs of the lowest-income New Yorkers."[27] In *Assessing De Blasio's Housing Legacy*, Samuel Stein of the Community Service Society also sees the de Blasio administration's record as "A Mix of Gains and Losses" and, like everyone else these days, decries "A Siloed Approach to Housing Planning."[28] In a section titled "Homelessness: The Ultimate Housing Issue, Sidelined," Stein does not see a record of dramatic change. He writes, "As a result of an inadequate commitment and behind-schedule supportive housing, undervalued vouchers, and limited housing construction targeted toward the homeless, the rate of placements in permanent housing remained flat, even as escalating housing costs pushed more and more New Yorkers into homelessness." He concludes that "the administration's political priority has instead been on providing very basic shelter, thus reducing the visibility of homelessness without resolving the conditions that are increasing it." Stein addressed the question of choices made by the city and commented, "While investing in shelters may be better than allowing shelter conditions to deteriorate further, the choice to continue spending on shelters rather than building permanent housing for the lowest-income New Yorkers assumes that homelessness will continue into the future."[29]

To these comprehensive analyses of the de Blasio/Banks records might be added a 2022 article from the *New York Times Magazine*, "The Man Who Fought Homelessness and Won (Sort Of)," which presented an overview of Banks's tenure at the HRA/DSS. The article convincingly characterizes him as "the most effective social-services director in New York City history" but nonetheless notes that "when he left office, there were still 45,000 people sleeping in shelters. Is that a success?" The passage below is relevant to an answer:

> When Banks left office, at the end of last year, conditions in some shelters remained dreadful, and investigations by journalists and the agency exposed financial irregularities and ethical concerns at some of the nonprofit organizations that partnered with the agency. Forty-five thousand New Yorkers remained in shelters. But under Banks, the average number of people in shelter declined for three years in a row, after rising for decades. Countless thousands were spared homelessness before they lost their housing, and New York became the first city in the country to guarantee that every tenant in housing court will have a lawyer. The department has been more effective than at any time in its history, yet still not effective enough.[30]

Suggestively, the article quotes a "long term colleague" of Banks's at Legal Aid as saying, "There's a part of him that almost feels responsible that he hasn't solved the problem."[31]

Banks did not solve the homelessness problem, but on his watch, a big dent was made in it. When de Blasio left office in December 2021, the shelter census had declined to 48,691 people.[32] Thus the administration's pledge in the March 2017 document *Turning the Tide on Homelessness in New York City* to reduce the shelter census by twenty-five hundred in five years was more than met. In fact, the census was reduced by 13,245 people for a 21.4 percent decrease. The last count under the de Blasio administration found that in January 2021, there were 2,376 unsheltered people in the city.[33] That was a decline since the start of his term in January 2014 of 981 people, or a 29 percent reduction. The administration also met its goal of ending the use of cluster site apartments, with the use of these units ending by October 30, 2021.[34] However, expenditures for homeless services remained high, and in fiscal year 2021, at the end of de Blasio's mayoralty, the DHS budget was about $2.88 billion.[35]

Change there was in homeless policy under Banks, good change, important change, but not the kind of nonincremental change that has been the principal focus of this book. The most striking example of nonincremental change in New York's homeless policy came under Mayor Koch, who approved the *Callahan v. Carey* consent decree that resulted in an operational right to shelter and began developing the city's shelter system. Thus, the old baseline of flophouses and no formal homeless policy at all was replaced with a legal entitlement to shelter provided by a growing bureaucracy. De Blasio and Banks accepted the baseline of a right to shelter, which Banks had done so much to establish, and rather than trying to end the shelter system, he wanted to make it work better. One might say that the homeless policy under de Blasio and Banks gave incremental change a good name.

New York City's Record of Innovation and Possible Future Directions in Homeless Policy

In some quarters the conviction lives on that homelessness, being entirely the result of unbridled neoliberal urban policy, is a completely unproblematic phenomenon, perfectly understood and susceptible to immediate cure if only well-known solutions were not blocked by political considerations. In a 2017 article, distinguished urban affairs scholar Peter Marcuse noted the lamentable fact that the New York City shelter census was at an all-time high and commented: "It is not lack of knowledge that is preventing us from solving the problem . . . the problem is implementing our knowledge."[36] What are the well-known solutions to homelessness that await implementation? Marcuse tells us that "public housing, housing subsidies, income subsidies, housing allowances, anti-speculation taxes, rent controls, community land trusts, inclusionary housing requirements, are all available tools."[37] Yet these tools, with the exception of antispeculation taxes, are not only available but already in place in New York City and in some cases have been for many decades. Furthermore, New York has deployed tools to solve homelessness not mentioned by Marcuse: shelters for families, singles, and victims of domestic violence; supportive housing; street outreach programs; antieviction assistance; and other forms of homelessness prevention. The city's spending for services to homeless people across all relevant agencies reached about $3 billion in fiscal year 2018, which was more than was spent on the fire department or sanitation services.[38] To these efforts must be added those of the city's highly developed nonprofit sector and homelessness policy network. If it is true that only an entirely new economic system will completely eliminate homelessness, New York City has not waited for that dawn of a new age and has instead thrown considerable resources into addressing the problem in the context of its admittedly limited but at least presently existing welfare state and independent sector.

Of course, we still have homelessness. In 2017, the city's total homeless population was about 63,333 people, consisting of a daily average of 59,441 shelter clients and an estimated 3,892 unsheltered people.[39] Should we conclude that the city's efforts have all been for naught and are mere window dressing to disguise the fact that the real solution to homelessness (i.e., socialism) remains untried? This is the obverse of the naive conservative critique of the Great Society, which concludes that because the poor are still with us, it must follow that poverty was the victor in the war on poverty. These arguments overlook the fact that without the Great Society programs or New York's homeless system, the problems they address would be much worse than they now are. Both critiques deploy what has been called the futility argument. The rightist knocks against the Great Society assume that the causes of poverty are so rooted in human nature that the struggle against them is futile. Leftist agnosticism toward the importance of New York's homeless system assumes that the capitalist structures of oppression are so powerful that anything short of total revolution is otiose. These criticisms assume that there is nothing new under the sun, that the problem of poverty is already fully understood and the responses to it are fully formulated. The only difference is that conservatives argue that the obvious solutions have already been tried and have utterly failed, whereas leftists argue they will never get a chance until revolution produces a new world. On the other hand, New York's tradition of political action in the context of a limited welfare state in effect declares: "Say not the struggle naught availeth."

It is notable that many of the central programs of New York's system of homeless services were *not* well-known policy solutions that simply sat on the shelf waiting for a progressive regime with the political will to fund and implement them. The three foundational initiatives in the development of city homeless policy have been a right to shelter, a paternalistic philosophy of shelter management, and a postpaternalistic direction that included prevention programs, Housing First, and a focus on the chronically homeless. None of these approaches were old hat at the time they were deployed. All were nonincremental innovations that responded to newly discovered social problems, path-breaking research, policy entrepreneurship, and creative implementation and management. The city's homeless service system arose in a highly fragmented political environment that fostered not gridlock but innovation by a wide range of players.

A brief overview of these nonincremental changes or paradigm shifts in city homeless policy confirms they were genuine innovations fostered by creative policy entrepreneurs. The entitlement phase of homeless policy crystallized in the late 1970s and early 1980s when path-breaking reform litigation led by legal advocates such as Robert Hayes and Steven Banks established what amounted to a right to shelter for the homeless. Rapid implementation of this right resulted in poor-quality shelters that offered few services or opportunities for rehabilitation. In the early 1990s, these concerns precipitated the paternalistic paradigm. The principal entrepreneur behind that approach was Andrew Cuomo. He led a commission on homeless policy that called for the nonprofitization of the shelter system and for requiring clients to participate in rehabilitation programs in return for being sheltered. Paternalism led to better-quality shelters and more services. But many homeless people declined to accept shelter services on these terms and rehousing rather than rehabilitating clients soon turned out to be a more doable task. After the turn of the millennium, groundbreaking work by researchers including Sam Tsemberis and Dennis Culhane resulted in the postpaternalistic paradigm. Policy focused on moving clients into permanent housing quickly and developing supportive housing. The point is that modern New York City homelessness policy has been characterized by innovation and policy learning.

Innovative ideas and determined policy entrepreneurship have marked the development of New York's network of homeless services. I make my own, highly speculative contribution to these ideas. Before I do, I would like to state plainly some conclusions that were implicit in my book *Homelessness in New York City*.

There I was clear that the long-running litigation to establish a de facto right to shelter in New York was essential to forcing the city to address the pressing social problem of homelessness. In addition, I want to be clear that the city's experience also illustrates the significant costs and serious limitations to institutional reform through litigation. Quantifying those costs is very difficult. It would require documenting the costs of a particular initiative—say, improving shelter conditions—under the process of institutional reform litigation and then comparing them with the counterfactual of what those costs would have been if the same effort had been made without those constraints. Here there can be only speculation, not quantification, about the costs (and benefits) of the litigation model. But a few episodes in the city's homeless policy suggest that the costs may be substantial. A small but suggestive example is that a queuing theory analysis of court-mandated ratios of bathroom fixtures to shelter clients showed that the court's approach did require an installation of too many fixtures, just as city administrators had unavailingly argued.[40] How typical this case is of shelter management under court direction is impossible to say because few other cases are capable of such an "objective" evaluation of alternatives. But the terms and conclusion of the plumbing ratio debate sound very much like those of many other shelter management issues debated in court, and the fact that the city is now spending about $3 billion for services to the homeless suggests that cost concerns are legitimate.

As for the limitations of institutional reform litigation, the 1992 episode in which Justice Helen E. Freedman found four city officials in contempt of court for repeated failures to correct violations of court mandates is telling. There were many mistakes and disappointments, which is not uncommon in public administration. But there were also the city's efforts outside of the courtroom to devise an entirely new approach to homelessness policy, one that was developed by the independent Cuomo Commission and ultimately implemented with considerable success under the Giuliani administration. Looked at from not a judicial but a citywide perspective, New York's efforts were diligent and ultimately fruitful, and the administrators who implemented them deserved respect, not condemnation.

Neither of these points denies that institutional reform litigation is an indispensable prod into action. The classic pluralistic account of urban politics, Sayre and Kaufman's *Governing New York City*, correctly noted that the city's myriad interest groups can produce a political status quo mired in stasis.[41] The heroic efforts of the city's highly organized public interest legal network have been indispensable in breaking that logjam through court action, thus giving other policy entrepreneurs a chance to innovate. As a result of these conditions, credit for the significant progress the city has made on homelessness is widely shared. Legal crusaders, public executives, nonprofit leaders, academic researchers, and others all made change possible.

The question then comes up: In such a city, what might be the next useful innovation in homeless policy? Based on my reading of recent literature and policy history, I suggest that a model that might be called a Home Stay or Host Home approach deserves consideration. Home Stay is a strategy that would combine digital technology with old-school social work to address homelessness by making housing markets more efficient and public service more personal.

Home Stay is based on the fact that in one very particular sense, New York City's homelessness problem is relatively small. In 2017, the city had a total housing stock of 3,469,240 units, of which 2,183,064, or 62.9 percent, were rental units.[42] Obviously, most of these rentals are unaffordable to the homeless, but surely there is enough unused space among those units to physically accommodate another 63,000 people, who amount to only 0.73 percent of the city's population of 8.623 million people. A significant number of shelter clients have a small income. In fiscal year 2024, 76.8 percent of shelter families with children received public assistance. And among shelter clients between 1990 and 2002, "38 percent of adults in families and 45 percent of single adults received wage income."[43] Why don't the owners of the unused space rent it out for perhaps very little and make at least something on their otherwise unproductive asset? After the San Francisco earthquake of 1906, there was no housing shortage even though half of the city's housing had been destroyed because owners of the remaining stock rented out all previously unused space.[44] San Francisco thus accommodated perhaps eighty thousand people who would otherwise have been homeless. Why doesn't the same thing happen in New York today?

Consider the following. After the earthquake, San Francisco's housing owners saw an obvious opportunity and ran advertisements for the new space they were rushing to make available at higher prices than they had formerly been able to charge. Homelessness in New York is a disaster, but not as obvious as a major earthquake, and as things currently stand, owners of spare space can hardly make a killing letting it out to homeless people, only a minority of whom have an income, and even those very little.

Let us do some back-of-the-envelope calculations for 2018, a typical year for homelessness under de Blasio, before the sharp rise under Adams brought on partly by the migrant crisis. If we look at shelter costs only, and count clients in both DHS and HPD (Housing Preservation and Development) shelters, we find about $2.1 billion in expenditures to shelter roughly sixty-three thousand homeless people, which comes to about $33,000 per homeless person a year.[45] Put aside obvious funding stream problems for a moment and imagine if that sum was offered to space owners willing to accept homeless renters. Placing the city's relatively "small" homeless population in an already existing space begins to sound plausible.

No doubt there are many people with spare spaces that might be rented out, such as an extra bedroom or attic or large closet that might be suitable. (Back in the very early 1980s, I lived in a converted closet—just large enough to fit a small mattress—of a Park Slope apartment.) There already exists a technology for linking up people with extra space and people with no place, which is Airbnb or similar services. Through a digital exchange, travelers and housing owners with no other connection are able to communicate and strike a deal, and the city is thus able to house many more tourists than it did previously.

But isn't the very idea of an Airbnb for the homeless absurd? There are obvious problems. Many homeless people have disabilities or may otherwise seem to be less-than-ideal tenants in the eyes of space owners. Certainly, many owners will simply be prejudiced against the homeless, the majority of whom are poor,

Black or Hispanic, have children, are disabled, or for other reasons are targets of discrimination.

Some years ago, one of my students documented the existence of an ethnic network that connected poor Chinese immigrants to restaurant employers and landlords of very cheap apartments.[46] But there is no network that connects, say, a Black, female-headed family with three children to white ethnic owners of spare space in the outer boroughs. Airbnb connects employed, middle-class tourists with their home-owning counterparts. Can technology alone bridge the spatial and social distance that would separate the homeless—even if they had money— from potential renters? Probably not, but a human touch might succeed where technology alone cannot.

A program known as Host Homes, designed to find temporary accommodations for homeless LGBTQ youth, suggests what is needed. The idea of the program is to link this cohort of young people to homeowners with extra space they are willing to see occupied. A document from the US Department of Health and Human Services explains how a Host Homes program run by the Chicago nonprofit UCAN works:

> There is a need to provide safe, supportive housing paired with caring adults to model healthy home environments. The UCAN Host Home Program sought to respond to this need by creating an alternative to the shelter system for LGBTQI2-S[47] youth. The Host Home model was pioneered by The GLBT Host Home Program in Minneapolis, MN. Host Home programs recruit, screen, train, and support adults who open their homes to LGBT youth in need of safe and stable housing.... Both the youth and prospective host families are screened extensively. Host Homes are provided with training and support by UCAN's clinical staff.[48]

Nonprofits implementing Host Homes employ a program manager to find, evaluate, keep in contact with, and otherwise support hosts and a case manager to provide similar services to the guests. All staff members provide advice and mediation to help hosts and guests get along. Host home staff can provide the social work interventions necessary to help youths inured to street living learn to get along with their new hosts. More intense social work support might help people with disabilities succeed in host homes.

Host Home programs are good at providing the human interventions necessary to help the people they match up but are less sophisticated at recruiting hosts. Program handbooks recommend recruiting techniques such as handing out flyers at flea markets and making presentations to groups of retirees and church organizations.

Imagine if a nonprofit provided the social work services of a Host Home program, the digital networking of Airbnb, and a subsidy to hosts equivalent to the sum that New York City spends in sheltering its shelter clients. It is a suggestion that deserves to be explored at greater length than is possible here. Whether this particular idea flies or goes over like a lead balloon, New York City's homeless policy community will continue to be a fertile source of policy innovation.

10
DE BLASIO, CUOMO, AND TRUMP

As discussed earlier, under the federal constitution, city mayors are the lowest authority in the US intergovernmental hierarchy. In New York City as elsewhere, mayors seeking to make major changes need to find a way to deal with the chief executives above them: the state governor and the president. John Lindsay's mayoralty and career were eventually ruined by his inability to get along with Governor Nelson Rockefeller (among other things). Lindsay's early success depended on support from President Lyndon Johnson, just as Rudy Giuliani's welfare reforms benefited from a sympathetic President Bill Clinton.

One might think that a New York City mayor on the outs with both the governor and the president would be in a very unfavorable position to achieve much of anything, let alone major reforms. Mayor Bill de Blasio was in that unhappy position. He was notoriously at odds with Governor Andrew Cuomo and President Donald Trump. Even so, de Blasio implemented his Career Pathways welfare policies, achieved other notable reforms in pre-K education and supportive housing, and did not end up being destroyed as Lindsay was. How did de Blasio manage to be relatively much more successful despite the opposition of the governor and the president?

De Blasio and Cuomo

De Blasio and Cuomo were frequently at loggerheads. As Joseph Viteritti notes, "The relationship between Bill de Blasio and Andrew Cuomo . . . would prove to be among the worst in recent memory, surpassing the famous animosity between Nelson Rockefeller and John Lindsay."[1] That hostility sometimes impeded de Blasio's implementation of his welfare policies. Chapter 8 discussed how a lack of cooperation from the governor led to an unnecessary delay in the city's development of the Living in Communities rent subsidies for homeless families. However, the tension between de Blasio and Cuomo, unlike that between Lindsay and Rockefeller, was sometimes productive, perhaps because de Blasio, despite his impeccable progressive credentials, was capable of being politically pragmatic in a way Lindsay was not.

Supportive housing was a welfare-related issue where conflict between de Blasio and Cuomo, as unpleasant as it might have been for all concerned, was ultimately productive. Chapter 9 recounts how these two politicians, unlike their predecessors, did not come to a state/city agreement to replenish the dwindling supply of supportive housing. De Blasio concluded that state cooperation would never come; on his own, he committed the city to building fifteen thousand supportive housing units over fifteen years. Apparently, because their rivalry drove the governor to one-upmanship, in January 2016, Cuomo committed the state to producing twenty thousand units of supportive housing over fifteen years. The supportive housing policy network hailed these developments, which may have represented a larger commitment to such housing than would have been achieved through a fourth city/state agreement.

Raising the minimum wage was another issue where competition between the mayor and governor led to unexpected change. In January 2016, de Blasio implemented a $15 minimum wage for city employees and nonprofit employees working under contract to the city. In so doing, he could claim credit for achieving a goal strongly desired by progressives of the Democratic Party, thereby dishing Cuomo. The ongoing rivalry made it difficult for the governor to just do nothing, so in April 2016, Cuomo signed off on a state $15 minimum wage law.

Universal pre-K (UPK) was a signature de Blasio campaign pledge and accomplishment that also revealed that strained city/state relations need not impede change. De Blasio wanted to make pre-K classes available to all people independent of income and pay for the program with a tax on millionaires. This plan would require cooperation from the governor and state legislature since only the state had the power to impose such a tax. Cuomo supported the expansion of pre-K but not the millionaires' tax. He offered to find funding for the program in the regular state budget. Here de Blasio faced a dilemma because for many progressives the tax on high earners was as important as the program itself. One observer judged, "Progressives clearly believed that getting the program passed without specifically tacking on a tax on the rich would be a failure."[2] Despite his strong progressive orientation, de Blasio showed he was willing to be pragmatic when necessary and accepted Cuomo's funding scheme to guarantee the implementation of UPK.

One might say that de Blasio's strategy for navigating the potentially treacherous city/state relation was to act as a policy entrepreneur. He attached himself to popular policy initiatives, such as the $15/hour minimum wage and UPK, promoted them to the state's electorate, and then provoked a bidding war with the governor to see who would be able to claim credit for realizing them. This was a tactic that Lindsay was never able to pull off against Rockefeller. Lindsay's superagencies, generous welfare policies, and other progressive policies were never popular outside of the city, which is where Rockefeller's voting base was.[3] Rockefeller did not have much to gain electorally by stealing credit for Lindsay's initiatives. He was content to allow Lindsay to take full credit for them and receive blame for them when things did not work out. In any case, the main point about de Blasio's conflicts with Cuomo is that a mayor who can function as an effective policy entrepreneur can get a recalcitrant governor to participate in producing positive change. Despite the great animosity between these two executives, de Blasio got more cooperation out of Cuomo than is sometimes appreciated, and he did so by playing the role of a policy entrepreneur hawking popular policy ideas.

De Blasio and Trump

How did de Blasio fare in dealing with the other chief executive that all would-be reforming mayors must somehow confront: the president of the United States? As noted earlier, Lindsay and Giuliani had good relations with Presidents Johnson and Clinton, respectively, who were supportive of their broad agendas and welfare policies. But de Blasio and Trump were about as diametrically opposed as two elective officials can be in US politics.

Soon after Trump's election, the *Nation*, a leftist magazine, published a feature article that conceptualized the president and mayor as locked in combat. Titled "NYC vs. Trump: Center Ring, Will Bill De Blasio and the People of NYC Land the First Blows Against Trumpism?" The article asserted: "Since Election Day, de Blasio has taken on a role as a leader of the official resistance to the coming Trump regime."[4] Indeed, during the presidential campaign, de Blasio attacked Trump's deportation proposals as "dangerous" and "un-American" and said the KKK's support for him was "disgusting."[5] Not to be outdone, candidate Trump tweeted that de Blasio was "the worst mayor in the U.S. and probably the worst mayor in the history of" New York City.[6]

Earlier we noted that there is little New York City mayors can do to influence presidents. The mutual hostility and ideological clash between Trump and de Blasio did not bode well for a mayor who wanted to make big changes in welfare policy and the city's economy overall. One observer noted, "Getting into a slug fest with the president of the U.S. can only end poorly for the city of New York... Trump can seriously undermine de Blasio and literally cut off the spigot of federal funds."[7] Indeed, from the beginning of his term until the end, Trump tried, very ham-fistedly, to cut funds to New York City in various ways.

Only days after he was sworn in, Trump signed Executive Order 13768, "Enhancing Public Safety in the Interior of the United States," which ordered that "sanctuary jurisdictions" (so-called sanctuary cities), which in various ways refused to cooperate with Immigration and Customs Enforcement (ICE), a federal agency, would not be "eligible to receive Federal grants, except as deemed necessary for law enforcement purposes" by the US Attorney General or Secretary of Homeland Security.[8] New York City qualified as such a jurisdiction when the City Council enacted laws in 2014 that limited cooperation between ICE and the city's police and corrections departments in the processing of undocumented immigrants. In late April, de Blasio responded to this executive order by allocating $16.4 million for legal services to immigrants held in detention, asylum seekers, and unaccompanied children.[9]

New York and other cities affected by Executive Order 13768 took the Trump administration to court. In early November 2017, federal judge William Orrick blocked the policy, finding that the order was "unconstitutionally broad." Orrick also found the order coercive, noting that Trump had described it as a "weapon" to be used against uncooperative cities.[10] Eventually, the order was rescinded by President Joe Biden on his first day in office.

The infamous sanctuary cities executive order lasted only a few months before it was overturned by a court that cited Trump's own incautious words against him. Neither did the other executive orders and memorandums that Trump directed against New York and other cities have much effect.

For example, just weeks before the 2020 presidential election, Trump issued to the Office of Management and Budget a "Memorandum on Reviewing Funding to State and Local Government Recipients That Are Permitting Anarchy, Violence, and Destruction in American Cities," which called for "restricting eligibility of or otherwise disfavoring, to the maximum extent permitted by law, anarchist jurisdictions in the receipt of Federal grants." The memo specifically discussed New York City as a jurisdiction whose grants might be cut, citing the fact that "Mayor Bill de Blasio and the New York City Council agreed to cut one billion dollars from the New York Police Department (NYPD) budget."[11] The memo did not note that much of that cut came from proposals to move school crossing guards out of the police department and to reduce police overtime hours, neither of which was likely to provoke anarchy.[12] De Blasio accurately characterized Trump's memo as merely part of his campaign strategy, and few others took it seriously.

Even Nicole Gelinas of the Manhattan Institute, a conservative think tank often critical of de Blasio, had had enough, saying: "We know if Trump wins [in 2020], we'll just get more of the same, which is a very unconstructive and antagonistic relationship on both sides.... The designation of the 'anarchist jurisdiction' is a good example of that. Under no definition is New York City any more violent or lawless than any other place in the country."[13] Biden won the 2020 election, and in his first weeks rescinded the anarchist jurisdictions memo.[14]

The action of the Trump administration most relevant to welfare policy was Executive Order 13828 of April 10, 2018: "Reducing Poverty in America by Promoting Opportunity and Economic Mobility." The order evoked the "bipartisan welfare reform enacted in 1996" but claimed that "the welfare system . . . is in need of further reform." Federal agencies were required to review the programs they administer and determine whether they were consistent with the nine "Principles of Economic Mobility," the first of which involved "strengthening existing work requirements for work-capable people and introducing new work requirements when legally permissible." The Treasury, Agriculture, Commerce, Labor, Health and Human Services (HHS), Housing and Urban Development (HUD), Transportation, and Education Departments were mandated to "review any public assistance programs of their respective agencies that do not currently require work for receipt of benefits or services, and determine whether enforcement of a work requirement would be consistent with Federal law and the principles outlined in this order."[15] In July, the Council of Economic Advisers issued a report that advocated for work requirements in Medicaid, the Supplemental Nutrition Assistance Program (SNAP), and housing programs.[16]

These proposals had little impact anywhere, and less in New York City. Partly this was because work requirements were already imposed in many noncash programs. For example, SNAP as legislated in 1964 and amended in 1971 included work requirements. As of 2017, SNAP recipients who were "able bodied adults without dependents" had to "work 20 hours a week in order to receive benefits for more than three months within three years."[17] Medicaid did not include work requirements as a condition of eligibility, but by December 2017, eight states had asked the Centers for Medicare and Medicaid Services for waivers to test such requirements. Observers noted that "the agency has already been so aggressive that there may not be much more it can do to promote work in Medicaid"; even Robert Doar, former Human Resources Administration commissioner under Mike Bloomberg and strong supporter of work requirements, "said he is not sure whether there is much more the [Trump] administration can do in Medicaid."[18]

Furthermore, Trump's proposals for work requirements met with strong opposition from states and the courts. New York City and the District of Columbia sued the administration when it proposed a rule that would make it harder to exempt SNAP clients from work requirements.[19] Arkansas and New Hampshire challenged the implementation of waivers that would have allowed Medicaid work requirements. So did Kansas, where a federal judge found that the secretary of HHS "never adequately considered . . . [the waiver] would in fact help the state furnish medical assistance to its citizens, a central objective of Medicaid. This signal omission renders his determination arbitrary and capricious."[20] An academic overview of the success of the Trump administration's use of executive orders, waivers, and other administrative tools to make social policy painted a portrait of the "Trump administrative presidency stymied."[21]

We can now answer the question of how a New York City mayor might achieve significant change in the face of an openly hostile president. The problem solves itself if the president in question is politically clumsy, legislatively ineffective, and administratively incompetent. Despite his apparently paradigm-shattering election, Trump never had the resources or capabilities necessary to pull off major changes that could significantly affect New York City's social policy in the way that Johnson's Great Society programs or the Clinton-era national welfare reforms did.

Further, Trump's whole effort to follow up on the Personal Responsibility and Work Opportunity Reconciliation Act (PRWORA) and 1990s welfare reform was misconceived. As has been discussed, 1990s welfare reform was based on a strong research and professional consensus that rapid labor force attachment policies were the most effective strategies for encouraging work by clients of Aid to Families with Dependent Children and Temporary Aid to Needy Families (TANF). No such research base or professional consensus supported the Trump initiatives in SNAP, Medicaid, and other noncash programs. On the contrary, analysis of these programs was mostly negative, and most experts were unimpressed.[22] The process of distilling a professional consensus into a popular public idea and policy entrepreneurs competing to implement and take credit for innovative reforms never crystallized under Trump. On the contrary, Trump's blustering and polarizing rhetoric did not encourage other political actors to compete with him but provoked them to respond in kind and emphasize their opposition. That is exactly what de Blasio did, winning credit in New York City as being anti-Trump. If he had been able to pass relevant legislation, Trump could have derailed de Blasio's welfare policies and imposed stricter work requirements. But Trump was mostly ineffective at social policy legislation. For example, he was unable to get work requirements for SNAP included in a 2018 farm bill passed by Congress and had to resort to an executive order that states and localities effectively resisted. This pattern was entirely different from the 1990s welfare reform, which was embedded in PRWORA and thus had an enduring effect on states and localities. Trump's executive order on reducing poverty was revoked early in the Biden administration and left no legacy.[23] In short, for de Blasio and Trump, opposition from a president in no way blocked a mayor's efforts to achieve dramatic change in welfare policy.

Mayors, Governors, and the Constitution

The main point that emerges from this review of mayor–governor relations is that cities' subordinate constitutional position relative to states need not always foil nonincremental change. Certainly, Lindsay did not play his hand well and a cagey governor destroyed his agenda and career. But the case of Cuomo and de Blasio shows that the constitutionally based conflict between the mayor and the governor can stimulate (rather than block) unexpectedly large, positive change.[24] What is needed is a mayor who can turn conflict into competition and provoke a bidding war with the governor to see who will claim credit for popular initiatives. A mayor also must be pragmatic enough to know when he has to settle for half a loaf and achieve something rather than nothing. Giuliani's experience shows that bipartisanship in the form of boldly crossing party lines is another technique for getting what a mayor needs out of a governor.

The ultimate solution to the weak position of cities in the US constitutional structure would be a constitutional amendment granting large cities the direct representation in Congress that states enjoy, under the proposition that it no longer makes sense that thinly populated states have two senators in Congress while the great metropoles have none. The situation we now have certainly can be a barrier to change. But creative New York City mayors have found a way to deal with the problem and achieve positive change.

In summation, the relatively weak constitutional position of New York City's mayor and their dependence on the governor and president need not derail ambitious reforms. A mayor who can effectively play the role of a policy entrepreneur can engage a hostile governor in a bidding-up process that facilitates change. The power of the presidency depends on the character and capabilities of the president. A mayor can easily work around and even derive support in opposing a president whose hostility is expressed mostly in empty bluster.

Conclusion

HOW CHANGE HAPPENS IN URBAN POLITICS

The main question this book has tried to address is whether US cities can deal effectively with "wicked" social problems,[1] or if they are prevented from doing so because the nature of urban politics is to be mired in stasis, gridlock, and bureaucratic paralysis, making policy change nearly impossible. Rephrased in political science terminology, the question is whether nonincremental change (change that breaks with baseline policy and creates a new baseline) can happen in urban politics, or whether incremental change (change that modifies the baseline but leaves it intact) is all that US cities can muster? Almost by definition, incremental change is more frequent than nonincremental change; this is not necessarily bad. But like all polities, cities must be able to confront crises; festering problems that threaten to explode; and new economic, social, and political imperatives. In these and other situations, a capacity for nonincremental change is needed.

This issue is important for several reasons. It has long been recognized that even from a conservative viewpoint seeking to maintain a status quo, the ability to change is essential. Edmund Burke famously wrote, "A state without the means of some change is without the means of its conservation."[2] Another iconic statement of conservatism endorses the need for nonincremental change specifically in saying: "If we want things to stay as they are things will have to change. . . . Then all will be the same though all will be changed."[3] More immediately relevant is the fact that in the United States today, large percentages of both major political parties believe nonincremental change is now needed. A recent poll sponsored by *The New Republic* for its special issue on "Democracy in Peril" found that 48 percent of Democrats and 44 percent of Republicans believed that "complete overhaul/major changes" were needed in the US constitutional system.[4] The inability of a political system to generate nonincremental change is a serious problem. Demographics are also an important consideration. Considering that 83 percent of the US population lives in urban areas,[5] the claimed abundance of barriers to such change in cities would be a major flaw in the political system.

This book set out to illuminate the main issue by looking at three attempts to achieve nonincremental change in the nation's largest city, New York, in an area that has often been subject to highly polarized contestation: welfare policy. These three episodes were Mayor John Lindsay's effort in the 1960s to coordinate the city's many poverty programs by founding the Human Resources Administration (HRA) superagency; Mayor Rudy Giuliani's work-first "welfare reform" of the 1990s; and—the main focus of the book—Mayor Bill de Blasio and Steven Banks's Career Pathways changes to welfare and workforce policy. Each was an attempt at classic nonincremental change that would end baseline policy and establish a new status quo. After covering these initiatives in earlier chapters, we can now summarize their success and draw conclusions about whether the city was capable of nonincremental change and, if so, how such change is possible.

Conclusions on Lindsay

Lindsay's attempt at nonincremental change in welfare policy and administration was discussed in chapter 1. It was a classic progressive attempt to achieve dramatic reform through a strategy of coordination that manifested itself in the creation of a superagency, the HRA. The effort was successful in the sense that the HRA was a break with the old baseline of many disparate welfare agencies and endured over the decades to become the centerpiece of the city's welfare system. But these successes were achieved at a high cost and over the long run. In its early years, the agency became (for good reason) a stock example of waste, fraud, and inefficiency in welfare programs. Once these problems were addressed through stronger eligibility determination processes and better administrative oversight, the HRA nonetheless remained a symbol of a Kafkaesque bureaucracy. This image of the HRA as an administrative nightmare has been memorialized in the 1975 documentary *Welfare* (dir. Frederick Wiseman, 1975) and dramatized in *The Joker* (dir. Todd Phillips, 2019), a film set in the early 1980s that depicts Batman's nemesis as being driven to madness by his experiences with the dysfunctional social services system of Gotham City, the comic book version of New York City.[6] Eventually, the HRA settled into the tasks of providing financial support to the city's poor and engaging them in work, with tolerable effectiveness. But given the agency's rocky start and the time it took to stabilize, one cannot point to the creation of the HRA as an ideal example of nonincremental change in an urban environment.

Conclusions on Giuliani

The next attempt to bring about nonincremental change in New York City's welfare policy was Giuliani's work-first welfare reform. This effort had many of the classic features of the ideational/entrepreneurial model for nonincremental change described by Marc K. Landy and Martin A. Levin. Giuliani's initiative rested on an expert consensus that the baseline welfare program of the federal Aid to Families with Dependent Children (AFDC) was not defensible in terms of professional values such as effectiveness, efficiency, and fairness. President Bill Clinton played the role of a policy entrepreneur and boiled down this expert consensus into a slogan-like public idea: "End welfare as we know it."

Giuliani was the policy entrepreneur who brought welfare reform to New York City. He was one of several state and local leaders who embraced the idea of welfare reform, instituted extensive changes to their jurisdictions' welfare programs, and hoped to claim political credit for fixing what was widely seen as a broken system. Governors Tommy Thompson of Wisconsin and William Weld of Massachusetts were also welfare reformers. These state-level welfare policy entrepreneurs were possible because the Omnibus Budget Reconciliation Act of 1981 gave states the option of implementing a range of work-related welfare programs, including job search, grant diversion, and nonmandatory workfare. States were allowed to implement a set of work or training programs, the Work Incentive Demonstrations. States thus developed experience with welfare-to-work programs. In the 1990s, governors begin requesting waivers from federal welfare regulations to experiment with (and take credit for) welfare reforms. As one scholar noted, "When waivers became the fashion, governors and state welfare administrations jumped on the bandwagon to write their own version. As a DHHS [US Department of Health and Human Services] official explained, 'Every waiver looks different because each governor wants to put his signature on it.' Welfare reform is also a competition."[7] The availability of waivers and the opportunity to get credit as welfare reformers created a bidding-up process in which states experimented with increasingly dramatic change to stand out from the crowd. US federalism is often viewed as a barrier to change because any proposal requiring state action has to overcome fifty veto points. The waiver process turned these potential veto points into opportunity points for state and local policy entrepreneurs.

As discussed in chapter 2, Giuliani did not take advantage of the waiver process to implement his version of welfare reform. He felt that the options open to him under the Family Support Act of 1988 were sufficient to make the changes he wanted. But he was very much aware of how subnational jurisdictions were leaping into the welfare reform arena and wanted to take his place there. The point is that welfare reform under Giuliani displayed certain classic features of ideational/entrepreneurial nonincremental change: expert consensus, leadership by a policy entrepreneur determined to follow up on that consensus, and political leaders bidding up reform initiatives to claim credit for dramatic change.

The most fundamental characteristic of nonincremental change is that it breaks with an old baseline and creates a new one rather than just modifying the old one. Again, Giuliani's changes took place under the Family Support Act of 1988 and did not break with it. So the New York City version of welfare reform was not a nonincremental change in the sense that the state reforms that relied on waivers or the substitution of Temporary Aid for Needy Families for AFDC were such baseline-breaking changes. Even so, in every other way, welfare reform under Giuliani counts as nonincremental change.

Another feature of New York City's welfare policy when Giuliani assumed office that can be considered a kind of baseline was the large size and rapid growth of the welfare rolls. In July 1993, 1,091,960 people were receiving public assistance in the city. By 1999, that number had shrunk to 572,100. After three years of a not terribly good national economy, by fiscal year 2004, the rolls had fallen to 437,500 people, a 60 percent decline since 1993.[8] Of course, welfare rolls had shrunk all over the country for reasons that are not clearly understood but that likely included the passage of the federal welfare reform law Personal Responsibility and Work Opportunity Reconciliation Act (PRWORA). Under PRWORA, welfare reform was implemented nationwide and might have contributed to the welfare caseload decline in New York City.

Unfortunately, the Giuliani administration would not allow research on its welfare reforms due to fear of criticism.[9] It is notable that some of the state-level welfare reforms of the 1990s were found to have an independent effect on caseload decline. William Weld's welfare reform in Massachusetts (known as Chapter 5), from the passage of the act in 1995 to February 1998, saw the basic caseload fall by 34 percent. Based on a time series analysis using administrative records, researchers found that "simply as a result of the improvements in the labor market and other factors a fall in the caseload of 21.8 percent over this period could have been expected. The decline in the caseload by another 12.2 percent—or more than one-third of the total decline—can be attributed to Chapter 5."[10]

Lawrence Mead's analysis of welfare policy in Wisconsin under Governor Tommy Thompson also suggested that work-oriented reform contributed to the decline in the rolls. Mead looked at the dramatic decline in the state's welfare caseload from 1986 through the implementation of Thompson's reform program,

W-2, in 1997–98. His analysis sought to explain not the overall decline but the degree to which county-level and intrastate variations in the decline were attributable to variations in work-oriented reforms. He found that "jurisdictions with the greatest caseload decline were those that enforced work and child support best, though economic conditions and other factors also mattered." Mead noted, "These results do not strictly prove that welfare reform drove the rolls down, but they are consistent with that view" and concluded, "Wisconsin enforced work and drove the rolls down through both politics and administration."[11]

The point here is that some subnational welfare reforms likely did contribute to breaking the long-standing baseline of high welfare rolls. It may be that New York City would not have seen these declines to the same extent had Giuliani's reforms not been implemented.

But the question of whether the decline in public assistance receipt was caused by Giuliani's changes may be beside the political point. The welfare explosion when Lindsay was mayor was not much greater than what happened in the rest of the country. Between 1965 and 1970, the number of people receiving public assistance in New York City rose 16.4 percent, but the nationwide increase was 15.8 percent.[12] Nonetheless, just as Lindsay and the HRA were blamed for the explosion, Giuliani and his reformed HRA were praised for the decline. Being able to claim credit plausibly for good outcomes is a policy entrepreneur's dream and an important motivation for undertaking nonincremental change.

Besides the great welfare slump, another development that can be counted as a nonincremental change in New York City's welfare system was the dramatic changes in the HRA's culture and operations. One feature of that organizational change that has not received the attention it deserves is the shift away from the coordination strategy on which the HRA was founded toward splitting off agencies to encourage the entrepreneurial pursuit of a new mission. Toward that end, Giuliani spun off services to children from the HRA to create the independent Agency for Children's Services (ACS) and accepted the establishment of the Department of Homeless Services (DHS) as a separate agency. According to Dennis Smith and William Grinker, the creation of these two freestanding entities had a marked effect on their provision of services and on the trimmed-down HRA:

> The creation of separate agencies to address homelessness and child welfare also appears to have contributed to the sharpening of focus on particular outcomes. It facilitated Mayoral access to agencies for the exertion of leadership; and agency leader access to the Mayor to encourage his attention and commitment. ACS under Mayor Giuliani is an example of the former, and DHS under Commissioner Linda Gibbs of

the latter. This clearer connection also heightens accountability. A more sharply focused HRA ... has probably come the farthest in the universal application of data usage and performance measurement at a management level.[13]

If we consider broad management philosophies as a sort of policy baseline, we can interpret Giuliani's shift away from coordination and toward entrepreneurialism, in the sense of creating independent, mission-driven agencies, as another example of nonincremental change.

In short, whatever one thinks of the work-oriented changes Giuliani made at the HRA, it is clear that they represented a break with the existing baseline organizational culture and management philosophy of the agency. His changes, even though they left the underlying legislation intact, for all practical purposes really did break with baseline policy. Welfare reform under Giuliani is a clear example of nonincremental change in an urban environment that is both highly pluralistic—in the sense of featuring a wide variety of players—and structurally constrained, and therefore potentially prone to gridlock.

This is true even if one disagrees with the substance of the policy direction Giuliani imposed on the HRA. At the end of Giuliani's administration, many people were critical of his brand of welfare reform. A 2002 report by the New York City Bar judged that "a close look at the harsh conditions faced by the poor in New York City belies the [Giuliani] administration's assertion that a reduction in the caseload may be equated with the successful implementation of welfare reform."[14] But even harsh critics of the results of work-first welfare reform acknowledged that Giuliani had accomplished change. As Giuliani left office at the turn of the millennium, a leftist publication ran an article frankly titled "Against the Giuliani Legacy," which acknowledged: "It is impossible not to give Giuliani credit for change. But it is the type of change that should be critically evaluated. It is ludicrous to mistake short-term policy aimed at alleviation of numbers with needed long-term policies for education and training. While the welfare system has problems, money must be spent on long-term solutions."[15]

Of course, it is true that any change should be critically evaluated. And in the de Blasio/Banks years, a welfare policy focusing on education and training got its chance. But no matter what one's preferred policy direction might be, achieving it involves understanding how the system can be changed. For this reason, the acknowledged reality of change (and nonincremental change for that matter) at the HRA under Giuliani, even though it came under a mayor who turned out to have all sorts of personal and political weaknesses, is a story that should be of interest to all would-be reformers, whatever their orientation. That story suggests a few lessons on how to achieve nonincremental change.

To begin with, the work-first reforms Giuliani introduced had previously undergone extensive testing and rigorous evaluation; they were found to be effective in bringing about their intended results. This point is relevant not because it proved that work-oriented reform was the right or best welfare policy option (which it did not). When a policy option holds up under rigorous evaluation, it is proven to likely produce a given outcome more effectively than some other alternative—not that the outcome is the most desirable outcome and not that the policy is better in some overall sense than all conceivable alternative policies. In the context of the present concern, how to achieve nonincremental change, validation by rigorous evaluation increases the chances that a radical new policy will be successfully adopted and implemented. Validation means the proposed change has at least one key constituency behind it: a community of experts. That community produces arguments to rebut skeptics, evidence to win over opponents, and ideas to disseminate to attentive observers. In the case of welfare reform in the 1990s, there is no doubt that political actors who preferred policies focusing on education and training, and who feared that a dramatic rejection of the status quo would damage a vulnerable clientele, were put on the defensive by the abundance of impressively documented studies validating that work-oriented reform was more effective in certain key respects than other potential options. Baseline-busting welfare reform made headway partly because its opponents could be answered by "objective" arguments developed by experts who were not overtly political and could plausibly be seen as representing the public interest.

Another reason the Giuliani reforms took hold is because the outcomes they sought to achieve were modest, in a certain sense. Work-oriented reform sought to put more clients to work and drive down the welfare rolls. These were not easily reachable goals. For decades, the general trend in the welfare rolls had been up, and at times—such as during the welfare explosion of the 1960s and during the David Dinkins administration—that trend seemed to be inexorable. Putting more clients to work looked very hard to accomplish when the organizational culture of welfare agencies focused on eligibility determination. Getting welfare clients working in some way was a much more ambitious goal than simply cutting checks with few errors.

On the other hand, putting clients to work was much less ambitious than developing their skills through education and training, placing them in the skilled jobs for which they then qualified, and moving them out of poverty through the higher income from the new and better jobs. The main alternative to the rapid labor force attachment reforms of the 1990s was the human capital development approach, which tackled those formidable goals head-on. It should have been unsurprising that when evaluated by the criterion of work placement, the rapid-attachment approach turned out to achieve its relatively limited goal, while the human capital development programs did not reach their ambitious goals of boosting income and poverty reduction. Putting people to work involved the challenging tasks of bureaucratic reorganization and changing organizational culture. But work-oriented reformers had (at least theoretically) immediate control over the bureaucracies and organizations they needed to change. The human capital approach involved struggling with labor markets, which were much harder to affect. The human capital approach also involved taking an optimistic position on whether educated workers do better in the labor market because of their education or because workers with the ability to do well in school and on the job self-select for education. Assuming education is as effective as could be hoped, human capital–oriented welfare reform requires finding a way to educate a welfare population that for the most part has not thrived under the existing education system and must be reached some other way. In short, the education and training approach to welfare policy was and is more ambitious than the already sufficiently ambitious work-first approach.

Thus the Giuliani welfare reforms were able to move the needle on their chosen goals of work participation and caseload decline. One can say what one will about the narrowness of these goals. The issue here is how to achieve nonincremental change. We can see that certain policy features foster this kind of change. The lessons to be drawn from Giuliani's welfare policy are that change that clearly and quickly achieves its stated goals, that makes a notable difference in terms that are plausibly relevant, and that reformers can take credit for will be feasible and endure in ways other efforts will not. It seems that nonincremental change requires a shrewd evaluation of what is and is not possible. Dramatic change can be achieved when what is needed is a tested strategy, political support, and institutional reform. Change that involves struggling with powerful social forces is much harder.

The purest example of nonincremental change in New York City's welfare policies has been the work-first welfare reform under Giuliani. But this claim requires some qualifications, and there are obvious objections that demand a response.

First, it is important to restate that classifying Giuliani's welfare reform as a nonincremental change brought about through an ideational/entrepreneurial process is not meant to imply that it was the best policy that could have been adopted then. It is true that the work-first policies implemented in New York during the mid-1990s were backed up by a consensus of expert opinion. This is not to say that the experts evaluated every possible policy alternative and picked the best one. John Kingdon has described the complex process by which only some problems and some solutions become part of the "list of subjects to which officials are paying some serious attention at any given time."[16] The agenda-setting process is political and mostly not meritocratic. There is no guarantee that the best policy—however that might be determined—will always make it onto the public agenda, let alone that it will be implemented. For this book, what is intriguing about work-first welfare reform in New York City is not that it was the best possible policy but that it represented a major policy change and thus shows that urban nonincremental change is possible and suggests ways other changes, perhaps very different kinds of change, might be possible.

Nonetheless, it might be argued that while work-first welfare policies were thought to be a great success early on, over time, they have lost their luster and are seen in some quarters as having been positively bad.[17] If the result of the city's work-first policies was very negative, that might suggest that the process that produced them was no good either.

There are no studies of the longer-term results of welfare reform in New York City, but the impact of welfare reform nationwide has been studied. A good overview of these findings is a 2018 article by Robert Moffitt and Stephanie Garlow. They summed up their conclusions as follows:

> The welfare rolls indeed plummeted under the influence of welfare reform. If anything, some of the early studies underestimated the causal effect of welfare reform itself (as against the effects of economic expansion)....
>
> Although there remains some ambiguity on the relative importance of the EITC [Earned Income Tax Credit] and welfare reform in accounting for changes in employment, it is clear that welfare reform played an important role. In the initial years after reform, many more women joined the labor force than even the reform's most ardent supporters had hoped....
>
> It would appear that, while welfare reform assisted families with incomes close to the poverty threshold, it did less to help families in deep or extreme poverty. Under the current welfare regime, many single mothers are struggling to support their families without income or cash benefits. Even women who are willing to work often cannot find good-paying, steady employment.
>
> Is it time for another round of reform to address these remaining problems? The simple answer: Yes.[18]

Thus welfare reform was responsible for a decline in the rolls, for more women joining the labor force, and for assisting families close to the poverty line; families in deep or extreme poverty were not helped. In *$2.00 a Day: Living on Almost Nothing in America*, Kathryn Edin and Luke Shaefer focused on such families and argued that as a result of welfare reform, "welfare is dead," and the number of families with a daily cash income of $2.00 a day or less more than doubled by 2011 to 1.5 million households.¹⁹ But later studies, although they did "confirm that deep and extreme poverty in the United States remain significant and increasing social problems," also found that "levels of $2/day poverty are far lower than estimates that Edin and Shaefer (2015) provided."²⁰

The debate about the results of work-first welfare reform continues and while early positive evaluations have been balanced by more critical views, it is very far from accurate to say the whole enterprise has been discredited. Neither has the ideational/entrepreneurial process that made the reforms of the Giuliani era possible been impugned. The drive to improve welfare policy continues and was manifested in the efforts of de Blasio and Banks to reform the reform with Career Pathways policies. In the search for new ways to create major change, it remains true that professional consensus, public ideas, policy entrepreneurs, and related factors are important resources.

Another relatively recent development that possibly is relevant to the evaluation of welfare reform in New York City is the dramatic decline of Giuliani's reputation. Andrew Kirtzman refers to "the implosion of his once godlike reputation."²¹ Another observer writing in the *New York Times* is amazed that "as impossible as it is to imagine, Rudolph Giuliani—the yowling Gollum of basic cable, President Trump's Cain-raisingest enabler—was once one of the most steadying, reassuring men in the United States."²² One might argue that the personality flaws and later failures of a politician do not necessarily discredit their earlier achievements. But in this case, perhaps the Roman insight that "no man suddenly becomes base" applies. With Giuliani, there is a case to be made that he always had an excessively combative personality and a propensity for Machiavellianism and even that these dark aspects of his character were essential to making the major changes he sought.

A recent article argues, "It's clear that Giuliani's worst instincts have long been evident" and cites his fomenting of a near police riot against Dinkins in 1992 as a precursor of his reported incitement of the January 6, 2021, mob attacking the US Capitol, during which he urged, "So, let's have trial by combat."²³ A vulnerability study of Giuliani produced for his 1993 campaign acknowledged his "ruthlessness" and recognized that "he was viewed as 'the Machiavelli of the legal profession . . . [and] certainly pushed the envelope of the permissible.'"²⁴

Fred Siegel develops the thesis that Giuliani's Machiavellianism was not only positive but also essential to his success as a mayor and even as a welfare reformer. He argues that a "good way to understand New York's recent rebirth is to think of Rudy Giuliani as a Renaissance Prince who revived his republic with more than a touch of Machiavelli's 'corrupt wisdom.'"²⁵ According to Siegel, Giuliani's Machiavellianism was crucial to the success of welfare reform: "Machiavelli . . . spoke of 'pious cruelty' and 'the bad use of compassion.' An effective Prince will, he noted, 'by making an example or two . . . prove more compassionate than those who being too compassionate allow disorders which lead to murder and rapine.' Looking to make 'an example or two,' Giuliani made it clear that New York couldn't 'sustain a million people on welfare. You can't do it from the point of view of the amount of misery and hopelessness that it causes.'"[26] Whatever one makes of this justification for stricter welfare policy, Giuliani's approach to bureaucratic change might legitimately be criticized as Machiavellian because it evinced a willingness to knock heads and resort to scheming. Kirtzman convincingly concludes that his subject "was intent on blowing things up to effect change; every initiative became an over-the-top drama."[27] That predilection came to the fore in the reorganization process at the HRA, as discussed in chapter 3, which staff found "tumultuous" and "stressful," and recalled that the administration embraced a strategy of "First Break All the Rules."[28]

In short, the question we come to is: Was Giuliani able to achieve welfare reform only because of his character flaws and moral duplicity, which later came to dominate his personality? If the answer is yes, must we conclude that nonincremental change in urban bureaucracies and policies can only be achieved by Machiavellian means? In that case, perhaps nonincremental change is not worth the moral cost.

The first step in answering this charge is to admit there is something to it: Giuliani's willingness to provoke tumult, inflict pain, and use guile to get his way was central to his governing style and enabled him to shake up the HRA and welfare policy generally in a way not seen before or since. But was this Machiavellianism entirely bad, and is it necessary to achieve nonincremental change?

There is considerable literature on Machiavellianism as a legitimate management technique and political strategy. An early example of such work from the 1960s defined the "Machiavellian administrator" as "one who employs aggressive, manipulative, exploiting, and devious moves in order to achieve personal and organizational objectives. These moves are undertaken according to perceived feasibility with secondary consideration . . . to the feelings, needs, and/or 'rights' of others." The article concluded, "Machiavellian moves may be warranted and even necessary under many circumstances in today's organizations."[29]

But these defenses of Machiavellianism often explain that it is something quite different from the willingness to do evil that it is popularly thought to be. In his biography of Machiavelli, Maurizio Viroli points out: "Machiavelli never taught that the end justifies the means or that a statesman is allowed to do what is forbidden to others, . . . he taught, rather, that if someone is determined to achieve a great purpose—free a people, found a state, enforce the law and create peace where anarchy and despotism reign—then he must not fear being thought cruel or stingy but must simply do what is necessary in order to achieve the goal."[30] A defense of the Machiavellian administrator is possible and might justify Giuliani turning the HRA inside out to make his reforms, but it does not excuse his later mendacious behavior as a Trump acolyte.

Giuliani certainly used Machiavellian techniques while he was mayor. But were these actions essential for achieving nonincremental changes in welfare reform? Since we are looking at only three case histories and just one of them involved this sort of problematic behavior, it is hard to generalize and say whether nonincremental change always requires aggression, manipulation, exploitation, and so on. Desmond King argues that a policy process that involves a strong expert consensus can be used to justify unethical means and negative ends. He maintains that "policies driven by strong expertise arguments are particularly likely to effect illiberal consequences because a robust evidential basis cannot easily be ignored." He notes that "this feature has strengths and drawbacks." On one hand, it "is desirable in that it reflects values in our society which respect rationality and scientific results. It is problematic, however, because it can produce policies without consideration of their political and social effects."[31]

The ideational/entrepreneurial policy process does rely on the existence of an expert consensus, so King's concerns could be well placed concerning policies developed by that process, including 1990s welfare reform. An expert consensus can give would-be reformers confidence and help overcome opposition; it can also produce overconfidence and bulldoze opposition. In fact, as discussed in chapter 3, the expert consensus on work-first programs was in some ways overly optimistic, and the Giuliani administration did run roughshod over opponents at the HRA, even when they had valid points to make.

Thus the ideational/entrepreneurial process has a dark side that bears acknowledgment. This approach to nonincremental change can involve overblown promises and stubbornness. King suggests how such propensities can be checked. He observes that "one useful response is a rigorous process of scrutiny followed by political choices." He also observes that while a "weak civil society removes potential constraints upon state intervention . . . in liberal democracies, however civil society is strong, policy and political legacies about the appropriate sphere of government are consequential, and electoral dynamics require politicians to defend their policy choices and political decisions. This does not, as we have seen, remove the potential for illiberal policy . . . but it does translate into significant strictures upon such ambitions."[32]

Perhaps one way to think about Giuliani's degeneration from an energetic and legitimate leader in the 1990s to the dangerous and mendacious demagogue of the 2020s is to consider what happened to US civil society over that period. As I described elsewhere, starting with the terrorist attacks of September 11, 2001, US political life has been hit with a series of shocks that weakened its liberal-democratic political culture and facilitated the rise of antidemocratic or illiberal actors and ideas, not least of which are Donald Trump and Trumpism. And Giuliani. When the guardrails and gatekeepers of civil society were strong, actors with illiberal propensities were kept in check. Trump remained a real estate deal maker and shady New York personality, and Giuliani was known as a bull-headed and hot-tempered but effective mayor. When civil society was weakened by political crises, the rise of unmoderated digital media, and other developments, the nasty impulses of Trump, Giuliani, and similar actors were unrestrained, with shocking consequences.

To sum up, the ideational/entrepreneurial road to nonincremental change may involve (but does not necessarily require) Machiavellian tactics, but it need not lead to illiberal consequences. Welfare reform in 1990s New York City depended on a forceful but not absolutely immoral chief executive. It did not involve the horrors of the truly illiberal social policies described by King, such as Soviet collectivization and involuntary sterilization. If Giuliani was a Machiavellian prince, he was tamed by the strictures of a healthy democratic political culture. The whole ideational/entrepreneurial political process behind the city's welfare reform also needs to be bounded by a strong civil society that keeps experts, policy entrepreneurs, media, and other actors from misbehaving.

Conclusions on de Blasio

The final and principal case history in attempted nonincremental change considered in this book is the Career Pathways reforms implemented under de Blasio and Banks. An important feature of this effort that could be considered a nonincremental change is the ending of the work-oriented programs and the beginning of the Career Pathways programs: Career Compass, Youth Pathways, and Career Advance. There is no question that this shift represented a distinct change in direction for the HRA away from the rapid-attachment approach and toward a human capital development approach based on a more in-depth evaluation of clients' abilities and needs and on placement into appropriate education and training programs.

Homeless policy also took a new direction under de Blasio and Banks when the rent subsidies that were ended under Bloomberg and resulted in a rise in the shelter census were reinstated in several programs. These programs were eventually combined into the City Fighting Homelessness and Eviction Prevention Supplement (CityFHEPS) in July 2018. This change was especially striking in that it represented a repudiation of the concern over perverse incentives that dominated city policy for a long time and led Bloomberg to dramatically end all rent subsidies in 2004, only to see the shelter census climb for the rest of his administration.

Another significant change that de Blasio and Banks wrought at the HRA was making its administration of welfare much less punitive than it had been under Bloomberg and Giuliani, with fewer sanctions imposed on clients and fewer fair hearings during which clients challenged agency decisions. In a 2015 testimony to the City Council, Banks took credit for imposing fewer sanctions, thus reducing "the number of preventable and inappropriate negative outcomes that trigger unnecessary fair hearings that subject us to a potential $10 million State penalty."[33]

De Blasio and Banks also made an important reorganization of welfare services. In the early days of the administration, Banks was commissioner of the HRA, while Gilbert Taylor was commissioner of the DHS. When Taylor did not work out, Banks and First Deputy Mayor Anthony Shorris conducted a review of city homelessness policy that resulted in the end of the DHS as an independent agency and its reabsorption into the larger welfare bureaucracy from which it had been spun off under Dinkins. More specifically, Banks became commissioner of the Department of Social Services (DSS) with the HRA and DHS now reporting to him. The relationship that had been established between the HRA and DSS in the Lindsay years was thus reversed. Before then, the DSS was the city's main welfare agency, responsible for administering such programs as the AFDC. With Lindsay's reorganization, the HRA was created as a new entity and the DSS became an office within the HRA along with the city's other antipoverty and related programs. For a time, the HRA was the umbrella agency and the DSS was a principal unit under it. With the Banks/Shorris reorganization and Banks's ascension to DSS commissioner, the DSS became the overhead agency with the HRA beneath it, along with the DHS. The reorganization reversed Giuliani's policy under which units of the HRA were spun off to create independent and presumably more entrepreneurial, mission-driven agencies.

Finally, one might say that Banks's appointment as HRA and then DSS commissioner represented one of the most startling changes ever to happen in the city's welfare bureaucracy. As noted, HRA staff who first heard the news of Banks's appointment on television were literally left gasping.[34] Before Banks, no HRA commissioner had made a decades-long career of suing the city's welfare agencies. De Blasio's choice of Banks was similar to choices made by President Jimmy Carter, who gave leadership positions in regulatory agencies to members of Ralph Nader's consumer advocate network. For example, Joan Claybrook was appointed as administrator of the National Highway Traffic Safety Administration after her work lobbying with Nader for the successful passage of the country's first auto safety laws.[35] But Banks as HRA commissioner was more radical than Carter's choices, being analogous to Nader himself becoming Secretary of Commerce.

CONCLUSION

Banks was not the only outsider to city government to become a key player in homeless affairs during the de Blasio years. Early in his career, Andrew Cuomo created the private HELP USA system of shelters. Precisely because he was an outsider to government, Cuomo had been brought in to forge a new policy direction when the Dinkins administration was unable to do so on its own. Later, Cuomo held the noncity position of Secretary of Housing and Urban Development. As the Institute for Children, Poverty & Homelessness has noted, "Between Cuomo and Banks, many of the key players in the City's handling of social services were now those who, at times, had helped shape those social services from the outside."[36] The de Blasio-Banks-Cuomo years might be thought of as a giant experiment in the strategy of making outsiders into insiders to achieve dramatic change.

The question is: Did all these developments under Banks and de Blasio represent what this book has described as nonincremental change? Several of these changes did feature an essential characteristic of such change in that they apparently broke with baseline policy and established a new baseline. The substitution of the Career Pathways education and training programs for the former work-first programs could be said to have created a new baseline. So did the introduction of the CityFHEPS rent subsidy programs for homeless families break decisively with Bloomberg's policy of eliminating these subsidies. The shift away from the punitive enforcement of work requirements and other client obligations to a more client-friendly approach that relied much less on sanctions was also a change in baseline policy. The reorganization of the welfare bureaucracy to improve coordination by consolidating agencies broke with the baseline of creating independent agencies to foster mission-oriented entrepreneurialism.

Yet all of these apparently nonincremental changes wrought by de Blasio and Banks were in a certain sense much less radical than those that Giuliani instituted and Bloomberg maintained. Giuliani's rapid labor force attachment reforms took the HRA in a direction it had never gone before. From the mid-1970s up to Giuliani, HRA policy and organizational culture emphasized eligibility determination and income maintenance. The work-oriented direction Giuliani took the HRA brought the agency into uncharted territory. Similarly, breaking off the DHS and ACS as independent, entrepreneurial agencies was a departure from the original strategy of combining agencies under a single structure to encourage coordination.

In contrast, the de Blasio/Banks changes represented not so much the establishment of a new baseline as the return to a prior baseline. Reinstituting rent subsidies for homeless families was just a return to a policy that in various forms operated through the Dinkins and Giuliani years and was abandoned by Bloomberg. The less punitive approach to enforcing client obligations was a return to the policy of the Dinkins years, which focused on supporting client choices about which programs to participate in, rather than on mandating what those choices should be. The Career Pathways programs represented a return to the education and training orientation of Dinkins's welfare policy, although these programs tried to improve on earlier versions of that approach.

A look at the evolution of the HRA's mission statements shows that the direction de Blasio and Banks took the agency was not so much to a new baseline as a return to an older one. Under Banks, the HRA changed its mission statement to move away from the emphasis, under Giuliani and Bloomberg, on temporary aid and achieving economic independence and returned to the stress under Dinkins on open-ended income support and social services for the needy. As Grinker and Smith noted, the HRA mission statement in the 1993 Mayor's Management Report (MMR) reads: "The Human Resources Administration provides income support and social services to New York City's needy residents." The last MMR published under Bloomberg presented the following mission statement for the HRA: "The Human Resources Administration (HRA) assists individuals and families to achieve and sustain their maximum degree of self-sufficiency."[37] At the end of Banks's tenure, the mission statement of the HRA, of which he was in charge, read: "The New York City Human Resources Administration/Department of Social Services (HRA/DSS) is dedicated to fighting poverty and income inequality by providing New Yorkers in need with essential benefits such as Food Assistance and Emergency Rental Assistance."[38] The Banks mission statement speaks of supporting "New Yorkers in need," which is a return to the statement from the Dinkins years of providing for "New York City's needy residents." The main difference between the de Blasio/Banks mission statement and that of Dinkins is that the former adds to the relatively straightforward goal of supporting people in need the very ambitious goal of "fighting poverty and income inequality."

The goal of fighting poverty and income inequality raises another sense in which the changes of the de Blasio and Banks years were less dramatic than those brought about under Giuliani. Giuliani's HRA mission statement declared that the agency "assists individuals and families to achieve and sustain their maximum degree of self-sufficiency." If this is interpreted as putting clients in jobs that would allow them to leave the welfare rolls, it is a very ambitious goal that the agency did not achieve. But note that this goal is carefully hedged. The HRA only "assists" clients to achieve the "maximum degree" not of gainful employment but of the vaguer standard of "self-sufficiency." Thus qualified, the Giuliani administration could plausibly argue that the agency met its goal by putting more clients into some form of work and dramatically lowering the welfare rolls.

Certainly, de Blasio could claim considerable success in fighting poverty and income inequality. A city document, *The De Blasio Years: The Tale of a More Equal City*, lists many accomplishments, the most striking of which is a 12.5 percent decline in the city poverty rate between 2013 and 2019 to the lowest rate since the city began tracking that statistic in 2005.[39] The document also notes many policy initiatives that are plausibly relevant to that trend, including successfully lobbying the state to raise the minimum wage to $15 an hour. Also noted are Career Pathways and industry partnerships, described as "two programs with a focus on career development for New Yorkers, and creating feedback loops with employers."[40] Strikingly, no mention is made of the employment programs introduced at the HRA with much ballyhoo—Career Compass, Youth Pathways, and Career Advance—and almost nothing is said about the HRA or DSS.[41] One way a policy change can be considered nonincremental is if it moves a relevant indicator in a way that its developers can claim credit for. But oddly, in *The De Blasio Years*, the outgoing administration chose not to give any credit to its welfare employment programs for the notable decline in poverty on its watch. Nor have any sources outside the administration claimed that Career Compass, Youth Pathways, and Career Advance played a significant role in reducing poverty. During the de Blasio administration, an important baseline was broken in that poverty was considerably reduced. But no one, not even the mayor, seemed to want to attribute that change to the Career Pathways programs at the HRA.

This is not to say that the changes introduced at the HRA by de Blasio and Banks were failures or that they were unimportant. All of them count as significant changes in their own right regardless of whether one classifies them as incremental or nonincremental. If they were all modifications of baseline policy or returns to a previous baseline, they were nonetheless carefully thought out, were successfully implemented, and could plausibly be considered improvements on the policies they superseded. Moreover, to appreciate their importance, it is necessary to look at what did not happen. As discussed previously, in the early days of de Blasio's and Banks's tenures, many observers confidently predicted their policies would bring disaster. Education and training programs and a less punitive enforcement of client obligations would surely lead to more people on the welfare rolls and fewer clients working, were the claims. None of these predictions came true. Perhaps the most important thing to learn from the de Blasio/Banks years is that it is possible to run a welfare program that requires clients to be engaged in education and training programs as well as work assignments and does away with punitive sanctioning, without provoking perverse incentives, driving up the welfare rolls, or reducing levels of client engagement. This is a very important accomplishment no matter how one wants to classify it.

Chapter 4 described de Blasio as a pragmatic progressive and asked whether that philosophy could lead to a successful welfare policy. De Blasio can be thought of as a pragmatic progressive to the extent that he did not flatly reject the concept of an entrepreneurial city that crystallized under twenty years of conservative mayors but sought to strike a better balance between the imperatives of capitalism and democracy than his predecessors had done. If we accept the claim, noted in chapter 3, that a truly progressive welfare/work policy would not focus on training workers to fit into the labor market but on structuring labor markets to have "higher- and lower-skilled positions that reward skill," then de Blasio never challenged the "neoliberal theory of labor pricing."[42] Instead, de Blasio focused on what some consider the second-best approach, that of "education and training," which is to say he focused on what was doable and was, therefore, a pragmatist. He did not buckle to conservative critics who forecast disaster and, in that sense, he stayed true to progressive principles. When one evaluates de Blasio's welfare policies or categorizes the magnitude of the changes it wrought, it is fair to say those policies were a case of pragmatic progressivism.

Overall Conclusions

To sum up, much that was positive came out of the case histories of change in New York City's welfare policies considered in this book. It is also true that there were some negative results. If the question is "Which episodes represented a clear nonincremental change?" the answer is that Giuliani's work-first welfare reform was the one that did so. As for what factors made change of that magnitude possible, the most important were the development of a set of policy options backed up by a strong expert consensus and the presence of a mayor who was both an effective policy entrepreneur and a strong executive. How often these factors come together is hard to say. They did crystallize at least once in the modern history of welfare policy in New York City and may do so again.

The question of whether nonincremental change is possible in US cities concerns more than just narrow issues for political science and public administration theory. As noted earlier, the ability to change is relevant to the legitimacy of liberal democratic government because a system that cannot generate dramatic change when it is called for cannot long endure.

The story of change in New York City's welfare policies and administration is relevant to the current rise of antidemocratic ideologies, disinformation, and irrationalism in US political culture. These phenomena are dealt with in my earlier books.[43] These movements insist that US liberal democracy is a failure and unable to meet the challenges of the twenty-first century. But the fact that New York City was able to generate significant change in welfare policy—most strikingly in the unambiguously nonincremental change under Giuliani—challenges the nihilistic despair of the antidemocratic right.

In 2005, Smith and Grinker evaluated the impact of the Giuliani welfare reforms. They came to a prescient conclusion that anticipated the rise of illiberal irrationalism and gave a response to it: "For those who believe in the potential of using systematic thinking, evidence, and analysis in public policy and management, the trajectory in New York City is encouraging. Experience, however, warns against viewing the trend as irreversible. In a new period of budget crisis, or with another ideologically guided administration whose approach is, in effect, 'do not bother me with the facts; my mind is made up' a counter trend is not unimaginable."[44]

Today, US politics is faced precisely with an illiberal ideology that refuses to bother with facts and relies on factoids and fake news when reality is inconvenient. As one particularly radical online outlet of nihilistic illiberalism has recently proclaimed, "The United States is in crisis, the country's problems are profound, intrinsic, without solution and worsening."[45] Smith and Grinker were right to say that New York City's welfare policy vindicates the relevance of systematic thinking, evidence, and analysis in political affairs. These authors had in mind the experience of the Giuliani administration, and this book has shown that the welfare reforms of that period are the purest example of nonincremental change in New York's welfare policy.

But the experiences of the Lindsay and de Blasio administrations are also encouraging in their own ways. Lindsay's creation of the HRA needs to be put in the context of his mostly successful effort to introduce modern management techniques into city government. As discussed, the HRA got off to a very rocky start, but this was largely due to the excessively permissive eligibility policies and does not invalidate the underlying logic of modernizing and coordinating the city's confusion of welfare and antipoverty programs. Once later administrations stiffened the agency's lackadaisical eligibility policies, the HRA eventually came into its own and, in tandem with the network of community-based organizations spawned during the war on poverty years, became the backbone of the city's welfare system.

The reforms introduced under de Blasio and Banks did not amount to the radical change that could be hoped for from an administration that made fighting economic inequality its signature goal and that put the most salient critic of the city's welfare system in charge of policy. Even so, considerable good was done. On the homeless front, rental assistance programs for shelter clients were reintroduced, and forty-nine new shelters were opened as of November 2021.[46] Outreach to street dwellers was improved. Legal representation for low-income defendants in housing court became standard. In welfare policy, the eligibility and sanctioning processes were made much less punitive, with no uptick in the rolls or other moral hazards. A new set of welfare-work programs emphasizing education and training were substituted for the rapid-attachment programs, which likely resulted in greater client satisfaction, again without significant perverse effects. The welfare bureaucracy was reorganized on the plausible—though so far not proven—principle that eliminating administrative silos would improve service delivery.

However, as noted in a classic article, "wicked" problems "are never solved. At best they are only re-solved—over and over."[47] It should be acknowledged that under Mayor Eric Adams, New York City and its Department of Social Services continue to wrestle with daunting challenges. The most salient of these is a dramatic increase in migrants arriving in the city in need of shelter and other basic services. This uptick is only partly due to the border states with Republican governors sending busloads of border-crossers to New York. Between September 2022 and September 2023, the city received more than one hundred thousand such migrants, but only 13,100 arrived by buses sent by the state of Texas.[48]

However the migrants arrive, they put a strain on the social service system. In a letter to New York Supreme Court Justice Erika Edwards, the city noted, "This influx has increased the population within the City's care from approximately 45,000 on April 1, 2022, to over 116,700 on October 1, 2023, a 159% increase." The city asked for a modification in the *Callahan* right-to-shelter consent decree, arguing that "[c]ertainly, the *Callahan* Consent Judgment never intended the City to build and finance an endless supply of accommodations necessary to keep pace with the sudden influx of tens of thousands of migrants seeking shelter. . . . The City requires immediate relief with respect to the most intractable aspect of the present crisis—the global perception that the Consent Judgment extends a blanket right to obtain City-provided shelter to the world at large."[49]

New York City's housing and homeless advocacy network is pushing back against the Adams administration's request to be temporarily relieved of certain obligations under the *Callahan* decree. Indeed, the Coalition for the Homeless will oppose the administration in court, represented by none other than Steven Banks.[50] As of November 2023, it is not clear what the courts will decide and how the administration will respond. But it seems that New York is continuing to cope with crises and make policy through the networks of policy entrepreneurs and public agencies that have been in operation for some sixty years now.

After reviewing the efforts of three key administrations to deal with poverty, homelessness, and inequality, one comes away impressed with the steady determination of the city to make progress on these wicked problems and with the impressive levels of analysis and high-mindedness that were involved. These problems were not eliminated, but certainly, their severity and extent were less than they would have been without the city's efforts. It seems very unlikely that the irrational impulses of the Trumpist new right or of antidemocratic illiberals could do nearly as well. In that sense, New York's record of striving over the course of decades to do a better job of aiding the city's poorest and most vulnerable classes represents a vindication of US democratic government.

Notes

INTRODUCTION

1. Charles Lindbloom, "The Science of Muddling Through," *Public Administration Review* 19, no. 2 (1959): 79–88.
2. Wallace S. Sayre and Herbert Kaufman, *Governing New York: Politics in the Metropolis* (New York: Russell Sage, 1960).
3. Martin Shefter, *Political Crisis/Fiscal Crisis* (New York: Columbia University Press, 1992), emphasizes the "boundaries within which the game of urban politics is played and the imperatives confronting the players of that game" (xxviii). Similarly, Ira Katznelson, *City Trenches* (Chicago: University of Chicago Press, 1981), emphasizes the "boundaries and rules" of urban politics (6). In *City Limits* (Chicago: University of Chicago Press, 1981), Paul E. Peterson argues that "city politics is limited politics" (4).
4. J. J. Harrigan and R. J. Vogel, *Political Change in the Metropolis*, 6th ed. (New York: Longman, 2000), 15.
5. Blanche Blank, "Bureaucracy: Power in Details," in *Urban Politics New York Style*, edited by Jewel Bellush and Dick Netzer (Armonk, NY: M. E. Sharpe, 1990), chap. 5.
6. Charles Brecher and Raymond D. Horton, with Robert A. Cropf and Dean Michael Mead, *Power Failure: New York City Politics and Policy since 1960* (Oxford: Oxford University Press, 1993), 14.
7. Michael Lipsky, *Street-Level Bureaucracy: Dilemmas of the Individual in Public Services* (New York: Russell Sage, 1980), 192.
8. Preface, Marc K. Landy and Martin A. Levin, eds., *The New Politics of Public Policy* (Baltimore, MD: Johns Hopkins University Press, 1995), x.
9. Eugene Bardach, *Getting Agencies to Work Together: The Practice and Theory of Managerial Craftsmanship* (Washington, DC: Brookings Institution Press, 1998), 204. Bardach uses the term "strategic idea," which, being a "verbal formula or slogan," is essentially the same concept that is here called a public idea.
10. Martin A. Levin, Mark K. Landy, and Martin Shapiro, eds., *Seeking the Center: Politics and Policymaking at the New Century* (Washington, DC: Georgetown University Press, 2001).
11. Katznelson, *City Trenches*, 4.
12. Daniel P. Moynihan, *The Politics of a Guaranteed Income: The Nixon Administration and the Family Assistance Plan* (New York: Random House, Vintage Books, 1973), 7, emphasis in original.
13. Steven Kelman, *Making Public Policy: A Hopeful View of American Government* (New York: Basic Books, 1987), 248.
14. Timothy J. Conlan, David R. Beam, and Margaret T. Wrightson, "Policy Models and Political Change," in *The New Politics of Public Policy*, edited by Marc K. Landy and Martin A. Levin (Baltimore, MD: Johns Hopkins University Press, 1995), 142.
15. Thomas J. Main, *Homelessness in New York City: Policymaking from Koch to de Blasio* (New York: NYU Press, 2016).
16. What is positive change, and how is it different from negative change? Negative change not only does not accomplish the goals of a policy, it actually undermines those goals. Positive change achieves the goals of the policy and advances the public interest. Attempting to define the "public interest" would take us into questions of political theory

that are beyond the current policy-oriented inquiry. Perhaps it should also be noted that catastrophes like the fiscal crisis of 1975, the terrorist attacks of September 11, 2001, or the COVID-19 pandemic in the early 2020s are not the sort of nonincremental change this work is concerned with. These disasters certainly broke with the status quo baseline, but they don't represent anything that a sensible person could desire.

17. Charles R. Morris discusses "the almost total chaos that existed in the Human Resources Administration" by 1969: *The Cost of Good Intentions: New York City and the Liberal Experiment 1960-1975* (New York: W. W. Norton, 1980), 117-18. In 1973, The Scott Commission on New York City government operations concluded that "the superagency concept, which is difficult to fault in principle, has been far from the administrative panacea it originally appeared to be" (*Final Report of the Temporary State Commission to Make a Study of the Governmental Operation of the City of New York*, State Study Commission for New York City, Stuart N. Scott, chairman, April 1973, 16).

18. Thomas J. Main, "Nonincremental Change in an Urban Environment: The Case of New York City's Human Resources Administration," *Administration & Society* 37, no. 4 (2005): 483-503, doi.org/10.1177/0095399705277.

19. Richard R. Buery Jr., quoted in Andrew Rice, "How Are You Enjoying the de Blasio Revolution?," *New York Magazine*, December 28, 2015.

20. The Dillon rule is named after John F. Dillon, an Iowa Supreme Court justice and US Circuit judge. In *City of Clinton v. Cedar Rapids & Missouri River Railroad* (24 Iowa 455, 475, 1868), he ruled that

> municipal corporations [ex: cities] owe their origin to, and derive their powers and rights wholly from, the [State] legislature. It breathes into them the breath of life, without which they cannot exist. As it creates, so it may destroy. If it may destroy, it may abridge and control. Unless there is some constitutional limitation on the right, the legislature might, by a single act, if we can suppose it capable of so great a folly and so great a wrong, sweep from existence all of the municipal corporations in the State, and the *corporation* could not prevent it. We know of no limitation on this right so far as the corporations themselves are concerned. They are, so to phrase it, the mere *tenants at will* of the legislature.

1. THE HRA UNDER LINDSAY

1. Terry Pristin, "Mitchell Sviridoff, 81, Dies; Renewal Chief," *New York Times*, October 23, 2000.

2. Mitchell Sviridoff, "Developing New York City's Human Resources: Report of a Study Group of the Institute of Public Administration to Mayor John V. Lindsay," Vol. 1, June 1966, 7, accessed July 23, 2024, eric.ed.gov/?id=ED010783.

3. Sviridoff, "Developing New York City's Human Resources," 7.

4. Sviridoff, "Developing New York City's Human Resources," 7-8.

5. Sviridoff, "Developing New York City's Human Resources," 7-9.

6. Sviridoff, "Developing New York City's Human Resources," 45.

7. Quoted in Howard N. Mantel, "Reorganization of the New York City Government," *Public Administration* 48, no. 2 (1970): 198.

8. Laurin Hyde, review of "Developing New York City's Human Resources," *Social Service Review* 40, no. 4 (December 1966): 447-49.

9. Bertram M. Beck, "Organizing Community Action," *Proceedings of the Academy of Political Science* 29, no. 4 (1969): 173, accessed July 23, 2024, www.jstor.org/stable/1173695.

10. State Study Commission for New York City, Task Force on Social Services, *Social Services in New York City*, March 1973, 30-31.

11. State Study Commission for New York City, Task Force on Social Services, *Social Services in New York City*, March 1973, 30–31.
12. Beck, "Organizing Community Action," 175–76.
13. David Rogers, "Management versus Bureaucracy," in *Summer in the City: John Lindsay, New York, and the American Dream*, ed. Joseph P. Viteritti (Baltimore, MD: Johns Hopkins University Press, 2014), loc. 2531, Kindle.
14. Andrew M. Cuomo, chair, *The Way Home: A New Direction in Social Policy, A Report of the New York City Commission on the Homeless*, February 1992, 116.
15. Geoffrey Kabaservice, "On Principle a Progressive Republican," in *Summer in the City: John Lindsay, New York, and the American Dream*, ed. Joseph P. Viteritti (Baltimore, MD: Johns Hopkins University Press, 2014), loc. 1022, Kindle.
16. Kabaservice, "On Principle a Progressive Republican," loc. 866.
17. Vincent J. Cannato, *The Ungovernable City: John Lindsay and His Struggle to Save New York* (New York: Basic Books, 2001), 200, 497–98.
18. Alton A. Linford, "Review of *Social Services in New York City*," *Social Service Review* 48, no. 1 (March 1974): 136–38.
19. Cannato, *The Ungovernable City*, 546–47.
20. Martin Shefter, *Political Crisis/Fiscal Crisis: The Collapse and Revival of New York City* (New York: Basic Books, 1985), 111–12.
21. Dick Netzer, "The Budget: Trends and Prospects," in Lyle C. Fitch and Annmarie Hauck Walsh, *Agenda for a City: Issues Confronting New York* (Beverly Hills, CA: Sage, 1970), 652; *Final Report of the Temporary State Commission to Make a Study of the Governmental Operation of the City of New York*, State Study Commission for New York City, Stuart N. Scott, chair, April 1973, 16.
22. Joseph P. Viteritti, "Preface," in *Summer in the City: John Lindsay, New York, and the American Dream*, ed. Joseph P. Viteritti (Baltimore, MD: Johns Hopkins University Press, 2014), loc. 46, Kindle.
23. Howard N. Mantel, "Reorganization of the New York City Government," *Public Administration* 48, no. 2 (1970): 191.
24. Cannato, *The Ungovernable City*, 539.
25. Shefter, *Political Crisis/Fiscal Crisis*, 174.
26. William F. Buckley Jr., *The Unmaking of a Mayor* (New York: Encounter Books, 1977), loc. 419, Kindle.
27. Charles R. Morris, *The Cost of Good Intentions: New York City and the Liberal Experiment* (New York: W. W. Norton, 1989), 107–26.
28. Rogers, "Management versus Bureaucracy," loc. 2748.
29. Rogers, "Management versus Bureaucracy," loc. 2461.
30. Wallace S. Sayre and Herbert Kaufman, *Governing New York* (New York: Russell Sage Foundation, 1960), 716.
31. Rogers, "Management versus Bureaucracy," loc. 2424.
32. *Final Report of the Temporary State Commission*, Scott, chair, 16d.
33. Rogers, "Management versus Bureaucracy," loc. 2537.
34. Jack Krauskopf, "Sustaining Government/Nonprofit Initiatives: New York City Human Services in Transition from Bloomberg to de Blasio," n.d., accessed July 23, 2024, marxe.baruch.cuny.edu/wp-content/uploads/sites/7/2020/04/SustainingGovernment NonprofitInitiatives.pdf.
35. For a discussion of how Lindsay "acted to decentralize New York City's poverty program . . . to the community level" but also by "unifying the city's social service programs within one 'superagency,' the Human Resources Administration . . . attempted to maintain some degree of centralized control over the antipoverty programs," see Robert F.

Pecorella, *Community Power in a Postreform City: Politics in New York City* (Armonk, NY: M. E. Sharpe, 1994), 89–90.

36. Mantel, "Reorganization of the New York City Government," 210.

37. Horst W. J. Rittel and Melvin W. Webber, "Dilemmas in a General Theory of Planning," *Policy Sciences* 4, no. 2 (June 1973): 155.

38. Rittel and Webber, "Dilemmas in a General Theory of Planning," 160.

39. Mitchell Sviridoff, study director, cover letter to Lyle C. Fitch, president, Institute of Public Administration, June 27, 1966.

40. Rittel and Webber, "Dilemmas in a General Theory of Planning," 160.

41. Brian W. Head and John Alford, "Wicked Problems: Implications for Public Policy and Management," *Administration & Society* 47, no. 6 (2015): 732.

42. Quoted in Howard Husock, "Nathan Glazer's Warning," *City Journal* (Summer 2011): 6.

2. THE HRA UNDER GIULIANI'S FIRST TERM

1. Parts of chapters 2 and 3 use material from a previously published article, Thomas J. Main, "Nonincremental Change in an Urban Environment: The Case of New York City's Human Resources Administration," *Administration & Society* 37 (2005): 483–503.

2. "Welfare Reform in Action," *New York Daily News*, April 24, 1995, 20.

3. City of New York, Human Resources Administration, "Public Assistance Recipients in NYC 1955–2001," undated.

4. City of New York, Human Resources Administration, *A Time of Examination, [a] Time of Discovery, a Time of Accomplishment: January 2002—June 2003 Progress Report*, undated, 6, www.nyc.gov/html/records/pdf/govpub/865annual_progress_report.pdf.

5. General Accounting Office, *Welfare Reform, Work-Site Based Activities Can Play an Important Role in TANF Programs*, GAO/HEHS-00-122, 2000, 1–2.

6. A. S. Bush, S. Desai, and J. Weissman, "New York City's 'JobStat' Program: Managing for Performance in Large Welfare-to-Work Organizations," City of New York, Human Resources Administration, July 2000.

7. The Board of Estimate was not a purely legislative body. It had executive powers including approval of many land-use decisions and approval of contracts that were not competitively bid. No one was elected to the board; all of its members served ex officio. Nonetheless, Sayre and Kaufman in their historic analysis assert that "the Board is, in effect, the upper chamber in a bicameral city legislature." Wallace S. Sayre and Herbert Kaufman, *Governing New York City: Politics in the Metropolis* (New York: Russell Sage Foundation, 1960), 627.

8. Sayre and Kaufman, *Governing New York City*, 626, 652.

9. See Sayre and Kaufman, *Governing New York City*, 622, for a discussion of the weakness of the pre-1989 City Council. Similarly, Charles Brecher and Raymond D. Horton, with Robert A. Cropf and Dean Michael Mead, *Power Failure: New York City Politics and Policy Since 1960* (Oxford: Oxford University Press, 1993), 54, note that "historically, the city council has been characterized as a 'weak' legislature."

10. Sayre and Kaufman, *Governing New York City*, 627.

11. Sayre and Kaufman, *Governing New York City*, 650.

12. In the case of *Gray v. Sanders*, the Supreme Court found that "the conception of political equality from the Declaration of Independence, to Lincoln's Gettysburg Address, to the Fifteenth, Seventeenth, and Nineteenth Amendments can mean only one thing—one person, one vote." *Gray v. Sanders*, 372 US 368 (1963), supreme.justia.com/cases/federal/us/372/368/.

13. For an account of the charter revision process, see Joseph P. Viteritti, "The New Charter: Will It Make a Difference?," in *Urban Politics New York Style*, ed. Jewel Bellush and Dick Netzer (Armonk, NY: M. E. Sharpe, 1990), 413–28.

14. The Fiscal Control Board had been founded to oversee the city's finances after the crisis of 1975. This oversight function lapsed on June 30, 1986, after the city had produced several balanced budgets, recovered access to financial markets, and begun repaying debt. However, should the city produce an operating deficit of more than $100 million in any year, the Fiscal Control Board would by law reemerge with its full powers.

15. V. S. Toy, "A Move to Shift Balance of Power in New York City," *New York Times*, January 7, 1997, 1.

16. New York City Charter, section 1515, "Statement and Estimate by the Mayor," reads, in part: "The mayor shall prepare and submit to the council . . . an estimate of the probable amount of (1) receipts into the City treasury during the ensuing fiscal year from all the sources of revenue of the general fund and (2) all receipts other than those of the general fund and taxes on real property." See also section 254, subsection 16, and section 250, subsection 16.

17. P. F. Vallone, State of the City Address, Council of the City of New York, January 6, 1997.

18. For accounts of the 1975 fiscal crisis and its consequences, see Martin Shefter, *Political Crisis/Fiscal Crisis: The Collapse and Revival of New York City* (New York: Basic Books, 1985); Charles R. Morris, *The Cost of Good Intentions: New York City and the Liberal Experiment* (New York: W.W. Norton, 1980), 215–40; Brecher and Horton, *Power Failure*, 144–45, 166–67, 333–35; Robert F. Pecorella, *Community Power in a Post Reform City: Politics in New York City* (Armonk, NY: M. E. Sharpe, 1994), 112–15.

19. Ken Auletta, *The Streets Were Paved with Gold: The Decline of New York, an American Tragedy* (New York: Random House, 1979), 106.

20. Fred Siegel, *The Prince of the City: Giuliani, New York, and the Genius of American Life* (San Francisco: Encounter Books, 2005), 111.

21. Siegel, *The Prince of the City*, 127.

22. Siegel, *The Prince of the City*, 188.

23. Judith M. Gueron, "A Research Context for Welfare Reform," *Journal of Policy Analysis and Management* 15, no. 4 (Autumn 1996): 547.

24. For a discussion of the concept of policy feedback, see Margaret Weir, Ann Shola Orloff, and Theda Skocpol, "Introduction: Understanding American Social Politics," in *The Politics of Social Policy in the United States*, ed. Margaret Weir, Ann Shola Orloff, and Theda Skocpol (Princeton, NJ: Princeton University Press, 1988), 25.

25. Eugene Bardach, *Improving the Productivity of JOBS Programs* (New York: Manpower Demonstration Research Corporation, 1993), 12–13. Bardach goes on to observe that "in practice, however, this is not the idea communicated to the clients." This was the case in New York City up through the mid-1990s, for reasons that will be discussed later.

26. New York City Council, Finance Division, "Welfare Reform 1967–1994: History, Analysis and Alternatives. Part II—An Alternative Approach to Welfare Reform," 1994, 1.

27. City of New York, Human Resources Administration, *BEGIN: Begin Employment/Gain Independence; Report of the Inter-Agency Work and Welfare Task Force; The New York City Model for Implementing Welfare Reform*, 1989, ii, v, 14.

28. Under Dinkins, services to homeless families were restructured to provide quicker access to benefits such as permanent housing. For an account of Dinkins's restructuring of homeless services, see Thomas J. Main, "Hard Lessons on Homelessness: The Education of David Dinkins," *City Journal* (Summer 1993): 30–39, accessed December 27, 2024, https://www.city-journal.org/article/hard-lessons-on-homelessness.

29. C. W. Dugger, "New York Shifts on Welfare: Education Stressed over Jobs," *New York Times*, October 4, 1991, A1.

30. City of New York, *Mayor's Management Report*, September 1990, 368.

31. City of New York, *Mayor's Management Report*, Preliminary, January 30, 1991, 434–35.

32. Fran Sullivan, director, New York City Work Experience Management Program, interview by author, November 22, 1995.

33. Swati Desai, executive deputy commissioner, New York City Human Resources Administration, interview by author, October 3, 1996.

34. James Q. Wilson, *Bureaucracy: What Government Agencies Do and Why They Do It* (New York: Basic Books, 1989), 34.

35. N. De Mause, "Live Welfare Free or Die," *Z Magazine*, April 1995, 30; J. Rosenberg and S. Stern, "America Works: A Venture to End Dependency," *City Journal* 3, no. 3 (1993): 66.

36. New York City Council, Finance Division, "New York City's BEGIN Program: Current Outcomes, Future Directions," November 22, 1994, 11, emphasis added.

37. New York City Council, Finance Division, "Welfare Reform 1967–1994: History, Analysis and Alternatives. Part II—An Alternative Approach to Welfare Reform," 1994, Executive Summary.

38. Meg O'Regan, Testimony before the Council of the City of New York, Committee on General Welfare, November 22, 1994.

39. See M. Anne Hill and Thomas J. Main, *Is Welfare Working? The Massachusetts Reforms Three Years Later* (Boston: Pioneer Institute, 1998), chap. 6 for an interpretation of PRWORA and Massachusetts's welfare reform law and chap. 5 on nonincremental change. See Steven M. Teles and Timothy S. Prinz, "The Politics of Rights Retraction: Welfare Reform from Entitlement to Block Grant," in *Seeking the Center: Politics and Policymaking at the New Century*, ed. Martin A. Levin, Marc K. Landy, and Martin Shapiro (Washington, DC: Georgetown University Press, 2001), 215–38, for a similar but less radical interpretation of PRWORA.

40. At the passage of PRWORA, the federal government was divided between a Democratic president and a Republican legislature. In Massachusetts, at the passage of Chapter 5, the state's version of welfare reform, which included features that anticipated PRWORA, the government was divided between a Republican governor and a Democratic legislature. In Wisconsin at the passage of legislation establishing the Wisconsin Works program, both houses of the legislature and the governorship were held by Republicans. However, the Republicans controlled the state Senate by only a single vote, and crucial amendments to the reform legislation were proposed by Democrats. Thus, Wisconsin at that time represented the sort of highly competitive political environment that encouraged the bidding-up process associated with nonincremental change.

41. Anthony Coles, deputy mayor, interview by author, January 8, 1997.

42. See Timothy J. Conlan, David R. Beam, and Margaret T. Wrightson, "Policy Models and Political Change," in *The New Politics of Public Policy*, ed. Marc K. Landy and Martin A. Levin (Baltimore, MD: Johns Hopkins University Press, 1995), 126–29, for a discussion of "Old Style Reform: The Presidential-Majoritarian Perspective." In the present context of city politics, I refer to this model as "executive-majoritarian."

43. John Hull Mollenkopf, *A Phoenix in the Ashes: The Rise and Fall of the Koch Coalition in New York City Politics* (Princeton, NJ: Princeton University Press, 1992), 185.

44. Mollenkopf, *A Phoenix in the Ashes*, 219.

45. I. Marcus, interview by author, January 8, 1997.

46. Coles interview.

47. Coles interview.

48. Lawrence M. Mead, *Beyond Entitlement: The Social Obligations of Citizenship* (New York: Free Press, 1986), 218–40.

49. See J. Phillip Thompson, "The Failure of Liberal Homeless Policy in the Koch and Dinkins Administrations," *Political Science Quarterly* 11, no. 4 (1996–97): 639–60; and Main, "Hard Lessons on Homelessness." Michael Cragg and Brendan O'Flaherty, "Do Shelter Conditions Determine Shelter Population?: The Case of the Dinkins Deluge," *Journal of Urban Economics* 46, no. 3 (November 1999): 377–415, argue that Dinkins's policy of placing homeless families into subsidized housing did not result in a net increase in the number of homeless families. The main point for this chapter is that at the time, policy makers (including many in the Dinkins administration) and the attentive public thought the policy had had this effect.

50. New York City Commission on the Homeless, *The Way Home: A New Direction in Social Policy*, 1992, 11.

51. *The Way Home*, 15.

52. On how competitive political environments encourage policy entrepreneurship and facilitate the adoption of new policy ideas, see Marc K. Landy, "The New Politics of Environmental Politics," 211, and Marc C. Landy and Martin A. Levin, "The New Politics of Public Policy," in Landy and Levin, *The New Politics of Public Policy*.

53. Main, "Hard Lessons on Homelessness."

3. THE HRA UNDER GIULIANI'S SECOND TERM

1. Dennis C. Smith and William J. Grinker, "The Transformation of Social Services Management in New York City: 'CompStating' Welfare," *Seedco: Innovations in Community Development* (March 2005): 19–20.

2. James Q. Wilson, *Bureaucracy: What Government Agencies Do and Why They Do It* (New York: Basic Books, 1989), 38, 49.

3. Arthur L. Levine, "Changing the Organizational Culture," in *Managing Welfare Reform in New York City*, ed. E. S. Savas (New York: Rowman & Littlefield, 2005), 66–67.

4. James Clark, "Overcoming Opposition and Giving Work Experience to Welfare Applicants and Recipients," in *Managing Welfare Reform in New York City*, ed. E. S. Savas (New York: Rowman & Littlefield, 2005), 204.

5. Levine, "Changing the Organizational Culture," 67.

6. Demetra Smith Nightingale, "Overview of Welfare Reform," in *Managing Welfare Reform in New York City*, ed. E. S. Savas (New York: Rowman & Littlefield, 2005), 23.

7. "The United States Department of Agriculture (USDA) investigated New York City's diversion program as part of its mandate to oversee implementation of the Food Stamp program. The USDA concluded that New York's welfare offices, called 'Job Centers,' did not permit applicants to apply for benefits on the same day that they contacted the offices. Instead, they were required to complete a 'Job Profile' and meet with a financial planner, ostensibly to assist the agency in determining whether applicants had alternative sources of income. Applicants were told to reappear on another date to file an application." Matthew Diller, "The Revolution in Welfare Administration: Rules, Discretion, and Entrepreneurial Government," *New York University Law Review* 75, no. 5 (2000): 1121. See also Rachel Swarns, "New York City Admits Turning Away Poor," *New York Times*, January 22, 1999, B3.

8. Lisa Fitzpatrick, interview by author, October 20, 2017.

9. "Welfare Reform in New York City: The Measure of Success," New York City Bar, Committee Report, July 1, 2002, https://www.nycbar.org/member-and-career-services/committees/reports-listing/reports/detail/welfare-reform-in-new-york-city-the-measure-of-success#.

10. Wayne Barrett, *Rudy!: An Investigative Biography of Rudolph Giuliani* (New York: Basic Books, 2000), 297–300.

11. Barrett, *Rudy!*, 300.
12. Douglas Harbrecht, Larry Light, with Richard S. Dunham, "What Made Giuliani Jump Ship?" *Business Week*, November 7, 1994, 30.
13. Fred Siegel, *The Prince of the City: Giuliani, New York, and the Genius of American Life* (San Francisco: Encounter Books, 2005), 136.
14. Siegel, *The Prince of the City*, 138.
15. Barrett, *Rudy!*, 300. Steven Lee Meyers, "Giuliani Secures up to $200 Million for Buyout Plan," *New York Times*, April 2, 1994.
16. Celia W. Dugger, "Giuliani Relieved of an Obligation on the Homeless," *New York Times*, December 31, 1994. For a full discussion of this complicated regulatory episode, see Thomas J. Main, *Homelessness in New York City: Policymaking from Koch to de Blasio* (New York: New York University Press, 2016), 121–27.
17. "New York City and State: The Odd Couple," *Economist*, December 10, 1994, 24–25.
18. John Hull Mollenkopf, *A Phoenix in the Ashes: The Rise and Fall of the Koch Coalition in New York City Politics* (Princeton, NJ: Princeton University Press, 1992), 40.
19. For example, Krinsky writes that "In the analytic sensibility behind the block models I construct . . . there is a not-altogether-coincidental similarity in the language between blocks and 'blocs' in this chapter. For Gramsci, the key to establishing hegemony was the formation of effective political blocs across institutional settings that could steer interactions in specific ways." John Krinsky, *Free Labor: Workfare and the Contested Language of Neoliberalism* (Chicago: University of Chicago Press, 2007), loc. 2738–39, Kindle. Krinsky also remarks on how his diagramming of claims, actors, and contexts can align with Gramsci's terminology because "as Gramsci's trench metaphor suggests, trenches—here, ways of organizing and making claims—are held and guarded by actors." Krinsky, *Free Labor*, loc. 1353.
20. Krinsky graciously granted me an interview and very patiently reviewed his work with me. He admitted he had trouble explaining his diagrams partly because it had been quite a while since he had worked on them. But he also noted that chapter 5 of *Free Labor*, which features the block models, requires so much work from the reader to understand it that he was surprised his editors had allowed it to stay in the book.
21. The grand expression of the social network analysis used by Krinsky is Doug McAdam, Sidney Tarrow, and Charles Tilly, *Dynamics of Contention* (Stanford, CA: Stanford University Press, 2001). Some scholars were disappointed in this work. See James M. Jasper, "Social Movement Theory Today: Toward a Theory of Action?," *Sociology Compass* 4, no. 11 (2010): 965–76; and Ruud Koopmans, "A Failed Revolution—But a Worthy Cause," *Mobilization* 8, no. 1 (2003): 117. For other critical accounts of the social network analysis used in *Dynamics of Contention*, see Pamela E. Oliver, "Mechanisms of Contention," and Verta Taylor, "Plus ça Change, plus c'est la Même Chose," both in *Mobilization* 8, no. 1 (2003). The point here is not to discredit the work of these distinguished scholars and, still less, the whole methodology of social network analysis. The point is that the school of thought from which Krinsky derives his approach has sometimes produced hard-to-interpret results.
22. Chris Tilly, "Review, *Free Labor: Workfare and the Contested Language of Neoliberalism* by John Krinsky," *Contemporary Sociology* 38, no. 3 (May 2009): 265–66. In a section on "Through the Trenches: Neoliberalism and Mechanisms of Change," Krinsky offers some concrete examples of how opposition to work-first welfare reform was blocked by the operations of certain mechanisms identified by the network-analytical method. The rapid turnover in welfare rolls and workfare placements was a form of "time shift" that frustrated labor organizing efforts. Devolution of welfare policy making to state and local governments was a "scale shift" that "empowers the shrewdest policy entrepreneurs in search of national reputations" (228). "Certification" of claims against welfare reform was

fragmented when the opposition took up the argument that clients should receive training and education but mostly ignored feminist arguments noting that mothers with children were already working. A focus on managing properties rather than fighting for affordable housing spread through housing activist organizations, which was a form of "institutional spillover" that co-opted them. Whatever one thinks of these claims, they can be made without reference to Krinsky's block model diagrams, which do not much illuminate them.

23. John Krinsky, "The New Tammany Hall?: Welfare, Public Sector Unions, Corruption, and Neoliberal Policy Regimes," *Social Research* 80, no. 4 (2013): 1100.

24. Krinsky, "The New Tammany Hall?" 1104.

25. Tom Robbins, "A Maximus Postscript," *Village Voice*, June 17, 2003, www.villagevoice.com/a-maximus-postscript/.

26. Krinsky, "The New Tammany Hall?" 1104–5.

27. John Krinsky, "The Dialectics of Privatization and Advocacy in New York City's Workfare State," *Social Justice* 33, no. 3 (105) (2006): 164.

28. Krinsky, "The Dialectics of Privatization," 163.

29. Krinsky, "The Dialectics of Privatization," 165.

30. Krinsky, "The Dialectics of Privatization," 159.

31. Krinsky, "The Dialectics of Privatization," 169.

32. Judith M. Gueron, "A Research Context for Welfare Reform," *Journal of Policy Analysis and Management* 15, no. 4 (Autumn 1996): 553, www.jstor.org/stable/3326048.

33. Gueron, "A Research Context for Welfare Reform," 553.

34. Gueron, "A Research Context for Welfare Reform," 552.

35. Mary Jo Bane, "Foreword," in Andrew R. Feldman, *What Works in Work-First Welfare: Designing and Managing Employment Programs in New York City* (Kalamazoo, MI: W. E. Upjohn Institute for Employment Research, 2011), xvi.

36. Andrew R. Feldman, *What Works in Work-First Welfare: Designing and Managing Employment Programs in New York City* (Kalamazoo, MI: W. E. Upjohn Institute for Employment Research, 2011), 5.

37. Feldman, *What Works in Work-First Welfare*, 6.

38. R. Kent Weaver, *Ending Welfare as We Know It* (Washington, DC: Brookings Institution Press, 2000), 145.

39. Mark K. Landy and Martin A. Levin, "The New Politics of Public Policy," in *The New Politics of Public Policy*, ed. Mark K. Landy and Martin A. Levin (Baltimore, MD: Johns Hopkins University Press, 1995), 292.

4. BEGINNINGS OF DE BLASIO'S WELFARE POLICIES

1. Chris McNickle, *Bloomberg: A Billionaire's Ambition* (New York: Skyhorse, 2017), 134.

2. McNickle, *Bloomberg*, 134.

3. Alessandro Busà, *The Creative Destruction of New York City: Engineering the City for the Elite* (New York: Oxford University Press, 2017).

4. For a discussion of New York City's reform regime, see Robert F. Pecorella, *Community Power in a Post Reform City: Politics in New York City* (Armonk, NY: M. E. Sharpe, 1994), 44–56.

5. Joseph P. Viteritti, *The Pragmatist: Bill de Blasio's Quest to Save the Soul of New York* (New York: Oxford University Press, 2017), 219.

6. Viteritti, *The Pragmatist*, 21.

7. See Busà, *The Creative Destruction of New York City*, 216.

8. Regarding de Blasio's choice of Steven Banks as HRA commissioner, Joel Berg, CEO of Hunger Free America, wrote: "For anti-poverty advocates—and for the millions of struggling New Yorkers we represent—there has been a 180-degree change at the city's leading social service agency, the Human Resources Administration (HRA).

And all that change is for the better." Joel Berg, "De Blasio Admin. Making City's Safety Net More Humane," *City Limits*, September 5, 2014, citylimits.org/2014/09/05/de-blasio-admin-making-citys-safety-net-more-humane/.

9. Leslie Kaufman, "He Fought City Hall over the Homeless. Now He's Battling from the Inside," *New York Times*, October 9, 2015.

10. Michael M. Grynbaum, Majorie Connelly, and Marina Stefan, "Good Grade for the Mayor; Regret over His 3rd Term," *New York Times*, August 21, 2012, 17.

11. Michael Barbaro et al., "The Constituents Speak," *New York Times*, August 18, 2013, 9.

12. Eric Alterman, *Inequality and One City: Bill de Blasio and the New York Experiment, Year One* (New York: Nation, 2015), loc. 93–100, Kindle.

13. Viteritti, *The Pragmatist*, 176.

14. Lisa Fitzpatrick, interview by author, October 20, 2017.

15. Fitzpatrick interview, October 20, 2017.

16. Steven Banks, interview by author, January 31, 2018.

17. Banks interview, January 31, 2018.

18. Jason DeParle, "What Welfare-to-Work Really Means," *New York Times*, December 20, 1998, sec. 6, 50.

19. See Abt Associates, *Final Report: Evaluation of the Homebase Community Prevention Program*, June 6, 2013, static1.squarespace.com/static/572e5b621d07c088bf6663d9/t/573bd62df85082862032f27b/1463539246596/homebase+report.pdf.

20. Albert O. Hirschman, *The Rhetoric of Reaction* (Cambridge, MA: Harvard University Press, 1991), 124, 149–50.

21. McNickle, *Bloomberg*, 105.

22. The City of New York, Mayor Bill de Blasio, *Career Pathways: Progress Update*, n.d. 18, www.nyc.gov/assets/careerpathways/downloads/pdf/Career-Pathways-Progress-Update.pdf.

23. New York City Human Resources Administration Press Release, testimony of Commissioner Steven Banks, New York City Human Resources Administration, Oversight: Review of HRA's Employment Plan Concept Papers before the New York City Council General Welfare Committee, September 22, 2015, 7.

24. Christian González-Rivera, *Building the Workforce of the Future*, Center for an Urban Future, 2014, 3.

25. This paragraph is based on personal communication from Brad Hershbein, senior economist and deputy director of research, W. E. Upjohn Institute for Employment Research, June 13, 2023.

26. Andrew R. Feldman, *What Works in Work-First Welfare: Designing and Managing Employment Programs in New York City* (Kalamazoo, MI: W. E. Upjohn Institute for Employment Research, 2011), 7.

27. Feldman, *What Works in Work-First Welfare*, 9.

28. Feldman, *What Works in Work-First Welfare*, 116.

29. Banks interview, January 31, 2018.

30. Lashawn Richburg-Hayes, *Helping Low-Wage Workers Persist in Education Programs: Lessons from Research on Welfare Training Programs and Two Promising Community College Strategies* (New York: MDRC, 2008), iii, www.mdrc.org/work/publications/helping-low-wage-workers-persist-education-programs.

31. Gayle Hamilton and Susan Scrivener, "Facilitating Postsecondary Education and Training for TANF Recipients," Urban Institute, Brief no. 7, March 2012.

32. Vanessa Martin and Joseph Broadus, *Enhancing GED Instruction to Prepare Students for College and Careers: Early Success in La Guardia Community College's Bridge to Health and Business Program* (New York: MDRC, 2013).

33. Mary Jo Bane, "Introduction," in Andrew R. Feldman, *What Works in Work-First Welfare: Designing and Managing Employment Programs in New York City* (Kalamazoo, MI: W. E. Upjohn Institute for Employment Research, 2011), xviii.

5. OVERVIEW OF THE CAREER PATHWAYS EMPLOYMENT PROGRAMS

1. Fred Siegel and Robert Doar, "De Blasio's Welfare-Reform Reversal," *City Journal* (Spring 2015), www.city-journal.org/article/de-blasios-welfare-reform-reversal.
2. "Rolling Back Welfare Reform in New York," *New York Post*, December 6, 2015, nypost.com/2015/12/06/rolling-back-welfare-reform-in-new-york/.
3. Samar Khurshid, "In Departure from Predecessors, De Blasio Administration Overhauls City Welfare System," *Gotham Gazette*, February 19, 2016, www.gothamgazette.com/index.php/city/6177-in-departure-from-predecessors-de-blasio-administration-overhauls-city-welfare-system.
4. Khurshid, "In Departure from Predecessors."
5. Heather MacDonald, "New York's Welfare Reactionaries," *City Journal* (May 21, 2014), www.city-journal.org/article/new-yorks-welfare-reactionaries.
6. Siegel and Doar, "De Blasio's Welfare-Reform Reversal."
7. Quoted in Khurshid, "In Departure from Predecessors."
8. Rachel L. Swarns, "De Blasio's Plan to Eliminate Workfare Lifts Hopes for Job Seekers," *New York Times*, November 3, 2014.
9. Mayor's Management Report, September 2020, 178, www.nyc.gov/assets/operations/downloads/pdf/mmr2020/2020_mmr.pdf.
10. Citizens Budget Commission, "What Will the Mayor's Management Report Tell Us about Progress on the De Blasio Administration's Priorities?," September 12, 2016, 6–7, cbcny.org/research/what-will-mayors-management-report-tell-us-about-progress-de-blasio-administrations.
11. Citizens Budget Commission, "What Will the Mayor's Management Report Tell Us," 7.
12. Citizens Budget Commission, "What Will the Mayor's Management Report Tell Us," 7.
13. Citizens Budget Commission, "What Does the MMR Reveal about Progress on the De Blasio Administration's Priorities? An Update," September 19, 2016, 2, cbcny.org/research/what-does-mmr-reveal-about-progress-de-blasio-administrations-priorities-update.
14. Independent Budget Office, "Have Changes to a Key City Job-Training Program for Cash Assistance Recipients Affected the Number of Placements?," November 13, 2018, ibo.nyc.ny.us/cgi-park2/2018/11/have-changes-to-a-key-city-job-training-program-for-cash-assistance-recipients-affected-the-number-of-placements/.
15. Mayor's Management Report, September 2018, 187–88. www.nyc.gov/assets/operations/downloads/pdf/mmr2018/2018_mmr.pdf.
16. Mayor's Management Report, September 2018, 187–88. As discussed later in this chapter, a "logic flaw" in calculations by DSS resulted in the MMR of 2018 reporting incorrect figures for placements made in May and June of 2017 and 2018. Placements made in these months were higher in 2018 than they were in 2017 but not by as much as the MMR reported. The calculations presented in this chapter are based on the corrected data provided to the author by Ellen Levine, chief program planning and financial management officer for DSS, in a personal communication of July 9, 2021.
17. Steven Banks, interview by author, November 14, 2018.
18. Banks interview, November 14, 2018.
19. Independent Budget Office, "After Expected Decline under New Employment Services Contracts, Are Job Placements Now Increasing for Cash Assistance Recipients?," November 26, 2019, ibo.nyc.ny.us/cgi-park2/2019/11/after-expected-decline-under-new

-employment-services-contracts-are-job-placements-now-increasing-for-cash-assistance-recipients/.

20. Mayor's Management Report, September 2019, 178, www.nyc.gov/assets/operations/downloads/pdf/mmr2019/2019_mmr.pdf.

21. Mayor's Management Report, September 2018, 187.

22. Ellen Levine, personal communication, July 9, 2021.

23. On June 15, 2021, I contacted Ellen Levine, chief program planning and financial management officer for DSS, noting that "since the MMR [of FY 2018] had compared vendor placements of May and June 2017 to those of May and June 2018 it would be illuminating to look at the placements of May and June 2019." Levine responded on June 22, 2021, with a set of numbers that "includes all placements associated with contract employment activity vendors, including WeCare, as it seems like this would be most relevant to your work." I requested and received from DSS data that separated out placements made by WeCare and placements made by the new employment services programs.

24. Khurshid, "In Departure from Predecessors."

25. Levine, personal communication, August 17, 2021.

26. Regression analysis provided by Sanders Korenman, personal communication, August 27, 2021.

27. Jeffrey L. Pressman and Aaron B. Wildavsky, *Implementation: How Great Expectations in Washington Are Dashed in Oakland: Or, Why It's Amazing That Federal Programs Work at All, This Being a Saga of the Economic Development Administration as Told by Two Sympathetic Observers Who Seek to Build Morals on a Foundation of Ruined Hopes* (Berkeley: University of California Press, 1973).

6. IMPLEMENTATION OF CAREER PATHWAYS WELFARE PROGRAMS

1. Diane Edelson, interview by author, May 21, 2018.
2. Goodwill Industries executives, interview by author, July 26, 2021.
3. Maximus executives, interview by author, July 6, 2021.
4. Gordon P. Whitaker, "Coproduction: Citizen Participation in Service Delivery," *Public Administration Review* 40, no. 3 (1980): 240.
5. Lawrence M. Mead, "The Interaction Problem in Policy Analysis," *Policy Sciences* 16, no. 1 (September 1983): 52.
6. Edelson interview, May 21, 2018.
7. Goodwill Industries executives, interview by author, February 11, 2018.
8. Goodwill Industries executives interview, July 26, 2021.
9. Lee Bowes, CEO of America Works, interview by author, July 27, 2018.
10. Andrew R. Feldman, *What Works in Work-First Welfare: Designing and Managing Employment Programs in New York City* (Kalamazoo, MI: W. E. Upjohn Institute for Employment Research, 2011), 113.
11. Feldman, *What Works in Work-First Welfare*, 114.
12. Edelson interview, May 21, 2018.
13. M. Bryna Sanger, *The Welfare Marketplace: Privatization and Welfare Reform* (Washington, DC: Brookings Institution, 2003), 79.
14. Goodwill Industries executives interview, February 11, 2018.
15. Goodwill Industries executives interview, July 26, 2021.
16. Jim Miller, Maximus, interview by author, November 11, 2021.
17. Miller interview, November 11, 2021.
18. Maximus executives interview, July 6, 2021.
19. Lee Bowes, interview by author, August 18, 2021.
20. Bowes interview, July 27, 2018.
21. Bowes interview, July 27, 2018.

22. Goodwill Industries executives interview, February 11, 2018.
23. Edelson interview, May 21, 2018.
24. Feldman, *What Works in Work-First Welfare*, 115.
25. Feldman, *What Works in Work-First Welfare*, 109.
26. Goodwill Industries executives interview, February 11, 2018.
27. Goodwill Industries executives interview, July 26, 2021.
28. Edelson interview, May 21, 2018.
29. Edelson interview, May 21, 2018.
30. Vanessa Preston, Grant Associates, interview by author, July 7, 2021.
31. Maximus executives interview, July 6, 2021.
32. Bowes interview, July 27, 2018.
33. Bowes interview, July 27, 2018.
34. Judith M. Gueron, "A Research Context for Welfare Reform," *Journal of Policy Analysis and Management* 15, no. 4 (Autumn 1996): 547.
35. David J. Fein, *Career Pathways as a Framework for Program Design and Evaluation: A Working Paper from the Innovative Strategies for Increasing Self-Sufficiency (ISIS) Project*, OPRE Report no. 2012-30, Office of Planning, Research and Evaluation, Administration for Children and Families, US Department of Health and Human Services, 2012, 4–5.
36. David Aguado, CEO of America Works, interview by author, January 5, 2022.
37. Aguado interview, January 5, 2022.
38. City of New York, *Career Pathways: One City Working Together*, n.d., 5, accessed July 21, 2024, s3.amazonaws.com/PCRN/docs/career-pathways-full-report.pdf.
39. David Mastran, *Privateer!: Building a Business, Reforming Government* (CreateSpace, 2012), loc. 124, Kindle.
40. Mastran, *Privateer!*, loc. 137.
41. Mastran, *Privateer!*, loc. 3845.
42. Mastran, *Privateer!*, loc. 644.
43. Feldman, *What Works in Work-First Welfare*, 119.
44. Feldman, *What Works in Work First Welfare*, 119, 121.
45. Feldman, *What Works in Work-First Welfare*, 123.

7. CAREER PATHWAYS AND THE DRIVE FOR COORDINATION

1. Richard Kazis, "MDRC Research on Career Pathways," Manpower Development Research Corporation, Issue Brief 2016, 1; emphasis in original. This source quotes from David Fein, *The Struggle for Coherence in Emerging U.S. Career Pathways Initiatives* (Bethesda, MD: Abt Associates, 2014), 24, and US Departments of Education, Health and Human Services, and Labor, joint career pathways letter, April 4, 2012, www.dol.gov/sites/dolgov/files/ETA/advisories/TEN/2012/ten_36_11_att.pdf.
2. David J. Fein, *Career Pathways as a Framework for Program Design and Evaluation: A Working Paper from the Innovative Strategies for Increasing Self-Sufficiency (ISIS) Project*, OPRE Report no. 2012-30, Office of Planning, Research and Evaluation, Administration for Children and Families, US Department of Health and Human Services, 2012, 4.
3. Fein, *Career Pathways as a Framework for Program Design and Evaluation*, 4–5.
4. "Mayor de Blasio Announces 'Jobs for New Yorkers,'" Per Scholas, June 22, 2014, perscholas.org/news/mayor-de-blasio-announces-jobs-for-new-yorkers-executive-director-angie-kamath-appointed-to-task-force/.
5. "Jobs for New Yorkers Task Force: Workforce Development Re-Imagined," n.d., accessed July 22, 2024, www.nyc.gov/html/ohcd/downloads/pdf/jobs_for_nyers_task_force_flyer.pdf.
6. Testimony of Commissioner Steven Banks, New York City Human Resources Administration Oversight: Review of HRA's Employment Plan Concept Papers before the

New York City Council General Welfare Committee, New York City Human Resources Administration, September 22, 2015.

7. "De Blasio Administration Announces Overhaul of Workforce Development to Focus on Good-Paying Jobs, Skill-Building, and Strengthening New York City's Economy," Office of the Mayor, November 21, 2014.

8. *Career Pathways: One City Working Together*, City of New York, n.d., 5, accessed July 22, 2024, www1.nyc.gov/assets/careerpathways/downloads/pdf/career-pathways-full-report.pdf.

9. *Career Pathways: One City Working Together*, 12.

10. J. J. Harrigan and R. J. Vogel, *Political Change in the Metropolis*, 6th ed. (New York: Longman, 2000), 15.

11. Harold Seidman and Robert Gilmour, *Politics, Position, and Power: From the Positive to the Regulatory State*, 4th ed. (New York: Oxford University Press, 1986), 219.

12. James Q. Wilson, *Bureaucracy: What Government Agencies Do and Why They Do It* (New York: Basic Books, 1989), 270, 271, 274.

13. Seidman and Gilmour, *Politics, Position, and Power*, 226, 222.

14. Kellie Lunney, "Crash Course in Homelessness," *National Journal* 37, no. 45 (November 5, 2005): 3454–55.

15. Douglas McGray, "The Abolitionist," *The Atlantic*, June 2004, 36–37.

16. Randall Kuhn and Dennis P. Culhane, "Applying Cluster Analysis to Test a Typology of Homelessness by Pattern of Shelter Utilization: Results from an Analysis of Administrative Data," *American Journal of Community Psychology* 26, no. 2 (1998): 226.

17. Sam Tsemberis, Leyla Gulcur, and Maria Nakae, "Housing First, Consumer Choice, and Harm Reduction for Homeless Individuals with a Dual Diagnosis," *American Journal of Public Health* 94, no. 4 (April 2004).

18. Christopher Swope, "Abolitionist Apostle: On a Mission to End Chronic Homelessness," *Governing*, November 2006.

19. Works documenting the importance of ideas in policy making include Steven Kelman, *Making Public Policy: A Hopeful View of American Government* (New York: Basic Books, 1987); Robert B. Reich, ed., *The Power of Public Ideas* (Cambridge, MA: Harvard University Press, 1988); Marc K. Landy and Martin A. Levin, eds., *The New Politics of Public Policy* (Baltimore, MD: Johns Hopkins University Press, 1995); and Martin A. Levin, Mark K. Landy, and Martin Shapiro, eds., *Seeking the Center: Politics and Policymaking at the New Century* (Washington, DC: Georgetown University Press, 2001).

20. J. Phillip Thompson, interview by author, November 19, 2020.

21. City of New York, *Career Pathways: Progress Update*, n.d., 7, accessed July 22, 2024, www1.nyc.gov/assets/careerpathways/downloads/pdf/Career-Pathways-Progress-Update.pdf.

22. Jesse Laymon, director of policy and advocacy at the New York City Employment and Training Coalition, testimony to the City Council Committees on Small Business and Civil Service and Labor, November 27, 2017.

23. David Jason Fischer, "Fulfilling the Promise of the Jobs for New Yorkers Task Force," Center for an Urban Future, December 2014, nycfuture.org/research/fulfilling-the-promise-of-the-jobs-for-new-yorkers-task-force.

24. Amy Peterson, interview by author, November 16, 2020.

25. Jacqueline Mallon, interview by author, January 29, 2021.

26. Eugene Bardach, *Getting Agencies to Work Together: The Practice and Theory of Managerial Craftsmanship* (Washington, DC: Brookings Institution, 1998), 204–5.

27. Bardach, *Getting Agencies to Work Together*, 7.

28. States News Service, "Mayor De Blasio Announces Community Hiring Economic Justice Plan," August 13, 2020.

29. Mayor's Management Report, "Career Pathways," "Increasing System and Policy Coordination," September 2019, 36.
30. Official Website of the City of New York, Office of the Mayor, "Mayor de Blasio Announces Community Hiring Economic Justice Plan," August 13, 2020, www.nyc.gov/office-of-the-mayor/news/588-20/mayor-de-blasio-community-hiring-economic-justice-plan.
31. Mayor's Management Report, "Collaborating to Deliver Results: Career Pathways," September 2020, 42.
32. Mayor's Management Report, "Career Pathways," "Increasing System and Policy Coordination," September 2019, 36.
33. Mayor's Management Report, "Collaborating to Deliver Results: Career Pathways," September 2020, 39.
34. Mayor's Management Report, "Collaborating to Deliver Results: Career Pathways," September 2020, 41.
35. Mayor's Management Report, "Collaborating to Deliver Results: Career Pathways," September 2020, 41.
36. David Berman, NYC Opportunity Response to Westat Evaluation of NYC Job Training Programs, from Joseph Gasper, Ben Muz, Dawn Boyer, Mayor's Office for Economic Opportunity Independent Evaluation, Return on Investment Analysis of Industry-Focused Job Training Programs, January 2020, 1.
37. Julie Strawn, "Career Pathways: A Strategy to Boost College Completion and Economic Mobility," MDRC, May 2022, 2; emphasis in original, https://www.mdrc.org/work/publications/career-pathways-strategy-boost-college-completion-and-economic-mobility.
38. Annie Garneva, "Career Pathways Is the Missing Piece of Mayor de Blasio's Promised 'Fairest Big City,'" *New York Nonprofit Media*, March 12, 2018, www.nynmedia.com/news/career-pathways-is-the-missing-piece-of-mayor-de-blasio-s-promise-of-the-fairest-big-city.
39. *Career Pathways: One City Working Together*, 13.
40. Sarina Trangle, "City Fails to Establish Retail Industry Training Partnership after More than 4 Years," *amNY*, May 15, 2019. www.amny.com/news/nyc-retail-training-1-31083639/.
41. Christian Gonzalez-Rivera, "CityViews: Despite De Blasio's Changes, There Are Still Barriers to Getting Good Jobs," *City Limits*, November 30, 2017, http://citylimits.org/2017/11/30/1968539/.
42. Jesse Laymon testimony to the City Council Committees.
43. Workforce Professionals Training Institute, Workforce Field Building Hub, www.workforceprofessionals.org/the-hub/overview, accessed July 22, 2024.
44. Stacy Woodruff, interview by author, July 5, 2018.
45. Steven Dawson and Stacy Woodruff, *Workforce Agenda for New York*, Workforce Professionals Training Institute, September 2018, 22.
46. Stacy Woodruff, "Thank You and Transition Message," email communication, October 9, 2020.
47. Dawson and Woodruff, *Workforce Agenda for New York*, 7.
48. Malcolm Gladwell, "Million-Dollar Murray," *New Yorker*, February 13, 2006.

8. EARLY CHALLENGES TO DE BLASIO'S HOMELESSNESS POLICY

1. See Diana R. Gordon, *City Limits: Barriers to Change in Urban Government* (New York: Charter House, 1973), 255–93.
2. For accounts of homeless policy under Giuliani, see Thomas J. Main, "Shelters for Homeless Men in New York City: Toward Paternalism through Privatization," in *The New Paternalism: Supervisory Approaches to Poverty*, ed. Lawrence M. Mead (Washington, DC: Brookings Institution, 1997), 161–81; Thomas J. Main, "Housing the Homeless," in *Man-*

aging Welfare Reform in New York City, ed. E. S. Savas (Lanham, MD: Rowman & Littlefield, 2005), 289–98.

3. Coalition for the Homeless, "Number of Homeless People in NYC Shelters Each Night," accessed July 8, 2022, www.coalitionforthehomeless.org/facts-about-homelessness.

4. "Number of Homeless People in NYC Shelters Each Night."

5. "Number of Homeless People in NYC Shelters Each Night."

6. New York City Department of Homeless Services, "Homeless Outreach Population Estimate (HOPE) 2015 Shows Five Percent Decrease in Unsheltered Population," accessed July 22, 2024, www.nyc.gov/site/dhs/about/hope-2015-results.page.

7. Quinnipiac University Poll, "Mayor Gets Negative 2-1 Marks on Poverty, Quinnipiac University Poll Finds," October 30, 2015, 2, http://poll.qu.edu/Poll-Release-Legacy?releaseid=2297.

8. Tom Wilson, "20 Years of Cleaning Up NYC Pissed Away," *New York Post*, July 10, 2015, nypost.com/2015/07/10/apparently-its-now-ok-to-pee-on-the-streets-of-new-york-city. For a discussion of the *Post*'s coverage of street homelessness during the early de Blasio years, see Gothamist Staff, "Ask a Native New Yorker: Has De Blasio Turned NYC into a Peeing Homeless Terrordome?" *Gothamist*, July 13, 2015, gothamist.com/news/ask-a-native-new-yorker-has-de-blasio-turned-nyc-into-a-peeing-homeless-terrordome.

9. Jeff Foreman, "Are There More Homeless People in New York City?," *City Limits*, August 2015, citylimits.org/2015/08/21/are-there-more-homeless-people-in-new-york-city/.

10. Michael Gartland, "De Blasio Is Underestimating the Homeless Population: Advocate," *New York Post*, October 19, 2015, nypost.com/2015/10/19/de-blasio-is-underestimating-the-homeless-population-advocate/.

11. Council of the City of New York, "Hearing on the Fiscal 2016 Preliminary Budget & the Fiscal 2015 Preliminary Mayor's Management Report, Department of Homeless Services," March 17, 2015, 1, council.nyc.gov/budget/wp-content/uploads/sites/54/2015/06/fy2016-dhs.pdf.

12. New York City Department of Investigation, *Probe of Department of Homeless Services' Shelters for Families with Children Finds Serious Deficiencies*, March 2015; Vivian Yee, "Homeless Families Endure Roaches, Mice and Failed Promises," *New York Times*, August 28, 2015, www.nytimes.com/2015/08/29/nyregion/new-york-relies-on-housing-program-it-deplores-as-homeless-ranks-swell.html.

13. New York City Department of Investigation, *Probe of Department of Homeless Services' Shelters*, 9.

14. For examples of negative coverage of the use of cluster apartments under de Blasio, see Yee, "Homeless Families Endure Roaches"; Yoav Gonen, "NYC Homeless Shelters Plagued with Vermin, Safety Hazards," *New York Post*, March 12, 2015, nypost.com/2015/03/12/nyc-homeless-shelters-plagued-with-vermin-safety-hazards/.

15. For a press account of the de Blasio administration's reliance on commercial hotels and the controversy surrounding that practice, see William Neuman, "Confronting Surge in Homelessness, New York City Expands Use of Hotels," *New York Times*, December 7, 2016, www.nytimes.com/2016/12/07/nyregion/homelessness-new-york-city-hotels.html.

16. Aaron Short, "De Blasio Deputy Quits: He Doesn't Care about City's Exploding Homeless Problem," *New York Post*, November 1, 2015, nypost.com/2015/11/01/fed-up-deputy-mayor-quits-after-being-ignored-by-de-blasio/.

17. Quinnipiac University Poll, "Mayor Gets Negative 2-1 Marks on Poverty," 1; Quinnipiac University Poll, "Cuomo, Stringer Top De Blasio among New Yorkers Quinnipiac University Poll Finds; City Voters Split on Mayor-Gov Albany Battle," August 5, 2015, 1, poll.qu.edu/Poll-Release-Legacy?releaseid=2266.

18. "Finally, Urgency on Homelessness," *New York Times*, December 23, 2015, www.nytimes.com/2015/12/23/opinion/finally-urgency-on-new-yorks-homeless.html.

19. Dina Temple-Raston, "Bloomberg Vows to Make Chronic Homelessness 'Extinct,'" *New York Sun*, June 24, 2004.

20. Supportive Housing Network of New York, *Taking Stock of the New York/New York III Supportive Housing Agreement: A Community View of the Achievements and Challenges Implementing the Nation's Largest Supportive Housing Initiative*, February 2014, 4, https://shnny.org/uploads/ny-ny-iii-network-report.pdf.

21. Regarding Home Base, see Abt Associates, *Final Report: Evaluation of the Homebase Community Prevention Program*, June 6, 2013. Regarding Housing First, see Sam Tsemberis, Leyla Gulcur, and Maria Nakae, "Housing First, Consumer Choice, and Harm Reduction for Homeless Individuals with a Dual Diagnosis," *American Journal of Public Health* 94, no. 4 (April 2004): 651–56; Ronni Michelle Greenwood, Nicole J. Schaefer-McDaniel, Gary Winkel, and Sam J. Tsemberis, "Decreasing Psychiatric Symptoms by Increasing Choice in Services for Adults with Histories of Homelessness," *American Journal of Community Psychology* 36, nos. 3/4 (December 2005): 223–38.

22. The City of New York, *Uniting for Solutions Beyond Shelter: The Action Plan for New York City*, n.d., 34, accessed July 22, 2024, www.nyc.gov/html/endinghomelessness/downloads/pdf/actionbooklet.pdf.

23. Coalition for the Homeless, "Number of Homeless People in NYC Shelters Each Night."

24. Leslie Kaurmann, "Mayor Urges Major Overhaul for Homeless," *New York Times*, June 23, 2004, www.nytimes.com/2004/06/24/nyregion/mayor-urges-major-overhaul-for-homeless.html.

25. Leslie Kaufman, "Homeless Families Blocked from Seeking U.S. Housing Aid," *New York Times*, October 20, 2004, www.nytimes.com/2004/10/20/nyregion/homeless-families-blocked-from-seeking-us-housing-aid.html.

26. Michael Cragg and Brendan O'Flaherty, "Do Homeless Shelter Conditions Determine Shelter Population? The Case of the Dinkins Deluge," *Journal of Urban Economics* 46 (1999): 379.

27. Coalition for the Homeless, "Number of Homeless People in NYC Shelters Each Night."

28. NYU Furman Center, Directory of NYC Housing Programs, Advantage, accessed July 22, 2024, furmancenter.org/coredata/directory/entry/advantage.

29. Coalition for the Homeless, "Number of Homeless People in NYC Shelters Each Night."

30. Kate Taylor and Thomas Kaplan, "Governor and Mayor Clashing Again, This Time Over Homelessness," *New York Times*, March 26, 2014, www.nytimes.com/2014/03/26/nyregion/andrew-cuomo-and-bill-de-blasio-clashing-again-this-time-over-homelessness.html.

31. Dennis P. Culhane, Stephen Metreaux, and Trevor Hadley, "Public Service Reductions with Placement of Homeless Persons in Supportive Housing," *Housing Policy Debate* 13, no. 1 (2002): 107–63.

32. See Michael Powell, "A Victory, and a Knife in the Side," *New York Times*, April 3, 2014; Alexander Burns, "Allies Perpetually at War: Cuomo and de Blasio," *New York Times*, February 12, 2015; Eric Alterman, "This Is the Real Battle for the Soul of the Democratic Party," *Nation*, July 16, 2015.

33. "Finally, Urgency on Homelessness."

34. Caroline Iosso and Max Rein, *Family Homelessness in New York City: What the Adams Administration Can Learn from Previous Mayoralties*, Institute for Children, Poverty & Homelessness, March 2022, 10.

35. Nikita Stewart, "Mayor de Blasio's Aide on Homeless Is Resigning Amid Crisis," *New York Times*, August 31, 2015, www.nytimes.com/2015/09/01/nyregion/de-blasios

-aide-on-homeless-is-resigning-amid-crisis.html; Brigid Bergin and Mirela Iverac, "Exit of de Blasio's Deputy Saddens, Alarms Advocates," WNYC News, September 2, 2015, www.wnyc.org/story/exit-de-blasios-deputy-saddens-alarms-advocates/.

36. Lilliam Barrios-Paoli, interview by author, November 7, 2016.
37. Barrios-Paoli interview, November 7, 2016.
38. Barrios-Paoli interview, November 7, 2016.
39. City of New York Department of Investigation, *Probe of Department of Homeless Services' Shelters for Families with Children Finds Serious Deficiencies*, March 12, 2015, www1.nyc.gov/assets/doi/reports/pdf/2015/2015-03-12-Pr08dhs.pdf.
40. *Probe of Department of Homeless Services*, i.
41. *Probe of Department of Homeless Services*, 5.
42. Steven Banks, interview by author, May 29, 2015.
43. Nikita Stewart, "New York Comptroller Clashes with Mayor de Blasio over Shelter Contracts," *New York Times*, September 12, 2015, www.nytimes.com/2015/09/12/nyregion/new-york-comptroller-clashes-with-mayor-de-blasio-over-shelter-contracts.html.
44. "HRA Now Reviewing Shelter Contracts, with DHS Approving," *Norwood News*, October 19, 2015, www.norwoodnews.org/hra-now-reviewing-shelter-contracts-with-dhs-approving.
45. Michael M. Grynbaum and Nikita Stewart, "Mayor, Facing Homelessness Crisis, Issues Plan to Fight It," *New York Times*, December 18, 2015. www.nytimes.com/2015/12/18/nyregion/mayor-de-blasio-unveils-plan-to-track-homeless-population.html.
46. Nikita Stewart, "Gilbert Taylor, New York City Homelessness Chief, Quits Post," *New York Times*, December 16, 2015, www.nytimes.com/2015/12/16/nyregion/gilbert-taylor-new-york-city-homelessness-chief-to-leave.html.
47. Nikita Stewart, "Chief Lost Influence Amid Criticism of Mayor's Policies on Homelessness," *New York Times*, December 19, 2015. www.nytimes.com/2015/12/19/nyregion/chief-lost-influence-amid-criticism-of-mayor-de-blasios-policies-onhomelessness.html.
48. David Neustadt, deputy commissioner, Communications, Marketing, Legislative Affairs, NYC Human Resources Administration, personal communication, November 6, 2015.
49. Testimony of Steven Banks, New York State Senate–Task Force on Social Service Delivery in New York City, October 7, 2015, 7.
50. See Jennifer Steinhauer, "A Jail Becomes a Shelter, and Maybe a Mayor's Albatross," *New York Times*, August 13, 2002, B1.
51. New York City Department of Homeless Services, Daily Report, October 30, 2015, accessed October 31, 2015, http://www1.nyc.gov/assets/dhs/downloads/pdf/dailyreport.pdf; Coalition for the Homeless, Advocacy Department, "New York City Homeless Municipal Shelter Population, 1983–Present," www.coalitionforthehomeless.org/wp-content/uploads/2020/03/NYCHomelessShelterPopulation-Worksheet1983-Present.pdf, accessed July 22, 2024.
52. N.Y. ADC Law § 21-124: NY Code, Section 21-124 B, which reads in part: "No homeless family shelter shall be established which does not provide a bathroom, a refrigerator and cooking facilities and an adequate sleeping area within each unit within the shelter and which otherwise complies with state and local laws."
53. Quoted in Christopher Barca, "Pan Am Hotel Turned into Homeless Shelter," *Queens Chronicle*, June 12, 2014, www.qchron.com/editions/queenswide/pan-am-hotel-turned-into-homeless-shelter/article_44589a97-0dfc-522b-8216-b7d35c1bd482.html.
54. Justice Freedman order, *McCain*, March 25, 1991 (index no. 41023/83).
55. Celia W. Dugger, "Judge Orders Relocation of Homeless Families," *New York Times*, March 26, 1991.
56. 18 NYCRR 352.3.

57. 18 NYCRR 352.3 (e) (2).
58. J. Freedman order.

9. LATER DEVELOPMENTS IN DE BLASIO'S HOMELESSNESS POLICY

1. Rudy Giuliani, "Giuliani: De Blasio's Progressivism Created City's Homeless Crisis," *New York Post*, September 6, 2015, nypost.com/2015/09/06/giuliani-to-de-blasio-the-citys-homeless-crisis-needs-tough-love.

2. Council of the City of New York, Briefing Paper on the Human Services Division, Committee on General Welfare, "Oversight: An Examination of the Department of Homeless Services 90-Day Review," April 21, 2016, 17, file:///C:/Users/tmain/Downloads/Committee%20Report.pdf.

3. "Tackling the Homeless Crisis, Alone," *New York Times*, November 20, 2015.

4. Quoted in Thomas J. Main, *Homelessness in New York City: Policymaking from Koch to De Blasio* (New York: NYU Press, 2016), 65–66.

5. "Political Rumble over Pre-K," *New York Times*, January 23, 2014.

6. Kevin Corinth, "New York Should Fight Homelessness with Support Services, Not Just Housing," *US News and World Report*, February 11, 2016.

7. Christine C. Quinn, "Let's Rethink Our Homeless Shelters," *New York Times*, January 2, 2016.

8. For a summary of the public administration literature on coordination, see James Q. Wilson, *Bureaucracy: What Government Agencies Do and Why They Do It* (New York: Basic Books, 1989), 270–74.

9. Hildy Dworkin, "Selected History and Evolution of the Human Resources Administration," n.d., 5, www.nyc.gov/assets/hra/downloads/pdf/about/history_of_welfare_and_hra.pdf.

10. Final Report of the Temporary State Commission to Make a Study of the Governmental Operation of the City of New York, State Study Commission for New York City, Stuart N. Scott, chairman, April 1973, 16.

11. Joan Malin, quoted in Main, *Homelessness in New York City*, 105.

12. Main, *Homelessness in New York City*, 105.

13. Nikita Stewart, "Homeless Crisis Stymies Official Hired to Halt It," *New York Times*, October 26, 2016.

14. Dennis C. Smith and William J. Grinker, "The Transformation of Social Services Management in New York City: 'CompStating' Welfare," *Seedco: Innovation in Community Development*, March 2005, 35.

15. William Grinker, interview by author, June 3, 2022.

16. *United for Housing from the Ground Up: Affordable Housing Recommendations for New York City's Next Mayor*, New York Housing Conference, 2021, 51.

17. *Right to a Roof: Demands for an Integrated Housing Plan to End Homelessness and Promote Racial Equity*, n.d., 7. file:///C:/Users/tmain/Downloads/20210208_Right_to_a_Roof_Report-%20(1).pdf.

18. Quoted in David Brand, "Advocates' Advice for Eric Adams? Better Coordination between NYC's Housing and Homelessness Agencies," *City Limits*, December 1, 2021, citylimits.org/2021/12/01/advocates-advice-for-eric-adams-better-coordination-between-nycs-housing-and-homelessness-agencies/.

19. See Dworkin, "Selected History and Evolution," 5–6.

20. City of New York, *Turning the Tide on Homelessness in New York City*, n.d., ii–iii, accessed July 22, 2024, www.nyc.gov/assets/dhs/downloads/pdf/turning-the-tide-on-homelessness.pdf.

21. *Review of Homeless Services Agencies and Programs*, April 11, 2016, 2, 3, www1.nyc.gov/assets/home/downloads/pdf/reports/2016/90-day-homeless-services-review.pdf.

22. City of New York, *Turning the Tide*, 1–2.

23. City Council of New York, *Our Homelessness Crisis: The Case for Change*, January 2020, 68–69, council.nyc.gov/data/wp-content/uploads/sites/73/2020/01/FINAL-PAPER.pdf, accessed July 22, 2024.

24. Caroline Iosso and Max Rein, *Family Homelessness in New York City*, Institute for Children, Poverty & Homelessness, March 2022, 3, www.icphusa.org/wp-content/uploads/2022/03/ICPH_Mayors-Report_WEB_030822.pdf.

25. Iosso and Rein, *Family Homelessness in New York City*, 18, 21.

26. Iosso and Rein, *Family Homelessness in New York City*, 18.

27. *Right to a Roof*, 7.

28. Samuel Stein, *Assessing De Blasio's Housing Legacy: Why Hasn't the "Most Ambitious Affordable Housing Program" Produced a More Affordable City?* (New York: Community Service Society, February 2021), 2.

29. Stein, *Assessing De Blasio's Housing Legacy*, 24.

30. Alex Carp, "The Man Who Fought Homelessness and Won (Sort Of)," *New York Times Magazine*, February 2, 2022.

31. Carp, "The Man Who Fought Homelessness."

32. Carp, "The Man Who Fought Homelessness."

33. New York City Department of Social Services, "Homeless Outreach Population Estimate 2021 Results," Key Findings, www1.nyc.gov/assets/dhs/downloads/pdf/hope-2021-results.pdf.

34. Rachel Holliday Smith "Steve Banks Had Big Goals for Shelters, and Hit the Mark on Some. Should He Stay?," *The City*, November 19, 2021, www.thecity.nyc/2021/11/17/22788703/steve-banks-had-big-goals-for-shelters-and-hit-the-mark-on-some-should-he-stay.

35. City of New York, *Mayor's Management Report*, September 2021, "Department of Homeless Services," Table: Agency Resources, 277, www1.nyc.gov/assets/operations/downloads/pdf/mmr2021/2021_mmr.pdf.

36. Peter Marcuse, "After Exposing the Roots of Homelessness—What?" *Urban Geography* 38, no. 3 (2017): 357, http://dx.doi.org/10.1080/02723638.2016.1247601.

37. Marcuse, "After Exposing the Roots of Homelessness," 358.

38. "A $3 Billion Problem: Homeless Services in New York City," Citizens Budget Commission, May 24, 2018, cbcny.org/research/3-billion-problem.

39. New York City Department of Homeless Services, "DHS Data Dashboard—Fiscal Year 2017," 1; New York City Department of Homeless Services, press release, "NYC Enhances Home-Stat Street Outreach Efforts amid Rise in Street Homeless Population," July 5, 2017.

40. See Main, *Homelessness in New York City*, 44–48.

41. Wallace Sayre and Herbert Kaufman, *Governing New York City: Politics in the Metropolis* (New York: Russell Sage Foundation, 1960).

42. New York City Rent Guidelines Board, *2018 Housing Supply Report*, May 24, 2018, 3.

43. Mayor's Management Report, September, 2024, 262. Stephen Metraux, Jamison Fargo, Nicholas Eng, and Dennis P. Culhane, "Employment and Earnings Trajectories During Two Decades among Adults in New York City Homeless Shelters," *Cityscape: A Journal of Policy Development and Research* 20, no. 2 (2018): 190.

44. Milton Friedman and George J. Stigler, *Roofs or Ceilings? The Current Housing Problem* (Irvington-on-Hudson, NY: Foundation for Economic Education, 1946).

45. The figure for 2018 shelter costs is from Table 1, "A $3 Billion Problem: Homeless Services in New York City," Citizens Budget Commission, May 24, 2018. Approximate homeless count for 2018 is based on the average monthly census for that year in DHS and

HPD shelters (62,739 people), calculated using figures from "Number of People Sleeping in DHS and HPD Shelters Each Night," Coalition for the Homeless.

46. Mari Kanai, "The Solution to the Crisis of Low-Cost Housing in New York City: Creating an 'Accessory Dwelling Unit' Category" (master's thesis, Baruch College, 2013).

47. LGBTQI2-S: Lesbian, gay, bisexual, trans, questioning, intersex, or two-spirit.

48. US Department of Health and Human Services, Substance Abuse and Mental Health Services Administration, *Learning from the Field: Programs Serving Youth Who Are LGBTQI2-S and Experiencing Homelessness*, n.d., 22, accessed July 22, 2024, www.homelesshub.ca/sites/default/files/attachments/lgbt_listening_tour_report_v.3.6.pdf.

10. DE BLASIO, CUOMO, AND TRUMP

1. Joseph P. Viteritti, *The Pragmatist: Bill De Blasio's Quest to Save the Soul of New York* (New York: Oxford University Press, 2017), 167.

2. Seth Barron, *The Last Days of New York: A Reporter's True Tale* (West Palm Beach, FL: Humanix Books, 2021), loc. 2627, Kindle.

3. An article noted: "In 1970, 44 percent of Rockefeller's vote was from the twenty swing counties, 34 percent from New York City, and 22 percent from Republican dominated counties." Looking at voting trends in the state, the article concluded that a "Republican gubernatorial candidate must still do well in New York City, but the center of the constituency that will determine his victory is in the suburbs of that city and its upstate sisters, and in the growing counties of the lower Hudson valley." See Gerald Benjamin, "Patterns in New York State Politics," *Proceedings of the Academy of Political Science* 31, no. 3 (May 1974): 31–44.

4. Jarrett Murphy, "NYC vs. Trump: Center Ring, Will Bill De Blasio and the People of NYC Land the First Blows against Trumpism?," *Nation*, January 30, 2017, 12–17.

5. Andrew Rice, "The Mayor Finally Found a Worthy Adversary," *New York*, December 12–25, 2016, 48. Regarding the KKK's support for Trump, see Peter Holley, "KKK's Official Newspaper Supports Donald Trump for President," *Washington Post*, November 2, 2016, https://www.washingtonpost.com/news/post-politics/wp/2016/11/01/the-kkks-official-newspaper-has-endorsed-donald-trump-for-president/. The Trump campaign repudiated the organization's support.

6. Katie Honan, "President Trump Calls Out New York City Mayor for Using Slogan; Popular Political Phrase 'Promises Made, Promises Kept' Sparks a War of Words on Twitter," *Wall Street Journal* (online), August 21, 2018.

7. Jonathan Turley, constitutional law professor at George Washington University Law School, quoted in Mara Gay, "New York City Officials Brace for Possible Federal Funding Cuts under Trump; Aides, Analysts Head to Washington to Try to Secure Critical Funds for Antipoverty Programs and Others," *Wall Street Journal*, December 15, 2016.

8. Executive Order 13768 of January 25, 2017, "Enhancing Public Safety in the Interior of the United States," *Federal Register* vol. 82 (January 30, 2017): 8799–8803, https://www.federalregister.gov/documents/2017/01/30/2017-02102/enhancing-public-safety-in-the-interior-of-the-united-states.

9. Liz Robbins, "New York's City Council Seeks to Bolster 'Sanctuary City' Status," *New York Times*, April 26, 2017.

10. Camila Domonoske, "Judge Blocks Trump Administration from Punishing 'Sanctuary Cities,'" NPR, November 21, 2017.

11. Presidential Memoranda, "Memorandum on Reviewing Funding to State and Local Government Recipients That Are Permitting Anarchy, Violence, and Destruction in American Cities," September 2, 2020, https://trumpwhitehouse.archives.gov/presidential-actions/memorandum-reviewing-funding-state-local-government-recipients-permitting-anarchy-violence-destruction-american-cities/.

12. Joe Anuta, "Crossing Guards Remain in NYPD Budget This Year, Despite Claims of $1B Cut," *Politico*, July 8, 2020, https://www.politico.com/states/new-york/albany/story/2020/07/08/crossing-guards-remain-in-nypd-budget-this-year-despite-claims-of-1b-cut-1298533.

13. Quoted in Samar Khurshid, "What's at Stake for New York City in the 2020 Presidential Election," *Gotham Gazette*, November 2, 2020, https://www.gothamgazette.com/city/9868-whats-at-stake-for-new-york-city-in-the-2020-presidential-election.

14. Nick Bowman, "Biden Administration Rescinds Seattle's 'Anarchist Jurisdiction' Label," *MyNorthwest*, February 24, 2021, https://mynorthwest.com/2630957/biden-administration-rescinds-seattle-anarchist-jurisdiction-label/.

15. Executive Order 13828, "Reducing Poverty in America by Promoting Opportunity and Economic Mobility," *Federal Register*, vol. 83, no. 72 (April 10, 2018), Presidential Documents.

16. Council of Economic Advisers, *Expanding Work Requirements in Non-Cash Welfare Programs*, July 2018,

17. Heather Han, Eleanor Pratt, Eva H. Allen, Genevieve M. Kenney, Diane K. Levy, and Elaine Waxman, *Work Requirements in Social Safety Net Programs: A Status Report of Work Requirements in TANF, SNAP, Housing Assistance and Medicaid*, Urban Institute, 2017, 4, 10.

18. James Romoser, "Experts Say CMS Can't Do Much More on Medicaid Work Requirements," *Inside CMS* 21, no. 15 (April 12, 2018): 20.

19. For a discussion of the de Blasio administration's opposition to Trump's proposed changes to SNAP work requirements, see Testimony of Steven Banks, Commissioner, Department of Social Services, Before the New York City Council General Welfare Committee the DSS, Fiscal Year 2020 Preliminary Budget, March 25, 2019, 7.

20. Memorandum Opinion, United States District Court for the District of Columbia, *Stewart v. Azar*, Civil Action No. 18-152 (JEB), June 29, 2018.

21. Michael K. Gusmano and Frank J. Thompson, "The Administrative Presidency, Waivers, and the Affordable Care Act," *Journal of Health Politics, Policy and Law* 45, no. 4 (August 2020): 644. The authors note: "If the courts support the Trump administration's work requirement" initiative, then "this portrait . . . might over time morph into a picture of 'Trump triumphant.'" But as discussed, the courts did not uphold the administration on this point.

22. Dorothy Rosenbaum and Ed Bolen, "SNAP Reports Present Misleading Findings on Impact of Three-Month Time Limit," Center on Budget and Policy Priorities, December 14, 2016; Han et al., *Work Requirements in Social Safety Net Programs*.

23. Executive Order 14018, "Revocation of Certain Presidential Actions," February 24, 2021.

24. See Viteritti, *The Pragmatist*, 198–99, for an account of the conflict over supportive housing that attributes the final positive outcome to the fact that "De Blasio had once again pushed the governor to take action on an issue more purposefully than he had first intended."

CONCLUSION

1. On "wicked" problems, see Horst W. J. Rittel and Melvin M. Webber, "Dilemmas in a General Theory of Planning," *Policy Sciences* 4, no. 2 (June 1973).

2. Edmund Burke, *Reflections on the Revolution in France* (1790; New York: Penguin Books, 1968), 106.

3. Giuseppe di Lampedusa, *The Leopard*, trans. Archibald Colquhoun (New York: Pantheon, 1960), loc. 741, 796, Kindle.

4. "TNR Poll: Americans Agree Democracy Is Doomed, but Not About Why," *New Republic*, April 14, 2022, newrepublic.com/article/166027/democracy-poll.

5. Center for Sustainable Systems, "U.S. Cities," University of Michigan, September 2021, http://css.umich.edu/publications/factsheets/built-environment/us-cities-fact sheet#:~:text=It%20is%20estimated%20that%2083,to%20live%20in%20urban%20areas.

6. *The Joker* depicts its protagonist as being cared for by a "Department of Health Social Worker." The office where the two meet looks exactly like the HRA offices of the early 1980s, with which the author is familiar.

7. Irene Lurie, "A Lesson from the JOBS Program: Reforming Welfare Must Be Both Dazzling and Dull," *Journal of Policy Analysis and Management* 15, no. 4 (Autumn 1996): 584, www.jstor.org/stable/3326050.

8. Demetra Smith Nightingale, "Overview of Welfare Reform," in *Managing Welfare Reform in New York City*, ed. E. S. Savas (New York: Rowman & Littlefield, 2005), 18.

9. Lawrence M. Mead, *Government Matters: Welfare Reform in Wisconsin* (Princeton, NJ: Princeton University Press, 2004), 222. See also Fred Siegel, *The Prince of the City: Giuliani, New York, and the Genius of American Life* (San Francisco: Encounter Books, 2005), 289.

10. M. Ann Hill and Thomas J. Main, *Is Welfare Working?: The Massachusetts Reforms Three Years Later*, Pioneer Institute for Public Policy Research, Boston, MA, 1998, 7.

11. Mead, *Government Matters*, 173, 192.

12. Vincent J. Cannato, *The Ungovernable City: John Lindsay and His Struggle to Save New York* (New York: Basic Books, 2002), 539.

13. Dennis C. Smith and William J. Grinker, "The Transformation of Social Services Management in New York City: 'CompStating' Welfare" *Seedco: Innovation in Community Development* (2005), 35, silo.tips/download/the-transformation-of-social-services-man agement-in-new-york-city-compstating-we.

14. New York City Bar, Committee Report, "Welfare Reform in New York City: The Measure of Success," July 1, 2002, www.nycbar.org/reports/welfare-reform-in-new-york -city-the-measure-of-success/.

15. Williams Cole, "Against the Giuliani Legacy," *Brooklyn Rail*, October–November 2001, https://brooklynrail.org/2001/10/local/against-the-giuliani-legacy-2.

16. John W. Kingdon, *Agendas, Alternatives and Public Policies*, 2nd ed. (New York: Longman), 196.

17. For later scholarship that is critical of PRWORA and welfare reform, see Stephen Pimpare, "Welfare Reform at 15 and the State of Policy Analysis," *Social Work* 58, no. 1 (January 2013): 53–62; Felicia Kornbluh and Gwendolyn Mink, *Ensuring Poverty: Welfare Reform in Feminist Perspective* (Philadelphia: University of Pennsylvania Press, 2019).

18. Robert A. Moffitt and Stephanie Garlow, "Did Welfare Reform Increase Employment and Reduce Poverty?," *Pathways*, Winter 2018, 17–21.

19. Kathryn J. Edin and H. Luke Schaefer, *$2.00 a Day: Living on Almost Nothing in America* (Boston: Houghton Mifflin Harcourt, 2015).

20. Z. Parolin and D. Brady, "Extreme Child Poverty and the Role of Social Policy in the United States," *Journal of Poverty and Social Justice* 27 (2019): 2376, 2369.

21. Andrew Kirtzman, *Giuliani: The Rise and Tragic Fall of America's Mayor* (New York: Simon & Schuster, 2022), loc. 74, Kindle.

22. Jennifer Senior, "As Trump Botches the Coronavirus Crisis, I Long for . . . Giuliani," *New York Times*, March 4, 2020.

23. Philip Elliott, "To Understand Rudy Giuliani's Actions on Jan. 6, Look at a 1992 Police Riot in New York," *Time*, February 22, 2023, time.com/6257682/rudy-giuliani -january-6-police-riot/.

24. Wayne Barrett, *Rudy!: An Investigative Biography of Rudolph Giuliani* (New York: Basic Books, 2000), 283.

25. Fred Siegel, *The Prince of the City: Giuliani, New York, and the Genius of American Life* (San Francisco: Encounter Books, 2005), xii.

26. Siegel, *The Prince of the City*, 159–60.

27. Kirtzman, *Giuliani*, loc. 53.

28. Lisa Fitzpatrick, interview by author, October 20, 2017.

29. Richard P. Calhoon, "Niccolo Machiavelli and the Twentieth Century Administrator," *Academy of Management Journal* 12, no. 2 (June 1969): 211–12.

30. Maurizio Viroli, *Niccolo's Smile: A Biography of Machiavelli*, trans. Antony Shugaar (New York: Farrar, Straus and Giroux, 2000), quoted in Claude Rochet, "The Common Good as an Invisible Hand: Machiavelli's Legacy to Public Management," *International Review of Administrative Sciences* 74, no. 3 (2008): 517.

31. Desmond King, *In the Name of Liberalism: Illiberal Social Policy in the United States and Britain* (Oxford: Oxford University Press 1999), 295–96.

32. King, *In the Name of Liberalism*, 296.

33. Testimony of Commissioner Steven Banks, New York City Human Resources Administration, Oversight: Review of HRA's Employment Plan Concept Papers before the New York City Council General Welfare Committee, September 22, 2015, 3.

34. "When City Hall announced Mr. Banks's appointment, Human Resources Administration officials were watching on television. 'There was an audible gasp,' said Lisa Fitzpatrick, a 30-year veteran of the agency who now serves as Mr. Banks's chief program officer." Leslie Kaufman, "He Fought City Hall over the Homeless. Now He's Battling from the Inside," *New York Times*, October 9, 2015.

35. Peter H. Schuck notes that "when the Carter Administration acceded to power in 1977, this regulatory establishment . . . was entrusted to many former (and perhaps future) public interest activists," including (besides Claybrook) Michael Pertschuk at the Federal Trade Commission and Carol Tucker Foreman as assistant secretary for Food and Consumer Affairs in the Department of Agriculture. See Peter H. Schuck, review of *The Politics of Regulation* by James Q. Wilson, *Yale Law Journal* 90, no. 3 (January 1981): 707.

36. Caroline Iosso and Max Rein, *Family Homelessness in New York City: What the Adams Administration Can Learn from Previous Mayoralties*, Institute for Children, Poverty & Homelessness, March 2022, 10.

37. City of New York, Mayor's Management Report, September 2013, 93.

38. "About the Human Resources Administration," New York City Human Resources Administration, Department of Social Services, accessed April 23, 2022, https://www1.nyc.gov/site/hra/about/about-hra.page.

39. *The De Blasio Years: The Tale of a More Equal City*, December 2021, 2, accessed July 25, 2024, www.nyc.gov/assets/home/downloads/pdf/press-releases/2021/Wealth-Transfer-Report.pdf.

40. *The De Blasio Years*, 8.

41. The only mention in *The De Blasio Years* of the HRA and DSS concerns the Parks Opportunity Program, which is run by the Department of Parks and Recreation and hires applicants from those agencies to clean city facilities. No program operated by the HRA or DSS receives any mention at all. *The De Blasio Years*, 7.

42. John Krinsky, "The Dialectics of Privatization and Advocacy in New York City's Workfare State," *Social Justice* 33, no. 3 (2006): 165.

43. See Thomas J. Main, *The Rise of the Alt-Right* (Washington, DC: Brookings Institution Press, 2018), and Thomas J. Main, *The Rise of Illiberalism* (Washington, DC: Brookings Institution Press, 2021).

44. Smith and Grinker, "The Transformation of Social Services Management in New York City," 8.

45. Fred Reed, "She's Gonna Blow," *American Renaissance*, June 2, 2022, www.amren.com/commentary/2022/06/shes-gonna-blow/.

46. Iosso and Rein, *Family Homelessness in New York City*, 12.

47. Rittel and Webber, "Dilemmas in a General Theory of Planning," 160.

48. Miriam Jordan and Edgar Sandoval, "Is Texas' Busing Responsible for the Migrant Crisis Across Cities?," *New York Times*, September 7, 2023.

49. Daniel R. Perez, New York City Assistant Corporation Counsel, letter to Honorable Erika Edwards New York Supreme Court Justice, "Re: *Callahan v. Carey*, Index No. 42582/1979," October 3, 2023.

50. Emma Whitford, "Former Homeless Services Head to Oppose City in Right-to-Shelter Litigation," *City Limits*, July 19, 2023.

Index

Abt Associates, 105
ACES, 78–79
Adams, Eric, 127, 165
Administration for Children's Services (ACS), 125
Advantage, 114, 115
Agency for Children's Services (ACS), 150–51
Aguado, David, 87
Aid to Families with Dependent Children (AFDC), 4, 28, 32, 52, 144, 148
Airbnb, 136–37
Alterman, Eric, 53
America Works, 73, 76–77, 83–84, 85t, 86t, 87–88, 89
Armlovivh, Alex, 64
Assessing De Blasio's Housing Legacy (Community Service Society), 129, 130–31
Auletta, Ken, 25

Back to Work, 83, 84
Baillargeon, Diane, 124
Baldwin, Beatriz, 76, 82
Bane, Mary Jo, 47, 62–63
Banks, Steven: approach to change at HRA, 54, 55; background of, 51–52, 111; and Career Pathways, 60, 93–94; on change in emergency housing regulation, 40–41; change in homeless policy under, 1, 158–59; and Coalition for the Homeless, 165; as commissioner of DSS, 159; as commissioner of HRA, 116, 118, 127–28, 159, 175n8, 190n34; and coordination vs. entrepreneurialism, 12; early critics of policies of, 64–65; HRA mission statement under, 161; impact of reforms of, 131–32, 164–65; and implementation of Career Pathways, 61; job placements under, 65–69, 90; on new direction of HRA, 57–58; *New York Times Magazine* article on, 131; predictions regarding policies of, 162; sanctioning process under, 76; on skill development and education approach, 61–62; sues city over family shelter quality, 120; trends in welfare rolls under, 69–72; as voice of de Blasio's homelessness policy, 125; welfare reform of, as nonincremental change, 91
Bardach, Eugene, 3, 102, 167n9, 171n25
Barrett, Wayne, 39–40
Barrios-Paoli, Lilliam, 116–18, 125
Beame, Abraham, 16
BEGIN, 29–31
Berg, Joel, 175n8
Berger, Steven, 14
Biden, Joe, 142, 143
bipartisanship, 39–41
Blank, Blanche, 2
block modeling analysis, 44, 174n19
Bloomberg, Michael: creates position of deputy mayor for HHS, 17; de Blasio and legacy of, 50–52, 55–56; de Blasio's attempts to recover from policies of, 122–32, 158–59; homelessness under, 113–14, 119, 120; incremental change under, 52; and New York/New York agreements, 115; and reaction against urban liberalism, 53; school system under, 57
Board of Estimate, 23–24, 35, 170n7
Bowes, Lee, 76–77, 80, 83–84
Brosnahan, Mary, 112
Buckley, William F., 16
Buery, Richard R. Jr., 6
Building the Workforce of the Future (Center for an Urban Future), 58–59
Burke, Edmund, 146

Callahan right-to-shelter consent decree, 165
Callahan v. Carey (1981), 111, 132
Cannato, Vincent J., 16
Career Advance, 58, 59. *See also* Career Pathways; Career Pathways, implementation of
Career Compass, 58, 59. *See also* Career Pathways; Career Pathways, implementation of

193

INDEX

Career Pathways: development and adoption of, 48, 57–63; evaluations of, 67, 104–5; job placements under, 65–69; literature on, 92–94; and poverty reduction, 162; as strategic idea, 103

Career Pathways, implementation of, 73–74, 90–91; client attitudes as obstacle to, 74–75; under de Blasio, 97, 158; effectiveness of ideational strategy for coordination concerning, under de Blasio, 103–9; fewer sanctions as obstacle to, 76–77; and mayor–governor relations, 139; new contract structures as obstacle to, 77–81; and organizational culture, 81–84; private-sector vendor interviews, 73, 74–84; vendor performance evaluations (VPEs), 73, 84–90

Career Pathways: One City Working Together (2014), 93–94, 99–100, 103, 105

Carter, Jimmy, 159, 190n35

Casey, David, 79–80

cash assistance, 66, 67, 69–72, 119

Center for an Urban Future, 58–59, 105–6

change: incremental vs. nonincremental, 4, 52; negative, 167n16; positive, 6, 91, 109, 141, 145, 167n16; as slow and incremental, 1–2; urban politics as resistant to, 2. *See also* executive-majoritarian model of change; ideational/entrepreneurial model of change; incremental change; nonincremental change; pluralist/incremental model of political change; presidential/majoritarian model of political change

charter revision, 23–25, 28, 42

Charter Revision Committee, 24–25

cities, positioning of, in US constitutional structure, 6–7, 14–15

Citizens Budget Commission (CBC), 65–66

City Fighting Homelessness and Eviction Prevention Supplement (CityFHEPS), 112, 158–59, 160

City Journal, 64

City of Clinton v. Cedar Rapids & Missouri River Railroad (1868), 168n20

Claybrook, Joan, 159

Clinton, Bill, 28, 32, 41, 139, 148

cluster apartments, 112, 128

Coalition for the Homeless, 165

Community Hiring Initiative, 98, 103

Community Progress, 9

Community Service Society, 129

Connelly, Patricia M., 75, 83

Construction Trades Council of Greater New York, 103

contract structures, and implementation of Career Pathways, 77–81

coordination: as disreputable, 11–12; effectiveness of ideational strategy for, under de Blasio, 103–9; vs. entrepreneurialism, 12; interviews with de Blasio officials on, 97–102; as key to HRA, 9–10; as Lindsay strategy, 17; skepticism regarding possibility of, 94–95; strategies for interagency, 94–97; vision and ideas in achieving, 97, 98, 99, 100, 101, 102–3

coproduction, 75

Corinth, Kevin, 124

corruption, 45

COVID-19 pandemic, 104

Cragg, Michael, 114, 173n49

Crowley, Elizabeth, 126

Culhane, Dennis, 96, 108, 134

Cuomo, Andrew: and coordination vs. entrepreneurialism, 12; and HELP USA, 160; and Living in Communities (LINC), 115; and mayor–governor relations, 7, 115–16, 122, 123–24, 139–41, 145; and New York/New York agreements, 115–16; and paternalistic paradigm, 134; and *The Way Home* report, 34–35

Cuomo, Mario, 7, 39–41, 115

de Blasio, Bill: attempts to recover from Bloomberg's homelessness policies, 122–32, 158–59; background of homelessness policy under, 111–16; and Bloomberg legacy, 50–52, 55–56; and Career Pathways, 57–63, 93–94; conclusions on, 158–63; contract structures under, 80; and coordination vs. entrepreneurialism, 12; early critics of policies of, 64–65; economic inequality as election issue of, 53, 91, 114, 128, 164; effectiveness of ideational strategy for coordination under, 103–9; effectiveness of reform campaign, 6; and history of HRA, 1; homelessness and personnel under, 116–20; HRA mission statement under, 161; impact of reforms of, 164–65; interviews with officials of, on coordination, 97–102; job placements under, 65–69, 90; and

INDEX 195

mayor–governor relations, 7, 115–16, 122, 123–24, 139–41, 145; and necessity arguments regarding homelessness, 120–21; paths to nonincremental change under, 52–57; as pragmatic progressive, 51, 162–63; predictions regarding policies of, 162; reduction in homelessness under, 131–32; sanctioning process under, 76; success in fighting poverty and income equality, 161–62; trends in welfare rolls under, 69–72; and Trump, 141–45; welfare reform of, as nonincremental change, 91

De Blasio Years, The: The Tale of a More Equal City, 161–62

Department of Homeless Services (DHS), 56, 110, 112, 116, 118–19, 125–28, 150–51, 159

Department of Inspections (DOI), 118

Department of Social Services (DSS), 67–68, 159

"Developing New York City's Human Resources," 9–10, 18–19

Dewey, John, 51

"Dilemmas in a General Theory of Planning" (Rittel and Webber), 18

Dillon, John F., 168n20

Dillon rule, 6–7, 168n20

Dinkins, David: BEGIN reorganization under, 29–31; and Cuomo Commission, 12; Giuliani's victory over, 33–34, 43; homeless policy of, 34–35, 114, 120, 121, 171n28; HRA mission statement under, 161; Job Club, 82; and New York/New York agreements, 115

Doar, Robert, 64, 65, 143

East River Development Alliance, Inc. (ERDA), 85t, 86t

economic inequality, as de Blasio election issue, 53, 91, 114, 128, 164

Edelson, Diane, 74, 78, 80–81, 82–83

Edin, Kathryn, 154–55

education, 61–63, 74, 162–63

Educational Data System, Inc. (EDSI), 85t, 86t

electoral college system, 14

Ellwood, David, 27

Emergency Financial Control Board (FCB), 26

emergency shelter system, 12, 35, 40–41, 112, 120

Empire State Supportive Housing Initiative (ESSHI), 124

entrepreneurial city, 50–51

entrepreneurialism, vs. coordination, 12

Executive Order 13768, "Enhancing Public Safety in the Interior of the United States," 142

Executive Order 13828, "Reducing Poverty in America by Promoting Opportunity and Economic Mobility," 143

executive-majoritarian model of change, 33, 55, 56

expert consensus, 27–28, 46–48, 59, 157

Family Assistance Plan, 3

Family Homelessness in New York City (ICPH), 129–30

Family Support Act (FSA, 1988), 27, 28, 29, 31, 48, 149

FedCap Rehabilitation Services, Inc. (FedCap), 85t, 86t

Fein, David J., 92–93

Feldman, Andrew R., 60, 77, 81, 89

Ferguson-Cousins, Sheree, 74–75, 76, 78–79, 80, 82

Field Building Hub, 107–8

Fiscal Control Board, 24, 171n14

fiscal crisis of 1975, 25–26, 171n14

Fitzpatrick, Lisa, 38–39, 54–55, 190n34

Foreman, Jeff, 111–12

Free Labor: Workfare and the Contested Language of Neoliberalism (Krinsky), 44

Freedman, Helen E., 40, 121, 135

Freidmutter, Cindy, 124

futility argument, 133

GAIN (Greater Avenues for Independence), 46, 47

Gardner, Jessica, 76

Garlow, Stephanie, 154

Garneva, Annie, 105

Gaul-Stigge, Katie, 97, 106

Gay Men's Health Crisis, Inc. (GMHC), 85t, 86t, 89, 90

GED programs, 62

Gelinas, Nicole, 143

Getting Agencies to Work Together (Bardach), 102

Gibbs, Linda, 114, 150–51

Gilmour, Robert, 94–95

Ginsberg, Mitchell, 11

INDEX

Giuliani, Rudy: change to work-oriented welfare reform under, 90; conclusions on, 148–58; criticism of, 151; decline in reputation of, 155–58; and history of HRA, 1; homelessness under, 110, 112, 114; HRA under, 160, 161; HRA under first term of, 21–35; HRA under second term of, 36–49; impact of reforms of, 6, 163–64; management approach of, 55; and Maximus contracts with NYC, 88–89; and mayor-governor relations, 7, 39–41, 139, 145; and New York/New York agreements, 115; restructuring of HRA under, 52, 54, 59, 156; welfare reform of, as example of ideational/entrepreneurial politics, 5; welfare reform of, as nonincremental change, 91; welfare reform of de Blasio vs., 54

Glazer, Nathan, 19

Goodwill Industries, 73, 74–75, 76, 78, 79, 81, 82, 85t, 86t, 89

Gotham Gazette, 64

Governing magazine, 96

Governing New York City (Sayre and Kaufman), 135

Gramsci, Antonio, 44, 174n19

Grant Associates, 73, 74, 82–83, 85t, 86t

Gray v. Sanders (1963), 170n12

Great Society, 15, 53, 63, 72, 133

Grinker, William, 29, 37, 126–27, 150–51, 161, 163–64

Gueron, Judith M., 27, 46, 47, 84

Gusmano, Michael K., 188n21

Hayes, Robert, 111

Head Start, 12

HELP USA, 160

Hevesi, Alan G., 45, 89

high school equivalency programs, 62

HireNYC: Human Services, 104

Hirschman, A. O., 56

Home Base program, 56, 119, 128

Home Stay, 135–38

Homeless Outreach Population Estimate (HOPE), 111

homelessness: background on policy, 111–16; under Bloomberg, 113–14, 119, 120; de Blasio's attempts to recover from Bloomberg policies, 56, 122–32, 158–59; under Dinkins, 114, 120, 121, 171n28; and emergency shelter system, 12, 35, 40–41, 112, 120; under Giuliani, 110, 112; and interagency coordination, 95–97; under Lindsay, 110; Mangano's strategic idea of ending chronic, 108–9; necessity arguments regarding, 120–21; New York's innovations and possible future policy regarding, 132–38; and 1993 mayoral election, 34–35; perceived increase in, under de Blasio, 111–16; and personnel under de Blasio, 116–20; phases in policies, 134; and right to shelter policy, 5, 34–35, 111, 120, 132, 133, 134, 165

Homelessness Prevention Administration, 119

Home-Stat program, 122–23

Host Home, 135, 137–38

hotel rooms, as emergency housing, 110, 112, 120–21

housing. *See* homelessness

Housing Court, 56

Housing First, 96, 108–9, 113

Housing Stability Plus, 114

human capital development (HCD) programs, 27, 46, 152–53

Human Resources Administration (HRA): ACS and DHS's effect on, 150–51; Banks as commissioner of, 116, 118, 127–28, 159, 175n8, 190n34; changes in culture and operations under Giuliani, 150; and conflict between Lindsay and Rockefeller, 13–14; contracts with work program providers, 77; creation of, 164; under de Blasio, 54–55, 57–58, 65–69, 159; early years of, 11–12; evaluating success of, under Lindsay, 15–20; evolution of mission statement of, 161; as focus of reform campaigns, 1; under Ginsberg, 11; under Giuliani, 52, 54, 59, 156, 160; under Giuliani's first term, 21–35; under Giuliani's second term, 36–49; impact of, 164; job placements under de Blasio, 65–69; as nonincremental change, 19, 91, 147–48; proposal for, 9–11; reintegration of DHS with, 125–28, 159; vendor performance evaluations (VPEs), 84–90; welfare employment service programs instituted at, 103. *See also* Career Pathways; Career Pathways, implementation of

hybrid contracts, 77–79, 80, 81

ideas: and achieving coordination, 97, 98, 99, 101, 102–3; effectiveness of coordination by, under de Blasio, 103–9; role of, in urban politics, 3. *See also* ideational/entrepreneurial model of change

INDEX

ideational/entrepreneurial model of change: and charter revision, 42; dark side to, 157; under de Blasio and Banks, 61; under Giuliani, 22, 148, 149, 153; limitation of, 48; and Machiavellianism, 157, 158; overview of, 4–5; public ideas as key element in, 3; and regime theory, 43–44; as relying on expert consensus, 157; used by Giuliani, 56
ideational-nonincremental model, 42
incremental change: under Banks and de Blasio, 131–32; vs. nonincremental change, 4, 52; in urban politics, 146
Independent Budget Office (IBO), 66, 67
industry partnerships, 100–2
Institute for Children, Poverty & Homelessness (ICPH), 116, 129–30
institutional reform litigation, 5, 51–52, 111, 121, 134–35
interagency commissions, 95
Inter-Agency Work and Welfare Task Force, 29

Job Centers, 36, 38, 39, 173n7
Job Club, 82
Job Opportunity and Basic Skills Training Program (JOBS), 28–30, 31
job opportunity specialist (JOS), 37–38
job placements: under de Blasio, 65–69, 90; interpretations of trends in, 72. *See also* Career Pathways; Career Pathways, implementation of
Jobs for New Yorkers Task Force, 66, 93
Job-Stat system, 21
Johnson, Lyndon B., 15, 53, 139
Joker, The (2019), 147, 189n6

Katznelson, Ira, 3, 167n3
Kaufman, Herbert, 17, 23–24, 135, 170n7
Kelman, Steven, 5
Kennedy, John F., 15
King, Desmond, 157
Kingdon, John, 153
Kirtzman, Andrew, 155, 156
Klein, Joel, 57
Koch, Ed, 17, 29, 120, 132
Krinsky, John, 44–46, 174nn19–22

La Guardia Community College, 62
La Guardia, Fiorello, 4
labor force attachment (LFA) welfare reform, 27, 46–48, 59
Lackman, Abe, 26
Landy, Marc K., 2, 4, 32, 42, 48, 148

Lane, Eric, 24–25
Layon, Jesse, 106
Levin, Martin A., 2, 4, 32, 42, 48, 148
Levine, Ellen, 71, 177n16, 178n23
LGBTQ youth, accommodations for homeless, 137
Lhorta, Joe, 26
liberal Republicanism, 13
Lindsay, John: conclusions on, 147–48; and creation of HRA, 164; decentralization of New York's poverty program under, 169n35; effectiveness of reform campaign, 6; and fiscal crisis of 1975, 25; and history of HRA, 1; homelessness under, 110; HRA under, 90; and mayor-governor relations, 7, 13–14, 139, 141, 145; reorganization of human resources as priority for, 9; success of HRA under, 15–20; welfare explosion under, 150
Lipsky, Michael, 2
Living in Communities (LINC), 112, 115, 140

MacDonald, Heather, 65
Machiavellianism, 155–57, 158
Malin, Joan, 125, 126
Mallon, Jacqueline, 97, 101–2
"Man Who Fought Homelessness and Won (Sort Of), The," 131
Mangano, Philip, 96, 108
Manpower Development Research Corporation (MDRC), 27, 62, 84, 92, 109
Manpower Training, 12
Mantel, Howard N., 15, 18
Marcuse, Peter, 132
Mastran, David V., 88–89
Maximus Human Services, 45, 73, 75, 78, 79–80, 83, 85*t*, 86*t*, 88–89
mayoral election (1993), 33–34
mayor-governor relations, 7, 13–14, 39, 40, 41, 115–16, 122, 123–24, 139–41, 145
Mayor's Committee on Management Survey (1953), 10
Mayor's Management Report (MMR): 1990, 29–30; 1993, 37, 161; 2016, 66; 2018, 66, 67, 68; 2019, 67; 2020, 65, 104
Mayor's Office of Workforce Development (WKDEV), 97, 99, 103–4, 106–7
McAdam, Doug, 174n21
McNickle, Chris, 50–51, 57
Mead, Lawrence, 27, 75, 149–50
Medicaid, 143, 144

INDEX

"Memorandum on Reviewing Funding to State and Local Government Recipients That Are Permitting Anarchy, Violence, and Destruction in American Cities," 142–43
migrants, influx of, in New York City, 165
Miller, Jim, 79
minimum wage, 140
Moffitt, Robert, 154
Mollenkopf, John, 43
Morris, Charles R., 16, 168n17
Moynihan, Daniel P., 3, 28
Municipal Assistance Corporation (MAC), 25–26, 40
mutual responsibility model, 34–35

Nader, Ralph, 159
Nation magazine, 141
National Association on Drug Abuse Problems, Inc. (NADAP), 85t, 86t, 89
negative change, 167n16
New Politics of Public Policy, The (Landy and Levin), 2–3, 19–20, 32, 42
New York Alliance for Careers in Healthcare (NYACH), 101, 104
New York City 15/15 Supportive Housing Initiative, 123–24
New York City charter, revision of, 23–25, 28, 42
New York City Council, 23, 24, 25, 31, 33, 53, 129
New York City's Supportive Housing Task Force, 124
New York/New York agreements, 113, 115–16, 123–25
New York/New York III Agreement (2005), 113, 123–24
New York/New York IV agreement, 115–16, 123–24
Nixon, Richard, 3
nonincremental change: achieving, 151–54; at agency level, 36; Aid to Families with Dependent Children as, 4; characteristics of, 149; de Blasio and New York City's capability of, 158–63; defined, 3–4, 91; establishment of HRA as, 19; frequency of, 5; under Giuliani, 21–25; Giuliani and New York City's capability of, 148–58; under Giuliani's first term, 28; under Giuliani's second term, 41–42; Giuliani's work-first programs as, 163; in history of US welfare policy, 4; impediments to, 44; vs. incremental change, 4, 52; issues relevant to urban, 6–7; under Koch, 132; Lindsay and New York City's capability of, 147–48; Machiavellianism and achieving, 156–57; paths to, under de Blasio, 52–57; perceived need for, 146–47; possibility of, 163; presidents as barrier to, 14–15, 141–42, 144; as relevant to democratic legitimacy, 5; revision of New York City charter and, under Giuliani, 23–25; and structural change in New York City charter, 28; underestimation of potential for, 3; in urban politics, 146
NYC Employment and Training Coalition (NYCETC), 105

Office of Temporary and Disability Assistance, 40
O'Flaherty, Brendan, 114, 173n49
Omnibus Budget Reconciliation Act (1981), 148
O'Regan, Meg, 31
organizational culture, and implementation of Career Pathways, 81–84
Orrick, William, 142
Our Homelessness Crisis: The Case for Change (City Council of New York), 129

Palacio, Herminia, 125
Pan Am Motel, 120
Parks Opportunity Program, 190n41
Pataki, George, 7, 39, 40, 41, 115
paternalistic paradigm, 134
Pecorella, Robert F., 169n35
performance-based models, 60, 77, 78–81
Personal Responsibility and Work Opportunity Reconciliation Act (PRWORA, 1996), 4, 5, 32, 48, 59, 144, 145, 149, 172n40
Pertschuk, Michael, 190n35
Peterson, Amy, 97, 99–100
pluralist/incremental model of political change, 4
policy legacies and feedbacks, 28–32
positive change, 6, 91, 109, 141, 145, 167n16
"poverty problem," 18
poverty reduction, under de Blasio, 161–62
pragmatism/pragmatic progressivism, 51, 162–63
pre-K, universal (UPK), 56, 140–41
presidential/majoritarian model of political change, 4
presidents, as barrier to nonincremental change, 14–15, 141–42, 144
Pressman, Jeffrey L., 72
Preston, Vanessa, 83

INDEX   199

Privateer!: Building a Business, Reforming Government (Mastran), 88, 89
Proceedings of the Academy of Political Science, 11–12
project labor agreement (PLA), 103

Quinn, Christine, 125, 127

Rachidi, Angela, 64
rapid attachment, 27, 47, 58, 82, 83. *See also* work-first programs
reciprocal obligation, 34–35, 42
regime theory, 43–44
rental subsidies, 112, 115, 129, 140, 158–59, 160
ResCare Workforce Services/Equus Workforce Services, 85t, 87t, 89
"Research Context for Welfare Reform, A" (Gueron), 27
Reynolds v. Giuliani (1999), 39
Right to a Roof: Demands for an Integrated Housing Plan to End Homelessness and Promote Racial Equity, 129, 130
right to shelter, 5, 34–35, 111, 120, 132, 133, 134, 165
Rittel, Horst W. J., 18, 19
Riverside, California, 109
Riverside GAIN program, 46, 47
Rockefeller, Nelson, 7, 13–14, 139, 141, 187n3
Rogers, David, 16–17

San Francisco, 136
sanctions, and implementation of Career Pathways, 76–77
Sanger, M. Bryna, 78, 79
Sayre, Wallace, 17, 23–24, 135, 170n7
Schuck, Peter H., 190n35
Schwartz, Richard, 55
Scott, Stuart, 13
Scott Commission (Temporary State Commission to Make a Study of Governmental Operation of the City of New York), 13–14, 168n17
Seidman, Harold, 94–95
Shaefer, Luke, 154–55
Shefter, Martin, 15, 16, 167n3
shelter system. *See* homelessness
Shorris, Anthony, 125, 159
Siegel, Fred, 26, 64, 155–56
Small Business Services (SBS) agency, 97, 100–1, 104, 106
Smith, Dennis, 37, 150–51, 161, 163–64

SNAP (Supplemental Nutrition Assistance Program), 143, 144
Social Security Act (1935), 4
Social Service Review, 10–11
Stein, Samuel, 130–31
Stewart B. McKinney Homeless Assistance Act (1987), 95–96
strategic idea, 102–3, 108–9
Stringer, Scott, 118
superagency concept, 17, 168n17
Supplemental Nutrition Assistance Program (SNAP), 143, 144
Sviridoff, Mitchell, 9–10, 11, 18–19
Swirin-Yao, Dolores, 76, 78
"Symposium on Welfare Reform," 27

Tarrow, Sidney, 174n21
Task Force for the Homeless, 95
Taylor, Gilbert, 116, 118, 119, 125, 159
Tech Talent Pipeline (TTP), 100–2, 104, 105
Temporary Aid to Needy Families (TANF), 4, 32, 52, 144, 149
Temporary State Commission to Make a Study of Governmental Operation of the City of New York (Scott Commission), 13–14, 168n17
Thompson, Frank J., 188n21
Thompson, J. Philip, 97–98, 103, 107
Thompson, Tommy, 28, 148, 149–50
Tilly, Charles, 174n21
trench warfare, 44, 174n19
Trump, Donald, 141–45, 155, 157, 158, 188n21
Tsemberis, Sam, 96, 108, 134
Turner, Jason, 36, 38, 45, 64, 88–89
Turning the Tide on Homelessness in New York City, 114–15, 128, 131

United Federation of Teachers (UFT), 57
United for Housing from the Ground Up, 127
United States Department of Agriculture (USDA), 173n7
United States Interagency Council on Homelessness (USICH), 95–97, 108
universal pre-K (UPK), 56, 140–41
US constitutional structure, 6–7, 14–15, 139, 145

Vallone, Peter, 25, 26
Viroli, Maurizio, 156
vision, and achieving coordination, 98, 100, 102–3
Viteritti, Joseph P., 15, 51, 53, 139–40

W-2, 149–50
waivers, 32–34, 143–44, 148–49
Way Home, The: A New Direction in Social Policy, 12, 34–35
Weaver, R. Kent, 48
Webber, Melvin M., 18, 19
WeCARE, 67–68, 69, 178n23
Weingarten, Randi, 57
Weld, William, 28, 148, 149
Welfare (1975), 147
welfare rolls: reduction in, under Giuliani, 152, 154; size and growth of, under Giuliani, 149–50; trends in, under de Blasio and Banks, 69–72
welfare-to-work programs, 27
Westat, 104–5
What Works in Work-First Welfare (Feldman), 89
Whitaker, Gordon P., 75
wicked problems, 18–19, 165
Wildavsky, Aaron B., 72
Williams, Charmaine, 76, 78

Wilson, James Q., 37, 95
Woodruff, Stacy, 106–7
Work Experience Program (WEP), 21, 36, 44–45, 47
workfare, 45, 46, 47, 63, 119, 148, 174n22
work-first programs: as begetting Career Pathways, 92–93; continuing debates on results of, 155; expert consensus on, 27–28, 46–48, 59, 157; under Giuliani, 90, 148, 151, 152–54; of Giuliani as nonincremental change, 163; under Giuliani's first term, 27; Krinsky on opposition to, 174n22; labor force attachment (LFA) welfare reform, 27, 46–48, 59; research base for, 60–61; as strategic idea, 109. *See also* rapid attachment
work-for-benefits programs, 47

Youth Pathways, 58, 59. *See also* Career Pathways; Career Pathways, implementation of

www.ingramcontent.com/pod-product-compliance
Lightning Source LLC
Chambersburg PA
CBHW020913230426
43666CB00008B/1436